OSINT Automation: Python & APIs for Intelligence Gathering

Algoryth Ryker

The field of Open-Source Intelligence (OSINT) is growing at an unprecedented rate. The sheer volume of publicly available data, from social media posts to domain records, from leaked databases to deep and dark web marketplaces, has made manual investigation methods obsolete. Analysts are facing a critical challenge: How can they efficiently collect, analyze, and interpret this flood of information while staying ahead of emerging threats?

The answer lies in automation. By leveraging Python, APIs, and machine learning, OSINT professionals can streamline data gathering, enhance intelligence workflows, and generate actionable insights in real-time. This book is designed to equip analysts, cybersecurity professionals, and investigators with the skills to automate OSINT processes—making intelligence gathering faster, more accurate, and more scalable than ever before.

This guide will take you step by step through the essential tools and techniques for OSINT automation. You'll learn how to scrape websites for intelligence, track social media activity with APIs, monitor the dark web with Python scripts, and even use artificial intelligence to detect patterns and threats.

By the end of this book, you'll have built a fully automated OSINT workflow, enabling you to gather, process, and visualize intelligence data like never before. Whether you're an investigator, researcher, journalist, or cyber threat analyst, mastering OSINT automation will give you a competitive edge in the digital intelligence landscape.

Let's dive in.

Chapter Breakdown

1. Introduction to OSINT Automation

- Why OSINT automation is essential for modern intelligence work
- The role of Python in OSINT investigations
- Overview of commonly used APIs and automation tools
- Setting up a Python environment for intelligence gathering
- Ethical and legal considerations in automated intelligence work

Case Study: How an OSINT team used automation to track a digital threat actor

2. Python Basics for OSINT Analysts

- **Key Python fundamentals**: variables, loops, functions
- Handling OSINT data formats (JSON, CSV, XML)
- Using regular expressions for data extraction
- Making API requests with Python
- Automating data collection and storage
- Best practices for writing efficient OSINT scripts

3. Web Scraping with Python & BeautifulSoup

- The ethics and legality of web scraping
- Setting up BeautifulSoup and Scrapy for intelligence gathering
- Extracting intelligence from public websites
- Handling dynamic content using Selenium
- Bypassing anti-scraping measures and avoiding detection

Case Study: Scraping government records to uncover financial fraud

4. Automating Google Dorking & Search Engine Queries

- Mastering Google Dorking for OSINT investigations
- Writing Python scripts to automate advanced search queries
- Scraping search engine results responsibly
- Customizing searches for deeper intelligence insights
- Integrating APIs from Google, Bing, and DuckDuckGo

Case Study: Automating reconnaissance on high-risk individuals

5. Extracting & Analyzing Social Media Data with APIs

- The power and limitations of social media APIs
- Automating Twitter OSINT with Tweepy
- Scraping Facebook & Instagram data responsibly
- Extracting intelligence from LinkedIn & Reddit
- Analyzing hashtags, mentions, and emerging social media trends

Case Study: Using Python to track a misinformation campaign

6. Automating Email & Domain Investigations

- Extracting email data from public breach databases

- Verifying emails and finding associated accounts
- Automating WHOIS and domain lookups
- Extracting DNS, IP, and hosting information programmatically
- Monitoring domain and email reputation with Python

Case Study: Tracking phishing campaigns using OSINT automation

7. Building OSINT Dashboards for Threat Intelligence

- Why dashboards matter in intelligence work
- Tools for building OSINT dashboards (Streamlit, Flask, Django)
- Automating data ingestion for real-time monitoring
- Visualizing intelligence reports dynamically
- Integrating live threat intelligence feeds

Case Study: Developing a real-time cyber threat intelligence dashboard

8. Image & Metadata Analysis with Automated Tools

- Understanding EXIF metadata in OSINT investigations
- Extracting image metadata using Python
- Automating reverse image searches (Google, Yandex, TinEye)
- AI-powered image recognition for object and face detection
- Geolocating images using metadata and satellite imagery

Case Study: Automating geospatial intelligence for tracking terrorist activity

9. Dark Web Monitoring with Python Scripts

- Challenges of monitoring the deep and dark web
- Automating Tor-based web crawling
- Extracting intelligence from onion sites via the Tor API
- Tracking cryptocurrency transactions on the dark web
- Monitoring marketplaces, forums, and leaked databases

Case Study: Automating dark web intelligence to track cybercriminals

10. Using Machine Learning for OSINT Insights

- How machine learning is transforming OSINT investigations

- Data classification and clustering for threat intelligence
- Using sentiment analysis to assess online activity
- AI-powered image recognition for OSINT investigations
- Automating threat detection with AI models

Case Study: Applying AI to detect and analyze disinformation campaigns

11. OSINT Data Visualization & Reporting

- The importance of data visualization in intelligence
- Using Matplotlib & Seaborn for intelligence graphing
- Creating interactive data reports with Plotly & Tableau
- Automating PDF report generation for OSINT findings
- Integrating geospatial data mapping

Case Study: Generating an automated OSINT intelligence report

12. Case Study: Automating an Intelligence Operation

- Defining the investigation scope and objectives
- Selecting the right OSINT automation tools
- Collecting and processing large-scale intelligence data
- Overcoming challenges in OSINT automation workflows
- Presenting findings with automated reports and dashboards
- Lessons learned and future trends in OSINT automation

Conclusion: The Future of OSINT Automation

As OSINT continues to evolve, automation will become an essential skill for intelligence analysts, investigators, and cybersecurity professionals. With Python and APIs, analysts can now monitor threats in real-time, automate complex investigations, and visualize intelligence like never before.

By mastering the techniques in this book, you will be equipped to build powerful OSINT automation tools, enhance your intelligence workflow, and gain a competitive edge in the ever-changing world of digital investigations.

Are you ready to transform the way you gather intelligence? Let's automate OSINT.

1. Introduction to OSINT Automation

In this chapter, we dive into the world of Open-Source Intelligence (OSINT) automation, a powerful approach to streamline and enhance intelligence gathering in the digital age. As the volume and complexity of online data grow exponentially, manual OSINT efforts can no longer keep pace with the demand for rapid, accurate insights. Here, we will explore the key concepts behind OSINT automation, its importance in modern intelligence workflows, and how leveraging Python and APIs can revolutionize data collection, analysis, and reporting. By the end of this chapter, you'll gain a solid understanding of how automation tools can empower OSINT analysts to maximize their productivity, efficiency, and effectiveness in an ever-evolving digital landscape.

1.1 Why Automate OSINT? Benefits & Use Cases

In today's digital world, Open-Source Intelligence (OSINT) has become an invaluable tool for a wide array of professionals, from cybersecurity experts and law enforcement agencies to journalists and business analysts. OSINT refers to intelligence that is gathered from publicly available sources, such as websites, social media platforms, forums, databases, and other online channels. However, as the volume of data on the internet continues to grow exponentially, the task of manually sifting through and analyzing this data has become increasingly difficult, time-consuming, and prone to human error. This is where automation comes into play. Automating OSINT collection, processing, and analysis offers numerous benefits that can significantly enhance the effectiveness and efficiency of intelligence-gathering operations.

In this section, we will explore why automating OSINT is crucial, the benefits it offers, and several real-world use cases that demonstrate its value.

1.1.1 The Growing Need for OSINT Automation

The internet today is a vast and ever-expanding network of data, with an estimated 5 billion internet users and trillions of web pages. Every second, massive amounts of new information are being generated, including social media posts, news articles, blogs, user reviews, academic papers, and much more. While this data provides valuable insights, it also presents significant challenges for analysts seeking to gather relevant intelligence.

Traditional methods of OSINT collection—such as manually searching websites, scrolling through social media feeds, or reading news articles—are simply not scalable. Analysts may need to monitor hundreds or even thousands of sources at any given time, and doing so manually becomes a tedious and inefficient process. Moreover, human error can lead to missed opportunities or incorrect conclusions, further diminishing the quality of intelligence gathered.

By automating OSINT processes, analysts can not only speed up data collection but also improve the accuracy, consistency, and comprehensiveness of their intelligence operations. Automation enables the continuous, real-time monitoring of vast amounts of data, allowing analysts to focus on interpreting and acting upon the findings rather than spending excessive time on data collection.

1.1.2 Key Benefits of Automating OSINT

The decision to automate OSINT offers several key advantages that can revolutionize the way intelligence is gathered and analyzed. These benefits can be broken down into the following categories:

1.1.2.1 Increased Efficiency and Speed

One of the most obvious benefits of automating OSINT is the significant increase in efficiency. Automated scripts and tools can process and analyze large volumes of data much faster than a human analyst could. For example, a script can continuously monitor a set of websites or social media platforms for specific keywords, extracting relevant data in real time. This allows analysts to receive up-to-the-minute intelligence without having to manually search and filter through massive amounts of content.

Automating tasks such as data scraping, data entry, and report generation allows analysts to spend more time analyzing the results and less time on tedious manual labor. The speed of automation also allows analysts to respond more quickly to emerging threats, such as cyberattacks, social media misinformation, or geopolitical developments.

1.1.2.2 Scalability

OSINT automation allows intelligence-gathering efforts to scale in ways that would be impossible with manual methods. Whether an analyst is tracking a few specific data points or monitoring thousands of websites and social media accounts, automation ensures that the scope of the operation can grow without additional manpower. This scalability is particularly valuable in situations where intelligence needs to be gathered from diverse sources, covering global or national-level developments.

For instance, an analyst may need to track specific indicators of cybersecurity threats across the dark web, or monitor trends and public sentiment surrounding a political event across multiple social media platforms. Automation makes it feasible to scale these operations efficiently, enabling real-time analysis of data from a vast array of sources.

1.1.2.3 Improved Accuracy and Consistency

Automated OSINT tools are not subject to the same limitations and biases as human analysts. By eliminating the risk of human error—such as overlooking key data points or making subjective judgments—automation enhances the overall accuracy and consistency of the intelligence-gathering process. Automation ensures that data collection is conducted according to predefined parameters and without bias, which is essential for maintaining the integrity of intelligence findings.

Additionally, automation can standardize the analysis process, ensuring that the same set of criteria is applied uniformly across all data sets. This consistency is particularly important when working with large datasets, where manual analysis may lead to inconsistencies or overlooked patterns.

1.1.2.4 Real-Time Monitoring and Alerts

Another critical advantage of automating OSINT is the ability to conduct real-time monitoring of online sources. Automation enables continuous surveillance of websites, social media, forums, and other data sources, so that analysts can be alerted to critical developments as they happen. For example, an automated script could track mentions of a specific event, person, or organization across news articles or social media, instantly notifying the analyst when new information is available.

Real-time alerts enable quick responses to emerging threats or issues, which is especially important in situations that require fast action, such as cybersecurity breaches, criminal activities, or public safety threats. The ability to stay on top of evolving situations without manually checking sources at regular intervals is a powerful tool for any OSINT analyst.

1.1.2.5 Cost-Effectiveness

Automating OSINT processes can also be a more cost-effective solution than relying on manual labor. By reducing the need for large teams of analysts to sift through data, organizations can save significant resources. Automation tools and scripts, once created, can be used repeatedly with minimal cost, making them an efficient long-term investment.

Additionally, automation can lower the likelihood of costly mistakes that might arise from human oversight, further reducing the potential for financial loss.

1.1.3 Use Cases for OSINT Automation

To better understand the impact of OSINT automation, it's important to examine how it can be applied in real-world scenarios. Below are several use cases where automating OSINT processes has proven to be invaluable:

1.1.3.1 Cybersecurity Threat Detection

Cybersecurity experts rely heavily on OSINT to monitor threats, detect vulnerabilities, and track hacker activities. Automating OSINT tasks such as scanning for leaked credentials on the dark web, identifying phishing sites, or monitoring hacker forums for mentions of specific targets can help detect threats early. Real-time alerts and automated threat feeds allow cybersecurity teams to respond quickly and mitigate risks before they escalate into major breaches.

1.1.3.2 Social Media Monitoring for Brand Protection

Companies can use automated OSINT tools to monitor social media platforms for mentions of their brand, products, or services. Automation allows them to track customer sentiment, identify potential PR crises, or spot fake reviews and fraudulent activities. By using advanced sentiment analysis and keyword tracking, companies can respond quickly to issues, engage with customers, and protect their reputation online.

1.1.3.3 Criminal Investigations and Law Enforcement

Law enforcement agencies and investigators can automate the collection of publicly available information from social media, websites, and online databases to support criminal investigations. By setting up automated searches for specific keywords or identifying patterns of criminal activity, agencies can track suspects, gather intelligence on organized crime, or identify human trafficking rings. Automation accelerates the investigation process and helps law enforcement stay ahead of criminals who may operate in the digital space.

1.1.3.4 Political and Geopolitical Analysis

Political analysts use OSINT to track trends, monitor public opinion, and evaluate geopolitical risks. Automating the collection of data from news sources, blogs, and social media platforms allows analysts to monitor shifting public sentiments, track political events, and predict potential conflicts or destabilizing events. Automation makes it possible to cover a wider range of data sources and identify emerging issues in real time, providing valuable insights for decision-makers.

1.1.4 Conclusion

Automating OSINT collection and analysis offers numerous benefits, from increasing efficiency and scalability to improving accuracy and enabling real-time monitoring. As the amount of data available online continues to grow, the need for OSINT automation will only become more critical. By embracing automation, intelligence professionals can streamline their operations, uncover valuable insights more effectively, and respond to threats and opportunities faster than ever before. Whether in cybersecurity, law enforcement, or business analysis, automation empowers OSINT analysts to stay ahead in an increasingly data-driven world.

1.2 Understanding Python's Role in OSINT Investigations

Python has become the go-to programming language for OSINT investigations due to its versatility, ease of use, and vast ecosystem of libraries. Whether you're gathering data from websites, analyzing social media trends, scraping dark web forums, or automating intelligence workflows, Python provides the tools necessary to efficiently collect, process, and analyze open-source intelligence. In this section, we will explore why Python is a preferred choice for OSINT, examine its key capabilities, and highlight real-world scenarios where Python-powered automation enhances intelligence operations.

1.2.1 Why Python is the Preferred Language for OSINT

There are several reasons why Python has gained widespread adoption in OSINT investigations:

1.2.1.1 Simplicity and Readability

Python's clean and readable syntax makes it an ideal language for both beginner and experienced OSINT analysts. Unlike lower-level languages, Python allows investigators to focus on solving intelligence problems rather than dealing with complex syntax. Even analysts with minimal programming experience can quickly learn Python and start building automation scripts for OSINT tasks.

1.2.1.2 Extensive Library Support

Python's vast ecosystem of libraries provides ready-made solutions for web scraping, data analysis, natural language processing, machine learning, and network investigations. Some of the most commonly used libraries in OSINT include:

- **Requests & BeautifulSoup** – For web scraping and extracting information from websites
- **Selenium** – For automating interactions with dynamic web pages
- **Tweepy** – For extracting Twitter data through the Twitter API
- **OpenCV & PIL (Pillow)** – For image analysis and metadata extraction
- **ExifTool** – For examining geolocation and metadata in images
- **Scikit-learn & TensorFlow** – For machine learning and pattern recognition in OSINT data
- **Pandas & Matplotlib** – For data processing, visualization, and reporting

By leveraging these libraries, OSINT analysts can automate repetitive tasks and focus more on extracting actionable intelligence.

1.2.1.3 Cross-Platform Compatibility

Python is platform-independent, meaning it runs smoothly on Windows, macOS, and Linux. This flexibility allows OSINT professionals to deploy their scripts across multiple environments, including cloud-based infrastructure, virtual machines, or local computers.

1.2.1.4 API Integration

Most OSINT investigations rely on APIs to access data from online services such as social media platforms, news aggregators, and cybersecurity databases. Python's built-in support for RESTful APIs enables analysts to automate data retrieval and integrate multiple sources into a unified intelligence workflow.

1.2.1.5 Scalability and Automation

Python allows analysts to scale their OSINT operations by automating tasks such as web scraping, data collection, and alert generation. Whether monitoring a single website or tracking thousands of data points across different platforms, Python scripts can handle large-scale OSINT tasks efficiently.

1.2.2 Key Capabilities of Python in OSINT Investigations

Python provides a wide range of capabilities that make it an essential tool for OSINT analysts. Below, we examine the most crucial areas where Python enhances intelligence gathering.

1.2.2.1 Web Scraping and Data Extraction

One of Python's most powerful features is its ability to extract data from websites. OSINT professionals frequently use web scraping to gather information from public sources such as news sites, forums, government databases, and company registries.

Example tools for web scraping:

- **BeautifulSoup** – Parses HTML and XML documents to extract relevant data.
- **Requests** – Sends HTTP requests to retrieve web pages.
- **Scrapy** – A more advanced web scraping framework for large-scale data extraction.
- **Selenium** – Automates interactions with dynamic, JavaScript-heavy web pages.

With Python-based web scraping, analysts can continuously monitor web pages for updates, extract intelligence, and process large amounts of unstructured data in a structured format.

1.2.2.2 Social Media Intelligence (SOCMINT)

Social media is a crucial source of intelligence, offering insights into public sentiment, emerging trends, and potential threats. Python simplifies social media intelligence gathering by interacting with platform APIs.

Example social media OSINT tasks with Python:

- Monitoring hashtags, keywords, and user activity on Twitter using Tweepy.
- Extracting comments and user profiles from Reddit using PRAW.
- Gathering Facebook and Instagram data via API integrations.
- Performing sentiment analysis to gauge public opinion.

By automating social media data extraction, OSINT analysts can track real-time developments and gain valuable intelligence from online communities.

1.2.2.3 Image and Metadata Analysis

Python's image-processing capabilities allow analysts to extract hidden metadata from images, track locations using geotags, and identify manipulated images.

Example tools for image analysis:

- **ExifTool** – Extracts metadata from images, including GPS coordinates, timestamps, and camera details.
- **OpenCV** – Identifies faces, objects, and patterns in images.
- **Pillow (PIL)** – Processes and analyzes image files.

By using Python for image forensics, OSINT analysts can verify the authenticity of images and trace their origins.

1.2.2.4 Dark Web and Cybercrime Monitoring

The dark web is a significant source of intelligence for tracking cybercriminal activity, leaked credentials, and illicit transactions. Python provides tools to access and analyze dark web content safely.

Example Python tools for dark web monitoring:

- Stem & Requests – Allows interaction with the Tor network to scrape .onion websites.
- Scapy – Analyzes network traffic for security investigations.
- Shodan API – Identifies exposed devices and vulnerable systems.

By automating dark web monitoring, cybersecurity professionals can detect threats early and take proactive measures against cyberattacks.

1.2.2.5 Machine Learning for OSINT

Python's machine learning capabilities enable analysts to detect patterns, classify data, and predict trends in OSINT investigations.

Example applications of machine learning in OSINT:

- **Sentiment analysis** – Understanding public sentiment on social media or news platforms.
- **Topic modeling** – Identifying trending topics from large datasets.

- **Anomaly detection** – Detecting suspicious behavior or irregular activities.

Libraries like Scikit-learn, TensorFlow, and NLTK allow OSINT professionals to apply machine learning techniques to enhance their investigative capabilities.

1.2.3 Real-World Use Cases of Python in OSINT

To demonstrate Python's effectiveness in OSINT investigations, let's explore some real-world scenarios where it plays a critical role.

1.2.3.1 Tracking Disinformation Campaigns

Python scripts can be used to track the spread of misinformation by monitoring social media platforms for fake news, coordinated bot activity, or propaganda campaigns. Analysts can automate the collection of posts, apply sentiment analysis, and detect trends in disinformation.

1.2.3.2 Cyber Threat Intelligence (CTI)

Python-based OSINT tools can track cyber threats, such as leaked credentials, malware indicators, and hacker discussions on dark web forums. Automated scripts can extract data from cybersecurity feeds and alert security teams about potential breaches.

1.2.3.3 Corporate Risk Assessment

Businesses use OSINT to monitor competitors, identify risks, and track public perception. Python automation allows companies to collect real-time data from news sources, financial reports, and social media to make informed decisions.

1.2.4 Conclusion

Python has revolutionized the field of OSINT by providing powerful tools for data collection, analysis, and automation. Its simplicity, extensive library support, and scalability make it the perfect programming language for intelligence professionals. Whether it's web scraping, social media monitoring, dark web investigations, or machine learning applications, Python enables OSINT analysts to efficiently extract valuable insights from vast amounts of open-source data. As OSINT continues to evolve, Python's role will only become more significant in streamlining intelligence operations and enhancing data-driven decision-making.

1.3 Overview of Common OSINT APIs & Tools

The field of Open-Source Intelligence (OSINT) relies on a vast array of tools and APIs to automate data collection, enhance investigations, and provide valuable intelligence from publicly available sources. By leveraging these tools, analysts can efficiently gather, process, and analyze large volumes of data from social media, websites, domain records, leaked databases, and even the dark web.

This section provides an overview of some of the most commonly used OSINT APIs and tools, categorized by their primary function.

1.3.1 Web Scraping and Search Engine Tools

1.3.1.1 Google Custom Search API

Google's search engine is one of the most powerful OSINT tools available. The Google Custom Search API allows analysts to automate Google searches and retrieve structured results programmatically. This API is particularly useful for Google Dorking—an advanced search technique that uncovers hidden or sensitive data.

- **Use case**: Automating Google Dorking to find exposed documents, login pages, and vulnerable websites.
- **Limitations**: API quotas and restrictions may apply; does not bypass Google's CAPTCHA challenges.

1.3.1.2 Scrapy

Scrapy is a powerful Python framework for web scraping, designed to efficiently extract data from websites and store it in structured formats.

- **Use case**: Large-scale web crawling for data collection, such as extracting company information or gathering articles from news websites.
- **Limitations**: Requires knowledge of HTML structures and may face challenges with dynamically loaded content.

1.3.1.3 BeautifulSoup & Requests

BeautifulSoup is a popular Python library for parsing HTML and extracting relevant data from web pages, while Requests simplifies sending HTTP requests.

- **Use case**: Scraping website content such as press releases, public profiles, or online databases.
- **Limitations**: Not ideal for large-scale scraping; struggles with JavaScript-heavy sites.

1.3.2 Social Media Intelligence (SOCMINT) APIs

1.3.2.1 Twitter API (Tweepy)

The Twitter API enables analysts to collect tweets, user data, hashtags, and trends in real time. Tweepy is a Python wrapper for this API, making data extraction easier.

- **Use case**: Monitoring political discourse, tracking emerging trends, and identifying bot activity.
- **Limitations**: Requires API keys and authentication; rate-limited for free users.

1.3.2.2 Facebook & Instagram Graph API

The Graph API allows analysts to collect publicly available data from Facebook and Instagram, including posts, pages, and interactions.

- **Use case**: Social media monitoring for brand protection, threat intelligence, or geopolitical analysis.
- **Limitations**: Strict privacy policies; requires permissions and API approvals.

1.3.2.3 Reddit API (PRAW)

The Reddit API (Python Reddit API Wrapper – PRAW) provides programmatic access to posts, comments, and user activity from Reddit.

- **Use case**: Extracting discussions on cybersecurity forums, tracking disinformation, or monitoring underground communities.
- **Limitations**: API limits and Reddit's content moderation policies can restrict data access.

1.3.3 Domain, DNS, and IP Intelligence APIs

1.3.3.1 WHOIS Lookup APIs (WhoisXML API, DomainTools, ViewDNS.info)

WHOIS APIs allow analysts to retrieve domain registration details, including owner information, creation dates, and hosting details.

- **Use case**: Investigating fraudulent websites, identifying potential phishing domains, and tracking domain ownership history.
- **Limitations**: Some domains use privacy protection to hide registrant details.

1.3.3.2 Shodan API

Shodan is a search engine for Internet-connected devices, allowing OSINT professionals to find exposed servers, webcams, routers, and other IoT devices.

- **Use case**: Identifying open ports, misconfigured databases, and vulnerable devices in cybersecurity investigations.
- **Limitations**: Requires API key; limited free queries available.

1.3.3.3 VirusTotal API

VirusTotal is a malware analysis platform that aggregates results from multiple antivirus engines. Its API allows users to check URLs, IPs, files, and domains for threats.

- **Use case**: Investigating phishing links, checking for malware-infected domains, and analyzing malicious file hashes.
- **Limitations**: Limited free access; does not guarantee full malware detection.

1.3.3.4 Censys API

Censys is an alternative to Shodan that provides real-time data on exposed hosts, certificates, and services across the internet.

- **Use case**: Mapping attack surfaces, identifying TLS certificates, and tracking infrastructure changes.
- **Limitations**: Requires API key; free tier has limited queries.

1.3.4 Dark Web & Cyber Threat Intelligence APIs

1.3.4.1 Tor Network Scrapers (OnionScan, Ahmia API)

The Tor network hosts hidden services (.onion websites), often used by cybercriminals. OnionScan and Ahmia provide ways to scrape and analyze dark web sites.

- **Use case**: Monitoring cybercrime activities, detecting leaked credentials, and investigating dark web marketplaces.
- **Limitations**: Accessing Tor requires special configurations; many .onion sites disappear frequently.

1.3.4.2 Have I Been Pwned (HIBP) API

HIBP allows analysts to check if an email address or password has been exposed in a data breach.

- **Use case**: Investigating compromised accounts and helping individuals secure their credentials.
- **Limitations**: Does not provide detailed breach data without a premium subscription.

1.3.5 Image and Metadata Analysis Tools

1.3.5.1 ExifTool

ExifTool extracts metadata from images, including geolocation, timestamps, camera details, and software modifications.

- **Use case**: Verifying the authenticity of images and tracing their origin.
- **Limitations**: Geolocation data may be stripped from images uploaded to social media.

1.3.5.2 Google Vision API

Google's Vision API can detect objects, faces, landmarks, and text within images.

- **Use case**: Analyzing images in OSINT investigations, such as identifying individuals or locations.
- **Limitations**: Paid API; accuracy varies depending on image quality.

1.3.5.3 TinEye Reverse Image Search API

TinEye allows analysts to perform reverse image searches to track the origins of an image.

- **Use case**: Verifying the authenticity of viral images and detecting manipulated content.
- **Limitations**: Database coverage may not include all images from the web.

1.3.6 Data Visualization & Reporting Tools

1.3.6.1 Maltego

Maltego is a powerful link analysis tool used for mapping relationships between domains, IPs, people, organizations, and social media accounts.

- **Use case**: Graph-based investigations into cyber threats, fraud networks, and online personas.
- **Limitations**: Requires licensing for full features.

1.3.6.2 Kibana & Elasticsearch

Kibana and Elasticsearch help analysts store, search, and visualize large datasets in an interactive dashboard format.

- **Use case**: Threat intelligence dashboards, log analysis, and network monitoring.
- **Limitations**: Requires setup and technical expertise.

1.3.7 Conclusion

Automating OSINT investigations with APIs and tools significantly enhances intelligence gathering, reduces manual workload, and provides analysts with real-time insights. Whether scraping websites, monitoring social media, tracking cyber threats, or analyzing images, Python-powered OSINT tools and APIs play a crucial role in modern intelligence operations.

By mastering these tools, analysts can streamline their investigations, stay ahead of emerging threats, and turn raw data into actionable intelligence.

1.4 Setting Up a Python Environment for OSINT

Before diving into OSINT automation, it is essential to set up a proper Python environment that includes the necessary tools, libraries, and configurations for intelligence gathering. This section will guide you through installing Python, setting up a virtual environment, installing OSINT-related libraries, and configuring essential tools for efficient investigations.

1.4.1 Installing Python

Python is a cross-platform language that runs on Windows, macOS, and Linux. The latest stable version of Python can be downloaded from the official Python website:

🔗 **Download Python**: https://www.python.org/downloads/

1.4.1.1 Verifying Python Installation

After installation, verify that Python is installed correctly by opening a terminal or command prompt and running:

python --version

or

python3 --version

If Python is installed, you should see an output similar to:

Python 3.x.x

1.4.2 Setting Up a Virtual Environment

A virtual environment allows you to create isolated Python environments for different projects, preventing conflicts between dependencies.

1.4.2.1 Creating a Virtual Environment

To create a virtual environment, navigate to your project directory and run:

python -m venv osint_env

or

python3 -m venv osint_env

1.4.2.2 Activating the Virtual Environment

Windows:

osint_env\Scripts\activate

macOS/Linux:

source osint_env/bin/activate

Once activated, your terminal prompt should change, indicating you are working within the virtual environment.

1.4.3 Installing Essential OSINT Libraries

After setting up the virtual environment, install the necessary Python libraries commonly used for OSINT investigations.

1.4.3.1 Installing Libraries for Web Scraping

Web scraping is a key technique in OSINT for gathering information from websites.

pip install requests beautifulsoup4 scrapy selenium

- **Requests** – Sends HTTP requests to web pages.
- **BeautifulSoup** – Parses and extracts data from HTML and XML.
- **Scrapy** – A framework for large-scale web scraping.
- **Selenium** – Automates interactions with dynamic websites.

1.4.3.2 Installing Libraries for Social Media Intelligence (SOCMINT)

pip install tweepy praw facebook-sdk

- **Tweepy** – Accesses the Twitter API.
- **PRAW** – Retrieves data from Reddit.
- **Facebook SDK** – Interacts with the Facebook Graph API.

1.4.3.3 Installing Libraries for Domain & IP Intelligence

pip install python-whois shodan virustotal-api censys

- **python-whois** – Fetches domain registration details.
- **Shodan** – Queries the Shodan API for exposed devices.
- **VirusTotal API** – Analyzes malicious files and URLs.
- **Censys** – Collects internet-wide scan data.

1.4.3.4 Installing Libraries for Data Processing & Visualization

pip install pandas matplotlib seaborn networkx

- **Pandas** – Handles structured data.
- **Matplotlib & Seaborn** – Creates visualizations.
- **NetworkX** – Builds relationship graphs for OSINT investigations.

1.4.3.5 Installing Libraries for Image & Metadata Analysis

pip install pillow opencv-python pyexiftool

- **Pillow** – Processes image files.
- **OpenCV** – Performs advanced image analysis.
- **PyExifTool** – Extracts metadata from images.

1.4.4 Configuring API Keys for OSINT Tools

Many OSINT APIs require authentication using API keys. Below are some commonly used APIs and how to set up their keys.

1.4.4.1 Obtaining API Keys

- **Twitter API**: https://developer.twitter.com
- **Shodan API**: https://account.shodan.io
- **VirusTotal API**: https://www.virustotal.com/gui/join-us
- **Censys API**: https://censys.io/register

1.4.4.2 Storing API Keys Securely

Instead of hardcoding API keys in scripts, store them in environment variables or configuration files.

Example: Using Environment Variables (Linux/macOS)

```
export SHODAN_API_KEY="your_api_key_here"
```

To access the stored key in Python:

```
import os
shodan_api_key = os.getenv("SHODAN_API_KEY")
```

1.4.5 Setting Up Jupyter Notebook for OSINT Analysis

Jupyter Notebook is a popular interactive coding environment for OSINT analysts. Install it using:

```
pip install jupyter
```

To launch Jupyter Notebook, run:

```
jupyter notebook
```

This opens a web-based interface where analysts can run Python code, visualize data, and document findings.

1.4.6 Using Docker for OSINT Automation

For complex OSINT projects, Docker can be used to containerize tools and dependencies.

1.4.6.1 Installing Docker

Follow installation instructions from https://www.docker.com.

1.4.6.2 Running an OSINT Tool in Docker

Example: Running Photon (a web crawler) in a container.

```
docker run -it --rm thehappydinoa/photon -u example.com
```

1.4.7 Testing the OSINT Environment

To verify that the Python environment is correctly set up, run the following script to perform a basic WHOIS lookup:

```
import whois

domain = "example.com"
info = whois.whois(domain)
print(info)
```

If successful, this should return domain registration details.

1.4.8 Conclusion

Setting up a Python environment for OSINT ensures that analysts have the necessary tools to automate intelligence gathering. By installing essential libraries, configuring API keys, and using tools like Jupyter Notebook and Docker, analysts can streamline their workflows and enhance their investigations. With this foundation in place, we can now move on to applying Python techniques for OSINT automation.

1.5 Ethical & Legal Considerations in OSINT Automation

As OSINT (Open-Source Intelligence) automation becomes increasingly sophisticated, it is crucial for analysts and investigators to understand the ethical and legal boundaries that govern data collection, processing, and usage. While OSINT relies on publicly available information, the methods used to gather and analyze this data can sometimes blur the line between legal intelligence gathering and unauthorized surveillance. This chapter explores the key ethical principles, legal frameworks, and best practices to ensure responsible OSINT automation.

1.5.1 Understanding the Ethical Responsibilities of OSINT Analysts

Ethics in OSINT revolves around responsible data collection and analysis. Just because data is publicly accessible does not mean it should always be used, especially when dealing with personal information. Analysts must ensure that their work does not violate privacy rights, cause harm, or contribute to malicious activities.

1.5.1.1 Key Ethical Principles in OSINT

- **Respect for Privacy** – Avoid collecting or sharing sensitive personal data unless there is a legitimate investigative purpose.
- **Transparency & Accountability** – Clearly define the purpose of OSINT investigations and ensure that automated tools are used responsibly.
- **Minimization** – Collect only the necessary data needed for an investigation, avoiding excessive or intrusive data gathering.
- **No Harm Policy** – Ensure that OSINT findings do not contribute to harassment, doxxing, or illegal activities.
- **Consent Considerations** – While OSINT relies on publicly available information, obtaining explicit or implied consent where necessary can strengthen ethical standing.

1.5.1.2 Common Ethical Dilemmas in OSINT Automation

- **Mass Data Collection** – Using automated scripts to scrape large amounts of data from social media platforms or websites may violate terms of service (ToS).
- **De-anonymization Risks** – Unmasking individuals from anonymous profiles using correlation techniques can have serious ethical implications.
- **Third-Party Data Use** – Using OSINT tools to collect and analyze data for commercial or malicious purposes can cross ethical boundaries.

1.5.2 Legal Frameworks Governing OSINT Automation

While OSINT is legal when conducted within the boundaries of publicly available data, different countries have specific regulations that impact how data can be collected and used. Analysts must be aware of regional and international laws that govern digital investigations.

1.5.2.1 Global OSINT Legal Considerations

General Data Protection Regulation (GDPR) – European Union

- Prohibits collecting personal data without consent.
- Requires proper justification for processing personal data.
- Grants individuals the "right to be forgotten" (deletion of personal information).

Computer Fraud and Abuse Act (CFAA) – United States

- Criminalizes unauthorized access to protected computer systems.

- Scraping or accessing restricted databases without permission may violate this law.

UK Investigatory Powers Act

- Regulates government intelligence-gathering operations.
- Requires oversight and legal justification for automated intelligence collection.

Data Protection Acts in Various Countries

- Many countries, such as Canada, Australia, and India, have strict data privacy laws that impact how OSINT can be conducted.

1.5.2.2 Website Terms of Service (ToS) & Web Scraping Laws

Many websites explicitly prohibit web scraping in their Terms of Service agreements. Automated data collection using tools like Scrapy or BeautifulSoup may violate these terms, leading to potential legal action. Analysts should review a website's robots.txt file before scraping to determine what is legally permissible.

Example of a robots.txt file restricting scraping:

*User-agent: ***
Disallow: /private-data/
Disallow: /user-info/

Ignoring robots.txt and bypassing access controls (such as CAPTCHA) can be legally problematic in many jurisdictions.

1.5.3 Ethical & Legal Risks in OSINT Automation

1.5.3.1 Misuse of OSINT for Malicious Purposes

OSINT tools can be misused for activities such as:

- **Doxxing** – The unauthorized release of private information.
- **Stalking & Harassment** – Using automated tools to track individuals.
- **Cybercrime** – OSINT data being leveraged for phishing, fraud, or hacking attempts.

1.5.3.2 Unauthorized Data Collection

Even though data is publicly available, mass scraping can still be considered unauthorized in cases where:

- The data was not intended for bulk collection.
- The platform has explicitly forbidden automated access.
- The data is used in ways that harm individuals or organizations.

1.5.3.3 Legal Action & Consequences

Violating OSINT legal boundaries can result in:

- Cease-and-desist orders from website owners.
- Lawsuits under data protection laws.
- Criminal charges for unauthorized data access.

1.5.4 Best Practices for Ethical & Legal OSINT Investigations

To mitigate risks and ensure compliance, OSINT analysts should follow these best practices:

1.5.4.1 Conducting Ethical OSINT Research

✅ **Use open-source data responsibly** – Only gather information that is publicly available and legally accessible.

✅ **Respect privacy regulations** – Avoid collecting personally identifiable information (PII) without justification.

✅ **Obtain explicit consent where applicable** – Especially when conducting deep social media research.

✅ **Verify data sources** – Ensure that collected data is accurate and from legitimate sources.

1.5.4.2 Staying Legally Compliant

✅ **Check website terms of service** – Ensure web scraping activities do not violate policies.

✅ **Use APIs when possible** – Many platforms provide public APIs (such as Twitter and Reddit) that offer structured and legally permissible data access.

✓ **Do not bypass security controls** – Avoid actions like circumventing CAPTCHAs, logging into unauthorized accounts, or exploiting vulnerabilities.

✓ **Store and handle data securely** – Follow cybersecurity best practices to prevent data breaches.

1.5.4.3 Implementing Transparency & Accountability

✓ **Maintain documentation** – Keep records of data collection methods and sources.

✓ **Use disclaimers** – When publishing OSINT findings, disclose the methodology and ethical considerations.

✓ **Engage in responsible disclosure** – If OSINT investigations reveal security vulnerabilities or threats, report them to the appropriate authorities rather than exposing them publicly.

1.5.5 Ethical OSINT Tools & Alternative Approaches

For analysts who want to ensure compliance with ethical standards, there are tools and methods that facilitate responsible OSINT gathering:

Using Public APIs Instead of Scraping

- Instead of scraping Twitter, use the Twitter API for legally permissible data access.
- For domain lookups, use WHOIS APIs rather than scraping web registries.

Leveraging AI for Ethical Analysis

- AI tools can help anonymize sensitive data while still allowing for meaningful intelligence analysis.

Focusing on Open Data Sources

- Government records, news archives, and open datasets (such as Kaggle and Data.gov) provide legitimate intelligence sources without privacy concerns.

1.5.6 Conclusion

Automating OSINT investigations presents powerful opportunities for intelligence gathering, but it also introduces ethical and legal risks. Analysts must balance the need for data with responsible collection practices, ensuring that investigations remain lawful and ethical. By adhering to best practices, respecting privacy laws, and using tools responsibly, OSINT professionals can maintain integrity and credibility in their work.

By keeping ethical and legal considerations at the forefront, analysts can ensure that OSINT remains a force for good, aiding cybersecurity, law enforcement, and intelligence agencies while minimizing potential harm.

1.6 Case Study: How Automation Improved an OSINT Workflow

In this case study, we will explore how OSINT automation significantly improved the efficiency, accuracy, and scalability of an intelligence-gathering operation. We will examine a real-world scenario where manual OSINT processes were replaced with automated Python scripts and APIs, reducing investigation time and enhancing analytical capabilities.

1.6.1 The Challenge: Manual OSINT Investigations Were Slow and Inefficient

Scenario:

A cybersecurity analyst working for a threat intelligence firm was tasked with tracking malicious domains, leaked credentials, and potential cyber threats across social media and the dark web. Initially, this was a manual process that involved:

- Searching Google manually using advanced operators (Google Dorking).
- Visiting multiple OSINT websites to check domain reputation, WHOIS data, and DNS records.
- Manually monitoring Twitter, Telegram, and dark web forums for emerging cyber threats.
- Extracting and analyzing metadata from leaked documents and images one file at a time.

This approach was time-consuming, prone to human error, and difficult to scale. As cyber threats increased, the need for automation became clear.

1.6.2 Implementing Automation in the OSINT Workflow

To improve efficiency, the analyst developed a Python-based OSINT automation system. This included:

1.6.2.1 Automating Google Dorking for Faster Search Queries

Instead of manually performing Google searches, the analyst wrote a Python script to automate Google Dorking using the SerpAPI.

Python Script for Automated Google Dorking:

```
import requests

API_KEY = "your_serpapi_key"
query = "inurl:admin login site:.gov"

url = f"https://serpapi.com/search.json?engine=google&q={query}&api_key={API_KEY}"
response = requests.get(url).json()

for result in response.get("organic_results", []):
    print(result["title"], "-", result["link"])
```

✅ **Impact**: Reduced search time from hours to minutes and retrieved structured results efficiently.

1.6.2.2 Automating Domain & IP Intelligence

The analyst integrated the Shodan and VirusTotal APIs to quickly check if a domain or IP address was associated with malicious activity.

Python Script for Checking a Domain on Shodan:

```
import shodan

SHODAN_API_KEY = "your_shodan_api_key"
api = shodan.Shodan(SHODAN_API_KEY)

domain = "example.com"
result = api.search(domain)

for match in result['matches']:
```

```
    print(f"IP: {match['ip_str']} | Organization: {match.get('org', 'N/A')}")
```

✅ **Impact**: Instead of checking multiple OSINT websites manually, the script provided real-time results in seconds.

1.6.2.3 Automating Social Media Monitoring for Threat Intelligence

The analyst used the Tweepy API to automate Twitter searches for cyber threats, reducing manual monitoring efforts.

Python Script for Tracking Keywords on Twitter:

```
import tweepy

API_KEY = "your_twitter_api_key"
API_SECRET = "your_twitter_api_secret"
ACCESS_TOKEN = "your_access_token"
ACCESS_SECRET = "your_access_secret"

auth = tweepy.OAuthHandler(API_KEY, API_SECRET)
auth.set_access_token(ACCESS_TOKEN, ACCESS_SECRET)
api = tweepy.API(auth)

keyword = "cyber attack"
tweets = api.search_tweets(q=keyword, count=10)

for tweet in tweets:
    print(f"{tweet.user.screen_name}: {tweet.text}")
```

✅ **Impact**: The script continuously monitored real-time cyber threat discussions instead of requiring an analyst to search manually.

1.6.2.4 Automating Dark Web Monitoring

The analyst wrote a script to crawl dark web forums using Tor and BeautifulSoup for intelligence gathering.

Python Script for Scraping a Dark Web Forum:

```
import requests
```

```
from bs4 import BeautifulSoup

url = "http://exampledarkwebsite.onion"
session = requests.session()
session.proxies = {'http': 'socks5h://127.0.0.1:9050', 'https': 'socks5h://127.0.0.1:9050'}

response = session.get(url)
soup = BeautifulSoup(response.text, 'html.parser')

for post in soup.find_all("div", class_="post"):
    print(post.text)
```

✓ **Impact**: Enabled real-time monitoring of dark web threats, significantly reducing the risk of missing crucial intelligence.

1.6.2.5 Automating Metadata Extraction from Leaked Files

Instead of manually inspecting leaked documents, the analyst used ExifTool to extract metadata automatically.

Python Script for Extracting Metadata from Images:

```
import subprocess

file_path = "leaked_image.jpg"
output = subprocess.check_output(["exiftool", file_path])
print(output.decode())
```

✓ **Impact**: Allowed for instant extraction of hidden metadata from leaked files, such as camera model, GPS coordinates, and timestamps.

1.6.3 Results & Key Benefits of OSINT Automation

After implementing automation, the analyst's OSINT workflow improved significantly:

Task	Manual Process	Automated Process	Improvement
Google Dorking	2-3 hours for multiple queries	A few minutes via script	90% faster
Domain reputation checking	30+ minutes per domain	Instantly via APIs	95% faster
Social media monitoring	Constant manual searching	Real-time alerts from scripts	100% automated
Dark web monitoring	Manually browsing forums	Automated scraping & alerts	Reduced risk
Metadata extraction	Checking files one by one	Instant batch processing	99% faster

1.6.4 Lessons Learned & Best Practices

1.6.4.1 Key Takeaways from Automating OSINT

✅ **Automation Saves Time:** Investigations that took days could now be completed in minutes.

✅ **Reduces Human Error**: Scripts ensure accuracy by consistently following predefined processes.

✅ **Scalability**: OSINT analysts can monitor thousands of sources without being overwhelmed.

✅ **Real-Time Alerts**: Automated tools provide instant alerts on potential threats.

1.6.4.2 Challenges & How They Were Overcome

- **Legal & Ethical Considerations**: Ensured compliance by using only publicly available data and API-based access instead of unauthorized scraping.
- **API Rate Limits**: Used caching and scheduled API queries to avoid exceeding limits.
- **Dark Web Access Risks**: Used proper security measures (VPN, Tor) to avoid exposure.

1.6.5 Conclusion

This case study demonstrates how OSINT automation transformed an inefficient intelligence-gathering workflow into a fast, scalable, and real-time investigative process. By leveraging Python scripts, APIs, and automation tools, OSINT analysts can enhance their investigative capabilities while reducing manual effort.

As the volume of online threats continues to grow, automation is no longer optional—it is a necessity for modern OSINT professionals. By applying these techniques, analysts can stay ahead of emerging threats, streamline intelligence operations, and make data-driven decisions faster than ever before.

2. Python Basics for OSINT Analysts

In this chapter, we introduce the foundational concepts of Python, the programming language that has become a vital tool for OSINT analysts. Whether you're a complete beginner or have some programming experience, we'll guide you through Python's core syntax, data structures, and libraries that are essential for automating intelligence tasks. From understanding variables and loops to working with lists, dictionaries, and functions, this chapter provides you with the building blocks needed to write clean, efficient code. By the end of this chapter, you will be equipped with the Python basics required to start automating data collection, processing, and analysis, unlocking the full potential of OSINT in your intelligence operations.

2.1 Python Fundamentals: Variables, Loops & Functions

In OSINT automation, Python serves as a powerful tool for data collection, processing, and analysis. To effectively leverage Python for OSINT investigations, analysts must understand core programming concepts such as variables, loops, and functions. These fundamentals form the building blocks for automating intelligence-gathering tasks, from web scraping to API integrations.

2.1.1 Understanding Variables in Python

Variables store data that can be referenced and manipulated throughout a Python script. They are essential for holding values such as URLs, API keys, search queries, and extracted intelligence data.

2.1.1.1 Declaring Variables

Python does not require explicit data type declarations—variables are dynamically assigned based on their values.

```
# Example: OSINT-related variables
source_url = "https://example.com"
threat_level = 5
is_compromised = True
```

Data Type	Example	Use Case in OSINT
str (String)	"username123"	Storing names, emails, or domain names
int (Integer)	42	Counting occurrences, threat levels

float (Float)   4.5   *Storing confidence scores*
bool (Boolean)   *True / False   Indicating presence of a threat*

2.1.1.2 Working with Variables

Variables can be manipulated using operators:

```
# Example: Automating threat scoring
threat_score = 7
threat_score += 3  # Increases threat score by 3
print(threat_score)  # Output: 10
```

2.1.2 Loops: Automating Repetitive Tasks

Loops allow analysts to process large datasets, iterate through search results, or extract intelligence from multiple sources efficiently.

2.1.2.1 The for Loop

Used to iterate over a sequence, such as a list of URLs or user profiles.

```
# Example: Checking multiple domains for threats
domains = ["example.com", "malicious-site.com", "safe-site.org"]

for domain in domains:
    print(f"Scanning {domain} for threats...")
```

2.1.2.2 The while Loop

Used when the number of iterations is unknown beforehand, such as waiting for a response from an OSINT API.

```
# Example: Retrying an API request until a valid response is received
import time

response = None
attempts = 0

while response is None and attempts < 5:
    print("Attempting API request...")
```

```
    attempts += 1
    time.sleep(2)  # Simulate waiting for a response
```

2.1.3 Functions: Structuring OSINT Scripts

Functions allow analysts to reuse code, making OSINT scripts modular and efficient.

2.1.3.1 Defining Functions

A function is defined using the def keyword and can accept parameters.

```
# Example: Function to check if a website is up
import requests

def check_website(url):
    try:
        response = requests.get(url, timeout=5)
        return response.status_code == 200
    except requests.exceptions.RequestException:
        return False


# Checking multiple websites
websites = ["https://example.com", "https://darkweb.onion"]
for site in websites:
    print(f"{site} is up: {check_website(site)}")
```

2.1.3.2 Returning Values from Functions

Functions can return values for further processing.

```
# Example: Function to classify threat levels
def classify_threat(score):
    if score > 7:
        return "High"
    elif score > 4:
        return "Medium"
    else:
        return "Low"

print(classify_threat(8))  # Output: High
```

2.1.4 Practical Example: Automating OSINT Data Collection

By combining variables, loops, and functions, analysts can automate intelligence-gathering tasks.

```python
# Example: Automating email lookup using an OSINT API
import requests

def check_email_breach(email):
    api_url = f"https://haveibeenpwned.com/api/v3/breachedaccount/{email}"
    response = requests.get(api_url)

    if response.status_code == 200:
        return f"{email} has been found in breaches!"
    else:
        return f"{email} is safe."

emails = ["target@example.com", "hacker@darknet.com"]

for email in emails:
    print(check_email_breach(email))
```

✅ Impact: This script automates the process of checking multiple emails for breaches, saving time in investigations.

2.1.5 Conclusion

Mastering Python fundamentals such as variables, loops, and functions is essential for OSINT analysts looking to automate intelligence-gathering tasks. By understanding how to structure code efficiently, analysts can create scalable and reusable scripts to improve their investigative workflows. In the next section, we will explore how these concepts apply to web scraping—a critical skill for gathering open-source intelligence from websites.

2.2 Working with JSON, CSV & XML Data Formats

In OSINT investigations, data is often retrieved in different formats, such as JSON, CSV, and XML. These formats are widely used for storing and exchanging structured information. Understanding how to parse, manipulate, and store data in these formats is essential for automating intelligence-gathering tasks using Python.

2.2.1 Introduction to Data Formats in OSINT

Format	Description	Common Use Cases in OSINT
JSON (JavaScript Object Notation)	Lightweight and human-readable, structured as key-value pairs	API responses, threat intelligence feeds
CSV (Comma-Separated Values)	Tabular format, easy to read and write	Storing OSINT reports, domain lists, breached credentials
XML (eXtensible Markup Language)	Hierarchical and structured, often used in web feeds	RSS feeds, forensic reports, security logs

Each format has its strengths, and Python provides built-in libraries to handle them efficiently.

2.2.2 Working with JSON in OSINT

2.2.2.1 What is JSON?

JSON is the most common format for OSINT APIs and structured data sharing. It consists of key-value pairs and supports nested structures.

Example JSON Response from an OSINT API:

```
{
  "domain": "example.com",
  "status": "malicious",
  "last_seen": "2025-02-15",
  "related_ips": ["192.168.1.1", "10.0.0.5"]
}
```

2.2.2.2 Parsing JSON with Python

To process JSON data in Python, we use the json module.

```
import json
```

```python
# Example JSON data (as a string)
data = '''
{
    "domain": "example.com",
    "status": "malicious",
    "last_seen": "2025-02-15",
    "related_ips": ["192.168.1.1", "10.0.0.5"]
}
'''

# Convert JSON string to Python dictionary
parsed_data = json.loads(data)

# Accessing JSON values
print(f"Domain: {parsed_data['domain']}")
print(f"Status: {parsed_data['status']}")
print(f"Last seen: {parsed_data['last_seen']}")
print(f"Related IPs: {', '.join(parsed_data['related_ips'])}")
```

✅ **Impact**: Quickly extracts OSINT-relevant data from JSON responses.

2.2.2.3 Fetching JSON Data from an API

Most OSINT APIs return data in JSON format. Here's how to automate API calls:

```python
import requests

api_url = "https://api.shodan.io/shodan/host/8.8.8.8?key=your_api_key"
response = requests.get(api_url)

# Convert response to JSON
data = response.json()

print(f"IP: {data['ip_str']}")
print(f"Organization: {data.get('org', 'Unknown')}")
print(f"Open Ports: {data['ports']}")
```

✅ **Impact**: Automates intelligence collection from APIs.

2.2.2.4 Writing JSON to a File

For storing OSINT data:

```
with open("osint_results.json", "w") as file:
    json.dump(parsed_data, file, indent=4)
```

✅ **Impact**: Saves structured OSINT findings for future analysis.

2.2.3 Working with CSV in OSINT

2.2.3.1 What is CSV?

CSV files store tabular data in plain text. Each line represents a row, and values are separated by commas.

Example CSV Data:

```
username,email,status
john_doe,john@example.com,breached
alice_smith,alice@example.com,safe
```

2.2.3.2 Reading CSV Data in Python

Python's csv module is used to process CSV files.

```
import csv

with open("breached_accounts.csv", "r") as file:
    reader = csv.reader(file)

    # Skip the header row
    next(reader)

    for row in reader:
        print(f"User: {row[0]}, Email: {row[1]}, Status: {row[2]}")
```

✅ **Impact**: Extracts intelligence from leaked databases.

2.2.3.3 Writing Data to a CSV File

To store OSINT results in CSV format:

```
data = [
    ["john_doe", "john@example.com", "breached"],
    ["alice_smith", "alice@example.com", "safe"]
]

with open("osint_results.csv", "w", newline="") as file:
    writer = csv.writer(file)
    writer.writerow(["username", "email", "status"])  # Header row
    writer.writerows(data)
```

✅ **Impact**: Creates structured OSINT reports for analysis.

2.2.3.4 Working with CSV as Dictionaries

For improved readability, csv.DictReader allows access by column names:

```
with open("breached_accounts.csv", "r") as file:
    reader = csv.DictReader(file)
    for row in reader:
        print(f"{row['username']} - {row['email']} is {row['status']}")
```

✅ **Impact**: Enables flexible data processing.

2.2.4 Working with XML in OSINT

2.2.4.1 What is XML?

XML is a structured format used in RSS feeds, forensic logs, and security reports.

Example XML Data from a Threat Feed:

```
<breach>
  <account>
    <username>john_doe</username>
    <email>john@example.com</email>
    <status>breached</status>
  </account>
```

```
<account>
   <username>alice_smith</username>
   <email>alice@example.com</email>
   <status>safe</status>
</account>
</breach>
```

2.2.4.2 Parsing XML in Python

Python's xml.etree.ElementTree module makes XML parsing easy.

```
import xml.etree.ElementTree as ET

xml_data = """
<breach>
   <account>
      <username>john_doe</username>
      <email>john@example.com</email>
      <status>breached</status>
   </account>
   <account>
      <username>alice_smith</username>
      <email>alice@example.com</email>
      <status>safe</status>
   </account>
</breach>
"""

# Parse XML
root = ET.fromstring(xml_data)

for account in root.findall("account"):
   username = account.find("username").text
   email = account.find("email").text
   status = account.find("status").text
   print(f"User: {username}, Email: {email}, Status: {status}")
```

✓ **Impact**: Extracts intelligence from XML threat feeds.

2.2.4.3 Writing XML Data

For exporting OSINT findings in XML format:

```
root = ET.Element("breach")

account1 = ET.SubElement(root, "account")
ET.SubElement(account1, "username").text = "john_doe"
ET.SubElement(account1, "email").text = "john@example.com"
ET.SubElement(account1, "status").text = "breached"

tree = ET.ElementTree(root)
tree.write("osint_results.xml")
```

✓ **Impact**: Enables structured data storage in XML.

2.2.5 Conclusion

Understanding JSON, CSV, and XML is critical for OSINT analysts working with automated tools and APIs. Mastering these formats allows for efficient data processing, storage, and exchange.

Key Takeaways:

✓ JSON is the most common format for OSINT APIs.

✓ CSV is useful for storing and analyzing OSINT reports.

✓ XML is often found in RSS feeds and forensic reports.

In the next section, we will explore web scraping techniques to extract OSINT data from websites using Python.

2.3 Using Regular Expressions for OSINT Data Extraction

Regular Expressions (RegEx) are powerful tools for pattern matching in text, making them essential for extracting key intelligence from unstructured data. In OSINT investigations, RegEx is used to identify emails, IP addresses, URLs, phone numbers, and other structured data hidden within web pages, logs, and documents. Python's built-in re module provides robust functionalities for working with RegEx efficiently.

2.3.1 Introduction to Regular Expressions

Regular expressions are sequences of characters that define search patterns. These patterns can be used to search, extract, and validate data.

RegEx Concept	Description	Example Pattern	Use Case
Literals	Exact character matching	`osint`	Finds the word "osint" in text
Character Classes	Match sets of characters	`[0-9]`	Finds any digit
Quantifiers	Define repetition	`\d+`	Matches one or more digits
Anchors	Specify position	`^Hello`	Matches "Hello" at the beginning of a line
Groups	Capture specific data	`` `(abc ``	`` def)` ``

2.3.2 Extracting Emails Using RegEx

Email addresses are a key intelligence target in OSINT, often found in breach dumps, phishing campaigns, and leaked documents.

2.3.2.1 Writing a RegEx for Emails

A typical email format follows the pattern: username@domain.com

RegEx Pattern:

[a-zA-Z0-9._%+-]+@[a-zA-Z0-9.-]+\.[a-zA-Z]{2,6}

2.3.2.2 Extracting Emails with Python

import re

text = "Contact us at info@osint-tools.com or support@security.net for more details."

 # Define the email pattern
email_pattern = r"[a-zA-Z0-9._%+-]+@[a-zA-Z0-9.-]+\.[a-zA-Z]{2,6}"

 # Find all matches

emails = re.findall(email_pattern, text)

print("Extracted Emails:", emails)

✅ **Impact**: Quickly extracts multiple emails from raw text.

2.3.3 Extracting IP Addresses

IP addresses appear in network logs, security reports, and cyber threat intelligence feeds.

2.3.3.1 Writing a RegEx for IPv4 Addresses

Pattern:

\b(?:[0-9]{1,3}\.){3}[0-9]{1,3}\b

This matches standard IPv4 addresses such as 192.168.1.1.

2.3.3.2 Extracting IPs with Python

text = "Suspicious activity detected from IPs: 192.168.1.100, 10.0.0.25, and 8.8.8.8."

 # Define the IP pattern
ip_pattern = r"\b(?:[0-9]{1,3}\.){3}[0-9]{1,3}\b"

 # Extract all IPs
ips = re.findall(ip_pattern, text)

print("Extracted IPs:", ips)

✅ **Impact**: Automates the extraction of IPs from security logs.

2.3.4 Extracting URLs from Text

OSINT analysts frequently need to extract URLs from reports, web pages, or chat logs.

2.3.4.1 Writing a RegEx for URLs

Pattern:

https?://[^\s]+

This captures URLs that start with http:// or https://.

2.3.4.2 Extracting URLs with Python

text = "Visit https://osint-toolkit.com or http://darkwebmonitoring.net for more details."

 # Define the URL pattern
url_pattern = r"https?://[^\s]+"

 # Extract URLs
urls = re.findall(url_pattern, text)

print("Extracted URLs:", urls)

✅ **Impact**: Automates the collection of links from OSINT sources.

2.3.5 Extracting Phone Numbers

Phone numbers appear in threat reports, leaked databases, and investigation files.

2.3.5.1 Writing a RegEx for Phone Numbers

A basic US phone number format: (123) 456-7890 or 123-456-7890

Pattern:

\(?\d{3}\)?[-.\s]?\d{3}[-.\s]?\d{4}

2.3.5.2 Extracting Phone Numbers with Python

text = "Call our support team at (123) 456-7890 or 987-654-3210."

 # Define the phone number pattern
phone_pattern = r"\(?\d{3}\)?[-.\s]?\d{3}[-.\s]?\d{4}"

 # Extract phone numbers
phone_numbers = re.findall(phone_pattern, text)

print("Extracted Phone Numbers:", phone_numbers)

✅ **Impact**: Automates phone number extraction from data leaks.

2.3.6 Extracting Custom Intelligence Patterns

2.3.6.1 Identifying Credit Card Numbers

Credit cards follow the 16-digit pattern.

Pattern:

\b(?:\d[-]?){13,16}\b*

This matches numbers like 4111 1111 1111 1111.

2.3.7 Using RegEx in OSINT Automation

Regular expressions are often combined with web scraping and API responses for real-world intelligence gathering.

Example: Extracting Data from a Web Page

```
import requests
import re

# Fetch webpage content
url = "https://pastebin.com/raw/sampleleak"
response = requests.get(url)

# Define patterns
email_pattern = r"[a-zA-Z0-9._%+-]+@[a-zA-Z0-9.-]+\.[a-zA-Z]{2,6}"
ip_pattern = r"\b(?:[0-9]{1,3}\.){3}[0-9]{1,3}\b"

# Extract data
emails = re.findall(email_pattern, response.text)
ips = re.findall(ip_pattern, response.text)

print("Extracted Emails:", emails)
print("Extracted IPs:", ips)
```

✅ **Impact**: Automatically extracts OSINT data from live sources.

2.3.8 Conclusion

Regular expressions are essential for automating data extraction in OSINT investigations. By leveraging Python's re module, analysts can efficiently retrieve intelligence from raw text, logs, and web pages.

Key Takeaways:

✅ Emails, IPs, URLs, and phone numbers can be extracted with RegEx.

✅ Python's re module makes pattern matching simple and powerful.

✅ Automating OSINT data extraction improves efficiency in investigations.

In the next section, we will apply these concepts to web scraping techniques using Python and BeautifulSoup.

2.4 Handling API Requests with Python

Application Programming Interfaces (APIs) play a critical role in OSINT investigations by providing structured data from web services, databases, and intelligence feeds. Whether querying domain information, extracting social media data, or retrieving cyber threat intelligence, handling API requests efficiently with Python is an essential skill for automation.

Python's requests module is the primary tool for interacting with APIs, allowing analysts to send HTTP requests, process JSON responses, and integrate multiple sources of intelligence seamlessly.

2.4.1 Understanding APIs in OSINT

APIs enable structured data retrieval without manually browsing websites. Many OSINT tools provide API access for intelligence gathering.

API Type	Use Case in OSINT	Example Service
WHOIS APIs	Domain and IP lookups	`whoisxmlapi.com`
Threat Intelligence APIs	Malicious IP & domain data	`VirusTotal API`
Social Media APIs	Extracting public posts & profiles	`Twitter/X API`
Geolocation APIs	Tracking locations from IPs	`ipinfo.io`
Dark Web APIs	Searching dark web marketplaces	`DarkOwl API`

Python makes it easy to query these APIs, automate data retrieval, and process responses.

2.4.2 Sending API Requests with Python

2.4.2.1 Making a Basic GET Request

A GET request retrieves data from a server.

import requests

 # Define API URL
url = "https://api.ipify.org?format=json"

 # Send GET request
response = requests.get(url)

 # Print response data
print(response.json())

✅ **Impact**: Automates IP lookups for OSINT tasks.

2.4.3 Handling API Responses

Most APIs return JSON data, which Python can parse easily.

2.4.3.1 Extracting Data from a JSON API Response

```
import requests

# Query an IP intelligence API
url = "https://ipinfo.io/8.8.8.8/json"
response = requests.get(url)

# Convert response to dictionary
data = response.json()

# Extract and display intelligence
print(f"IP: {data['ip']}")
print(f"City: {data['city']}")
print(f"Country: {data['country']}")
print(f"ISP: {data.get('org', 'Unknown')}")
```

✅ **Impact**: Quickly retrieves OSINT intelligence on an IP address.

2.4.4 Handling API Authentication

Some APIs require API keys for authentication.

2.4.4.1 Using an API Key in a Request

```
api_key = "your_api_key_here"
url = f"https://api.shodan.io/shodan/host/8.8.8.8?key={api_key}"

response = requests.get(url)
data = response.json()

print(f"Open Ports: {data['ports']}")
print(f"ISP: {data.get('isp', 'Unknown')}")
```

✅ **Impact**: Accesses restricted intelligence sources with API authentication.

2.4.5 Handling POST Requests

A POST request sends data to an API, often used for searching or submitting data.

2.4.5.1 Sending Data with a POST Request

```
url = "https://api.example.com/search"
payload = {"query": "threat intelligence"}
headers = {"Authorization": "Bearer your_api_key"}

response = requests.post(url, json=payload, headers=headers)

print(response.json())
```

✅ **Impact**: Automates advanced OSINT queries.

2.4.6 Error Handling in API Requests

APIs can fail due to invalid requests, rate limits, or server issues. Handling errors ensures smooth automation.

2.4.6.1 Handling API Errors in Python

```
try:
    response = requests.get("https://api.example.com/data")
    response.raise_for_status()  # Raises an error for bad responses
    data = response.json()
    print(data)
except requests.exceptions.HTTPError as err:
    print(f"HTTP Error: {err}")
except requests.exceptions.ConnectionError:
    print("Connection Error! Check your internet.")
except requests.exceptions.Timeout:
    print("Request Timeout! API is slow or down.")
except requests.exceptions.RequestException as err:
    print(f"API Request Failed: {err}")
```

✅ **Impact**: Prevents script crashes and ensures smooth OSINT automation.

2.4.7 Automating API Queries in OSINT

Example: Automating WHOIS Lookups

```
domains = ["example.com", "malicious-site.net"]
api_key = "your_api_key"
base_url = "https://api.whoisxmlapi.com/v1"
```

```
for domain in domains:
    response = requests.get(f"{base_url}?apiKey={api_key}&domain={domain}")
    data = response.json()

    print(f"Domain: {domain}, Registrar: {data.get('registrar', 'Unknown')}")
```

✅ **Impact**: Automates bulk domain intelligence gathering.

2.4.8 Conclusion

APIs are essential for OSINT automation, enabling analysts to retrieve structured data efficiently. Python's requests module simplifies handling API requests, authentication, and error management.

Key Takeaways:

✅ APIs provide structured intelligence for OSINT tasks.

✅ Python handles API authentication, GET/POST requests, and JSON responses.

✅ Error handling ensures reliable OSINT automation.

In the next section, we will explore web scraping techniques using Python and BeautifulSoup to gather intelligence from websites.

2.5 Automating Data Collection & Storage

Efficient OSINT operations require not only extracting intelligence from multiple sources but also storing and organizing it for analysis. Automation plays a key role in reducing manual effort, ensuring data consistency, and enabling real-time intelligence gathering. This section explores techniques to automate data collection from APIs, web scraping, and open sources, followed by methods for structured storage using databases and file formats like JSON, CSV, and SQLite.

2.5.1 The Need for Automated Data Collection

Manual intelligence gathering is time-consuming and prone to errors. Automating OSINT collection has several benefits:

✅ Faster Processing: Automates repetitive data retrieval.

✅ Consistency: Reduces human error and ensures standardized formats.

✅ Scalability: Enables collection from multiple sources simultaneously.

✅ Real-time Updates: Ensures intelligence is always up to date.

Common OSINT Data Sources

Source	Automation Method	Example Use Case
APIs	Python `requests`	WHOIS lookups, IP tracking
Web Scraping	BeautifulSoup, Selenium	Extracting social media profiles
Dark Web	Tor network scraping	Monitoring illicit marketplaces
Threat Feeds	CSV, JSON, RSS	Cyber threat intelligence
Government Databases	Open data portals	Company or tax records

2.5.2 Automating Data Retrieval

2.5.2.1 Collecting Data from APIs

Python's requests module simplifies API automation.

```
import requests

# Example: Automating IP lookup
api_url = "https://ipinfo.io/8.8.8.8/json"
response = requests.get(api_url)

if response.status_code == 200:
    data = response.json()
    print(f"IP: {data['ip']}, Location: {data['city']}, {data['country']}")
else:
    print("Failed to retrieve data")
```

✅ **Impact**: Automates OSINT queries from structured sources.

2.5.2.2 Automating Web Scraping

Web scraping helps extract intelligence from websites when APIs are unavailable.

```
import requests
from bs4 import BeautifulSoup

# Example: Scraping headlines from a news site
url = "https://example.com/news"
response = requests.get(url)
soup = BeautifulSoup(response.text, "html.parser")

# Extract headlines
headlines = soup.find_all("h2")
for h in headlines:
    print(h.text.strip())
```

✅ **Impact**: Extracts intelligence when API access is restricted.

2.5.3 Automating Data Storage

Once OSINT data is collected, it must be stored efficiently for further analysis.

2.5.3.1 Saving Data in JSON Format

JSON is useful for storing structured OSINT data from APIs.

```
import json

data = {
    "domain": "example.com",
    "ip": "192.168.1.1",
    "registrar": "NameCheap"
}

with open("osint_data.json", "w") as file:
    json.dump(data, file, indent=4)
```

✅ **Impact**: JSON allows easy integration with OSINT dashboards and tools.

2.5.3.2 Saving Data in CSV Format

CSV is useful for tabular OSINT data like domain lists or threat feeds.

```
import csv

data = [
    ["IP", "Country", "Threat Level"],
    ["8.8.8.8", "US", "Low"],
    ["192.168.1.1", "Unknown", "High"]
]

with open("osint_report.csv", "w", newline="") as file:
    writer = csv.writer(file)
    writer.writerows(data)
```

✅ **Impact**: CSV enables easy import into spreadsheets and security tools.

2.5.3.3 Storing Data in SQLite Database

For large OSINT datasets, a database like SQLite is more efficient.

```
import sqlite3

# Connect to database (or create if it doesn't exist)
conn = sqlite3.connect("osint_data.db")
cursor = conn.cursor()

# Create table
cursor.execute("""
CREATE TABLE IF NOT EXISTS osint (
    id INTEGER PRIMARY KEY,
    domain TEXT,
    ip TEXT,
    country TEXT
)
""")
```

```
# Insert sample data
cursor.execute("INSERT INTO osint (domain, ip, country) VALUES (?, ?, ?)",
        ("example.com", "8.8.8.8", "US"))

conn.commit()
conn.close()
```

✅ **Impact**: Databases allow querying and managing large-scale intelligence data.

2.5.4 Automating Data Collection & Storage in a Pipeline

A complete OSINT automation pipeline integrates data retrieval, processing, and storage.

Example: Automating an Intelligence Gathering Workflow

```
import requests
import sqlite3

# 1. Fetch data from API
api_url = "https://ipinfo.io/8.8.8.8/json"
response = requests.get(api_url)
data = response.json()

# 2. Store data in SQLite database
conn = sqlite3.connect("osint_data.db")
cursor = conn.cursor()

cursor.execute("""
CREATE TABLE IF NOT EXISTS ip_intelligence (
    id INTEGER PRIMARY KEY,
    ip TEXT,
    city TEXT,
    country TEXT,
    isp TEXT
)
""")

cursor.execute("INSERT INTO ip_intelligence (ip, city, country, isp) VALUES (?, ?, ?,
?)",
        (data["ip"], data["city"], data["country"], data.get("org", "Unknown")))
```

```
conn.commit()
conn.close()

print("OSINT data stored successfully!")
```

✅ **Impact**: Fully automates OSINT intelligence gathering and storage.

2.5.5 Conclusion

Automating OSINT data collection and storage enhances efficiency and scalability in intelligence operations. Python provides powerful tools to retrieve, process, and store data from APIs, websites, and open sources.

Key Takeaways:

✅ APIs, web scraping, and threat feeds can be automated for intelligence gathering.

✅ Data should be structured using JSON, CSV, or databases for easy analysis.

✅ Automating OSINT pipelines ensures real-time data collection and storage.

In the next section, we will explore web scraping with Python & BeautifulSoup to gather intelligence from websites.

2.6 Best Practices for Writing OSINT Scripts

Writing efficient and reliable OSINT scripts is crucial for scalability, accuracy, and security in intelligence gathering. Poorly written scripts can lead to incomplete data, API bans, or even legal issues. In this section, we will cover best practices for writing clean, optimized, and ethical OSINT scripts.

2.6.1 Structuring Your OSINT Scripts

A well-structured script improves maintainability, readability, and debugging. Follow these guidelines:

✅ **Use Functions & Modular Code**: Break down scripts into reusable functions.
✅ **Follow PEP 8 Guidelines**: Maintain clean and readable Python code.

✅ **Use Configuration Files**: Store API keys and settings separately.

✅ **Implement Logging & Error Handling**: Capture errors instead of crashing.

Example: Structuring a Simple OSINT Script

```python
import requests
import json

# Function to fetch IP details
def fetch_ip_details(ip):
    url = f"https://ipinfo.io/{ip}/json"
    response = requests.get(url)

    if response.status_code == 200:
        return response.json()
    else:
        return {"error": "Failed to retrieve data"}

# Main function
def main():
    ip = "8.8.8.8"
    data = fetch_ip_details(ip)

    print(json.dumps(data, indent=4))

if __name__ == "__main__":
    main()
```

✅ **Impact**: Organized, reusable, and easy-to-maintain code.

2.6.2 Efficient API Usage

Many OSINT scripts rely on APIs for intelligence gathering. Follow these best practices:

✅ **Respect API Rate Limits**: Check documentation and implement delays if needed.

✅ **Use API Keys** Securely: Never hardcode API keys in scripts.

✅ **Handle API Errors Gracefully**: Avoid crashes when APIs fail.

Example: Handling API Rate Limits

```
import time
import requests

api_key = "your_api_key"
ips = ["8.8.8.8", "1.1.1.1"]

for ip in ips:
    response = requests.get(f"https://ipinfo.io/{ip}/json?token={api_key}")

    if response.status_code == 429:  # Too many requests
        print("Rate limit reached! Waiting before retrying...")
        time.sleep(5)  # Wait before retrying

    print(response.json())
```

☑ **Impact**: Prevents bans and ensures stable API access.

2.6.3 Handling Web Scraping Responsibly

If APIs are unavailable, web scraping may be required. Follow ethical scraping guidelines:

☑ **Respect Robots.txt**: Some websites prohibit automated access.
☑ **Use Headers & User Agents**: Prevent detection and blocking.
☑ **Implement Rate Limiting**: Avoid overloading servers.
☑ **Use Proxies for Anonymity**: Protect your identity when necessary.

Example: Scraping Responsibly with Headers & Delay

```
import requests
from bs4 import BeautifulSoup
import time

url = "https://example.com/news"
headers = {"User-Agent": "Mozilla/5.0"}

response = requests.get(url, headers=headers)
time.sleep(2)  # Respectful delay

soup = BeautifulSoup(response.text, "html.parser")
headlines = soup.find_all("h2")
```

```
for h in headlines:
    print(h.text.strip())
```

✅ **Impact**: Reduces chances of detection and blocking.

2.6.4 Secure Storage & Handling of Sensitive Data

OSINT investigations often involve sensitive intelligence that must be stored securely.

✅ **Never Store API Keys in Scripts**: Use environment variables or config files.
✅ **Encrypt Sensitive Data**: Use encryption for databases and logs.
✅ **Sanitize Input Data**: Prevent SQL injection and security vulnerabilities.

Example: Using Environment Variables for API Keys

```
import os
from dotenv import load_dotenv

load_dotenv()  # Load .env file

api_key = os.getenv("API_KEY")
print(f"Using API Key: {api_key}")
```

✅ **Impact**: Protects credentials from leaks and unauthorized access.

2.6.5 Logging & Error Handling

✅ Use Logging Instead of Print Statements

✅ Handle Exceptions Properly

✅ Store Errors for Debugging

Example: Implementing Logging in an OSINT Script

```
import logging

# Configure logging
```

```
logging.basicConfig(filename="osint.log", level=logging.INFO, format="%(asctime)s -
%(levelname)s - %(message)s")

try:
    # Simulating API call
    response_code = 500
    if response_code != 200:
        raise Exception("API request failed")
except Exception as e:
    logging.error(f"Error occurred: {e}")
```

✅ **Impact**: Helps track failures for troubleshooting.

2.6.6 Automating Data Storage & Retrieval

Ensure collected OSINT data is stored efficiently and securely.

✅ Use Databases for Large-Scale Data

✅ Structure Data for Quick Retrieval

✅ Automate Backups & Data Retention

Example: Automating Data Insertion into SQLite

```
import sqlite3

# Connect to database
conn = sqlite3.connect("osint_data.db")
cursor = conn.cursor()

# Create table if it doesn't exist
cursor.execute("""
CREATE TABLE IF NOT EXISTS ip_data (
    id INTEGER PRIMARY KEY,
    ip TEXT,
    country TEXT
)
""")

# Insert sample data
```

```
cursor.execute("INSERT INTO ip_data (ip, country) VALUES (?, ?)", ("8.8.8.8", "US"))

conn.commit()
conn.close()
```

✅ **Impact**: Organizes OSINT data for long-term intelligence use.

2.6.7 Ethical & Legal Considerations

OSINT analysts must follow ethical guidelines and legal regulations:

✅ **Respect Privacy Laws (GDPR, CCPA):** Do not collect personal data illegally.

✅ **Avoid Hacking & Unauthorized Access**: Only use publicly available data.

✅ **Do Not Spread Disinformation**: Verify intelligence before reporting.

Example: Checking if a Site Allows Scraping

```
import requests

url = "https://example.com/robots.txt"
response = requests.get(url)

if "Disallow" in response.text:
    print("Scraping is restricted on this website.")
```

✅ **Impact**: Ensures compliance with ethical OSINT practices.

2.6.8 Conclusion

By following best practices, OSINT scripts become efficient, secure, and scalable.

Key Takeaways:

✅ Write modular and structured code for better maintainability.

✅ Use logging and error handling to avoid script failures.

✅ Follow ethical and legal guidelines when collecting intelligence.

✅ Store OSINT data securely using encryption and databases.

In the next section, we will explore web scraping with Python & BeautifulSoup for intelligence gathering.

3. Web Scraping with Python & BeautifulSoup

In this chapter, we explore the powerful technique of web scraping, which allows OSINT analysts to extract valuable data from websites automatically. Using Python and the BeautifulSoup library, we'll walk through the process of navigating HTML structures, locating key information, and pulling that data into a structured format for analysis. You'll learn how to handle common challenges such as dealing with dynamic content, managing request headers, and avoiding scraping pitfalls like rate-limiting or IP blocking. By the end of this chapter, you'll have the skills to harness the power of web scraping to collect real-time information from the web, making your OSINT automation workflows faster and more effective.

3.1 Introduction to Web Scraping & Legal Implications

Web scraping is a powerful technique for automating data extraction from websites. OSINT analysts use it to gather intelligence from news sites, social media, government portals, and the dark web. However, while scraping can provide valuable insights, it also comes with legal and ethical considerations that must be carefully navigated.

3.1.1 What is Web Scraping?

Web scraping is the process of automatically extracting data from web pages. Unlike APIs, which provide structured access to data, scraping allows OSINT analysts to collect information from sites that do not offer official data feeds.

How Web Scraping Works

- **Send a Request** – The scraper requests a webpage's HTML using Python's requests library.
- **Parse the HTML** – The scraper extracts specific data using BeautifulSoup or lxml.
- **Store the Data** – Extracted data is saved in formats like JSON, CSV, or databases.

Example Use Cases in OSINT

Use Case	Example Data Collected
Monitoring News	Headlines, articles, metadata
Tracking Social Media	Usernames, posts, comments
Company Investigations	Business records, addresses
Dark Web Monitoring	Marketplace listings, forum posts

3.1.2 Ethical Considerations in Web Scraping

Before scraping a website, OSINT analysts must follow ethical guidelines:

✅ **Respect Robots.txt** – Websites define scraping rules in their robots.txt file.
✅ **Avoid Overloading Servers** – Too many requests in a short time may disrupt a site's operations.
✅ **Do Not Bypass Security Measures** – Circumventing CAPTCHAs, authentication, or firewalls is illegal.
✅ **Use Data Responsibly** – Do not misuse collected data for unethical purposes.

Checking Robots.txt Before Scraping

```
import requests

url = "https://example.com/robots.txt"
response = requests.get(url)

print(response.text)  # Shows scraping rules
```

✅ **Impact**: Ensures compliance with website policies.

3.1.3 Legal Implications of Web Scraping

Web scraping laws vary across jurisdictions. Analysts must be aware of legal risks and regulations:

Key Legal Considerations

Law/Regulation	Implication for Web Scraping
Computer Fraud & Abuse Act (CFAA) (USA)	Unauthorized access can lead to legal consequences.
General Data Protection Regulation (GDPR) (EU)	Personal data collection requires consent.
Digital Millennium Copyright Act (DMCA)	Copying copyrighted content may violate laws.
Terms of Service (ToS)	Scraping against ToS may result in bans or lawsuits.

Case Study: LinkedIn vs. HiQ Labs

In HiQ Labs v. LinkedIn, LinkedIn sued HiQ Labs for scraping public profiles. Courts ruled that scraping public data does not violate the CFAA but still violates LinkedIn's ToS.

3.1.4 How to Legally & Ethically Scrape Websites

To minimize legal risks, follow these best practices:

✓ Scrape Publicly Available Data Only

✓ Check Website Terms of Service (ToS)

✓ Implement Rate Limiting to Avoid Server Overload

✓ Anonymize Requests When Necessary

Example: Scraping with Rate Limiting

```
import requests
from bs4 import BeautifulSoup
import time

url = "https://example.com/news"
headers = {"User-Agent": "Mozilla/5.0"}

response = requests.get(url, headers=headers)
soup = BeautifulSoup(response.text, "html.parser")

articles = soup.find_all("h2")
```

```
for article in articles:
    print(article.text.strip())
    time.sleep(2)  # Respectful delay
```

✓ **Impact**: Reduces detection risk and prevents server overload.

3.1.5 Conclusion

Web scraping is a valuable OSINT tool, but analysts must follow ethical and legal guidelines. Before scraping a site, always check its policies, avoid collecting personal data without consent, and respect rate limits.

Key Takeaways:

✓ Web scraping allows OSINT analysts to collect intelligence from websites.

✓ Ethical considerations include respecting robots.txt, avoiding overloading servers, and using data responsibly.

✓ Legal risks depend on jurisdiction, and scraping private data without permission may violate laws.

3.2 Setting Up BeautifulSoup & Scrapy for OSINT

Web scraping is a critical skill for OSINT analysts, allowing them to automate the collection of valuable intelligence from websites. Two of the most powerful Python libraries for web scraping are BeautifulSoup and Scrapy. In this section, we'll cover how to set up these tools, their differences, and how to use them effectively in OSINT investigations.

3.2.1 Choosing Between BeautifulSoup & Scrapy

Both BeautifulSoup and Scrapy serve different purposes in web scraping. Here's a comparison:

Feature	BeautifulSoup	Scrapy
Best For	Small-scale, static pages	Large-scale, dynamic sites
Ease of Use	Simple & easy to learn	More complex but powerful
Speed	Slower (relies on `requests`)	Faster (asynchronous)
Built-in Crawler	No (needs `requests` or `selenium`)	Yes
Handling JavaScript	No (needs `selenium`)	No (needs `scrapy-splash`)

When to Use Each Tool

- Use BeautifulSoup for quick extractions from simple, static websites.
- Use Scrapy when scraping multiple pages, large datasets, or complex websites.

3.2.2 Installing BeautifulSoup & Scrapy

Before using these tools, install the required libraries.

Installing BeautifulSoup & Requests

pip install beautifulsoup4 requests lxml

Installing Scrapy

pip install scrapy

After installation, verify by running:

python -c "import bs4, scrapy; print('Libraries installed successfully!')"

3.2.3 Setting Up BeautifulSoup for Web Scraping

Fetching & Parsing HTML with BeautifulSoup

import requests
from bs4 import BeautifulSoup

```
# Define target URL
url = "https://example.com/news"
headers = {"User-Agent": "Mozilla/5.0"}

# Fetch webpage content
response = requests.get(url, headers=headers)
soup = BeautifulSoup(response.text, "html.parser")

# Extract headlines
headlines = soup.find_all("h2")

for h in headlines:
    print(h.text.strip())
```

Key Features of BeautifulSoup

✓ Parses HTML & XML easily

✓ Allows searching with .find() & .find_all()

✓ Supports CSS selectors with .select()

3.2.4 Setting Up Scrapy for Large-Scale Scraping

Creating a Scrapy Project

1⬜ Generate a new Scrapy project

scrapy startproject osint_scraper

2⬜ Navigate to the project folder

cd osint_scraper

3⬜ Create a new Scrapy spider

scrapy genspider example example.com

This creates a spiders folder with a new Python script for the spider.

Writing a Scrapy Spider

Open example.py inside osint_scraper/spiders/ and modify the spider:

```
import scrapy

class ExampleSpider(scrapy.Spider):
    name = "example"
    start_urls = ["https://example.com/news"]

    def parse(self, response):
        for article in response.css("h2"):
            yield {"headline": article.css("::text").get()}
```

Running the Scraper

Execute the spider with:

```
scrapy crawl example -o results.json
```

✅ **Impact**: Scrapy extracts and stores data faster than BeautifulSoup.

3.2.5 Handling JavaScript-Rendered Pages

Some sites load content dynamically using JavaScript, making traditional scraping ineffective. Solutions:

- Use Selenium for Browser Automation
- Use Scrapy-Splash for JavaScript Execution

Using Selenium with BeautifulSoup

```
pip install selenium webdriver-manager

from selenium import webdriver
from bs4 import BeautifulSoup
from webdriver_manager.chrome import ChromeDriverManager

# Set up Selenium
options = webdriver.ChromeOptions()
```

```
options.add_argument("--headless")
driver = webdriver.Chrome(ChromeDriverManager().install(), options=options)

# Load the page
driver.get("https://example.com/dynamic-content")

# Parse HTML with BeautifulSoup
soup = BeautifulSoup(driver.page_source, "html.parser")

print(soup.text)
```

✅ **Impact**: Allows scraping JavaScript-heavy sites.

3.2.6 Conclusion

BeautifulSoup is great for quick, lightweight scrapers, while Scrapy excels at large-scale crawling. For JavaScript-heavy pages, Selenium or Scrapy-Splash is required.

Key Takeaways

✅ Use BeautifulSoup for small-scale scraping

✅ Use Scrapy for large-scale automation

✅ Use Selenium for JavaScript-heavy pages

3.3 Extracting Data from Public Websites

Extracting data from public websites is a fundamental OSINT technique that enables analysts to gather intelligence from news sites, social media, business directories, and government portals. This section explores how to extract structured and unstructured data using BeautifulSoup and Scrapy, including methods for handling HTML elements, dealing with pagination, and exporting collected data for further analysis.

3.3.1 Understanding HTML Structure for Data Extraction

Before scraping a website, it's crucial to understand its HTML structure. Every web page consists of elements such as:

- **\<div\>** – Used for containers
- **\<h1\>, \<h2\>, etc**. – Headings
- **\<p\>** – Paragraph text
- **\<a\>** – Links
- **\<table\>** – Tabular data

Example HTML Code from a Public Website

```
<div class="news-article">
   <h2>Breaking News: Cyber Threats on the Rise</h2>
   <p>Published: <span class="date">Feb 22, 2025</span></p>
   <a href="https://example.com/news/article1">Read more</a>
</div>
```

To extract information, we need to identify the relevant HTML tags and classes.

3.3.2 Extracting Data Using BeautifulSoup

Installing Required Libraries

```
pip install beautifulsoup4 requests lxml
```

Extracting News Articles from a Website

```
import requests
from bs4 import BeautifulSoup

# Define the target website
url = "https://example.com/news"
headers = {"User-Agent": "Mozilla/5.0"}

# Fetch the HTML content
response = requests.get(url, headers=headers)
soup = BeautifulSoup(response.text, "html.parser")

# Extract news articles
articles = soup.find_all("div", class_="news-article")

for article in articles:
    headline = article.find("h2").text.strip()
```

```
date = article.find("span", class_="date").text.strip()
link = article.find("a")["href"]

print(f"Title: {headline}\nDate: {date}\nLink: {link}\n")
```

✅ **Impact**: This script extracts headlines, dates, and links from the target website.

3.3.3 Extracting Data Using Scrapy

For large-scale scraping, Scrapy is more efficient than BeautifulSoup.

Creating a Scrapy Project

```
scrapy startproject osint_scraper
cd osint_scraper
scrapy genspider news example.com
```

Writing the Scrapy Spider

Edit news.py inside spiders/:

```
import scrapy

class NewsSpider(scrapy.Spider):
    name = "news"
    start_urls = ["https://example.com/news"]

    def parse(self, response):
        for article in response.css("div.news-article"):
            yield {
                "headline": article.css("h2::text").get(),
                "date": article.css("span.date::text").get(),
                "link": article.css("a::attr(href)").get()
            }
```

Running the Scraper

```
scrapy crawl news -o results.json
```

✅ **Impact**: Extracts structured news data efficiently and saves it in a JSON file.

3.3.4 Handling Pagination in Web Scraping

Many websites display data across multiple pages (e.g., page 1, page 2, etc.). To extract all data, we must handle pagination.

Example of a Paginated URL Structure

https://example.com/news?page=1
https://example.com/news?page=2

...

Scraping Multiple Pages with BeautifulSoup

```
for page in range(1, 6):  # Scrape first 5 pages
    url = f"https://example.com/news?page={page}"
    response = requests.get(url, headers=headers)
    soup = BeautifulSoup(response.text, "html.parser")

    articles = soup.find_all("div", class_="news-article")
    for article in articles:
        print(article.find("h2").text.strip())
```

✓ **Impact**: Extracts data from multiple pages automatically.

Scraping Multiple Pages with Scrapy

Modify the parse function in Scrapy:

```
def parse(self, response):
    for article in response.css("div.news-article"):
        yield {
            "headline": article.css("h2::text").get(),
            "date": article.css("span.date::text").get(),
            "link": article.css("a::attr(href)").get()
        }

    # Follow the "Next Page" link
    next_page = response.css("a.next::attr(href)").get()
    if next_page:
```

yield response.follow(next_page, self.parse)

✓ **Impact**: Scrapy automatically follows next-page links.

3.3.5 Exporting Extracted Data

Saving Data as CSV

With BeautifulSoup:

```
import csv

with open("news_data.csv", "w", newline="", encoding="utf-8") as file:
    writer = csv.writer(file)
    writer.writerow(["Headline", "Date", "Link"])

    for article in articles:
        writer.writerow([article.find("h2").text.strip(),
                    article.find("span", class_="date").text.strip(),
                    article.find("a")["href"]])
```

With Scrapy:

scrapy crawl news -o news_data.csv

✓ **Impact**: Data is structured and ready for analysis.

3.3.6 Conclusion

Extracting data from public websites is a crucial OSINT skill. BeautifulSoup is best for small projects, while Scrapy is ideal for large-scale data extraction. Analysts must also handle pagination and export data in usable formats like CSV or JSON.

Key Takeaways:

✓ Understand HTML structure before scraping

✓ Use BeautifulSoup for small-scale extractions

✓ Use Scrapy for large-scale and automated extractions

✅ Handle pagination to extract full datasets

✅ Export data to CSV or JSON for analysis

3.4 Handling Dynamic Content with Selenium

Many websites rely on JavaScript to load content dynamically, meaning traditional web scraping methods using requests and BeautifulSoup won't work. In these cases, Selenium—a browser automation tool—enables OSINT analysts to interact with and extract content from JavaScript-heavy websites. This section covers setting up Selenium, handling dynamic elements, and automating browsing for intelligence gathering.

3.4.1 Why Use Selenium for OSINT?

Selenium is useful when dealing with:

✅ **JavaScript-rendered content** (e.g., social media feeds, stock data)
✅ **Websites requiring interactions** (e.g., login, search bars, clicking buttons)
✅ **Infinite scrolling pages** (e.g., Twitter, LinkedIn)
✅ **Sites blocking traditional scrapers** (Selenium mimics human browsing)

However, Selenium is slower than Scrapy or BeautifulSoup and should be used only when necessary.

3.4.2 Setting Up Selenium

Install Selenium and WebDriver Manager

pip install selenium webdriver-manager

Selenium requires a web driver to automate a browser. The recommended approach is using webdriver-manager to automatically install and update the correct driver.

Launching a Headless Browser

A headless browser runs without a visible window, making it ideal for automated scraping.

from selenium import webdriver

```
from webdriver_manager.chrome import ChromeDriverManager

options = webdriver.ChromeOptions()
options.add_argument("--headless")  # Run without opening a window

driver = webdriver.Chrome(ChromeDriverManager().install(), options=options)

driver.get("https://example.com")
print(driver.title)  # Get page title

driver.quit()
```

✅ **Impact**: Allows automated browsing without a visible browser window.

3.4.3 Extracting Dynamic Content

Example: Scraping JavaScript-Rendered News Headlines

```
from selenium import webdriver
from selenium.webdriver.common.by import By
from webdriver_manager.chrome import ChromeDriverManager

options = webdriver.ChromeOptions()
options.add_argument("--headless")

driver = webdriver.Chrome(ChromeDriverManager().install(), options=options)
driver.get("https://example.com/news")

# Extract headlines using XPath
headlines = driver.find_elements(By.XPATH, "//h2")

for headline in headlines:
    print(headline.text)

driver.quit()
```

✅ **Impact**: Extracts JavaScript-generated headlines that BeautifulSoup would miss.

3.4.4 Interacting with Web Elements

Selenium allows analysts to simulate user actions such as:

- Clicking buttons
- Filling out forms
- Scrolling pages

Example: Automating a Search Query

```
from selenium.webdriver.common.keys import Keys

driver.get("https://example.com/search")

search_box = driver.find_element(By.NAME, "q")  # Find search bar
search_box.send_keys("cybersecurity news")
search_box.send_keys(Keys.RETURN)  # Press Enter

results = driver.find_elements(By.CLASS_NAME, "result")

for result in results:
    print(result.text)

driver.quit()
```

✓ **Impact**: Automates searching for intelligence on a website.

3.4.5 Handling Infinite Scrolling

Websites like Twitter, Facebook, and LinkedIn load new content when the user scrolls. Selenium can simulate scrolling to extract more data.

Example: Scrolling to Load More Tweets

```
import time

driver.get("https://twitter.com/explore")

last_height = driver.execute_script("return document.body.scrollHeight")

while True:
    driver.execute_script("window.scrollTo(0, document.body.scrollHeight);")
```

```
time.sleep(2)  # Wait for new content to load

new_height = driver.execute_script("return document.body.scrollHeight")
if new_height == last_height:  # Stop if no new content loads
    break
last_height = new_height


tweets = driver.find_elements(By.CSS_SELECTOR, "article div span")
for tweet in tweets:
    print(tweet.text)


driver.quit()
```

✅ **Impact**: Extracts all tweets from a feed, even those loaded dynamically.

3.4.6 Logging into Websites with Selenium

Some intelligence gathering requires accessing authenticated content. Selenium can log into websites by entering credentials automatically.

Example: Logging into a Website

```
driver.get("https://example.com/login")

username = driver.find_element(By.NAME, "username")
password = driver.find_element(By.NAME, "password")

username.send_keys("your_username")
password.send_keys("your_password")
password.send_keys(Keys.RETURN)  # Submit login form

print("Logged in successfully!")
```

✅ **Impact**: Enables OSINT analysts to access protected content legally.

⚠️ **Ethical Note**: Always follow legal guidelines and the site's Terms of Service.

3.4.7 Exporting Extracted Data

After extracting dynamic content, store it for analysis.

Example: Saving Data to a CSV File

```
import csv

data = [["Headline", "URL"], ["Cyber Threats Rising", "https://example.com"]]

with open("scraped_data.csv", "w", newline="", encoding="utf-8") as file:
    writer = csv.writer(file)
    writer.writerows(data)

print("Data saved successfully!")
```

✅ **Impact**: Saves extracted OSINT data for further investigation.

3.4.8 Conclusion

Selenium is a powerful tool for handling JavaScript-heavy websites, automating browsing, and interacting with web elements. However, it should be used strategically due to its slower performance compared to Scrapy or BeautifulSoup.

Key Takeaways

✅ Use Selenium when traditional scrapers fail (JavaScript-heavy sites)

✅ Automate interactions like searching, logging in, and clicking buttons

✅ Simulate scrolling for infinite-scrolling pages

✅ Extract and export OSINT data for intelligence analysis

In the next section, we'll explore automating Google Dorking and search engine queries for OSINT investigations.

3.5 Avoiding Detection & Bypassing Anti-Scraping Measures

Many websites employ anti-scraping mechanisms to detect and block automated data collection. These protections include CAPTCHAs, IP blocking, user-agent detection, and bot behavior analysis. OSINT analysts must ethically and legally navigate these defenses to gather intelligence efficiently. This section covers techniques for avoiding detection while adhering to ethical guidelines.

3.5.1 Common Anti-Scraping Techniques

Websites use several methods to detect and prevent automated access:

- **IP Blocking**: If too many requests come from the same IP, it gets banned.
- **User-Agent Detection**: Websites block browsers with missing or unusual headers.
- **CAPTCHAs**: Requiring human verification to block bots.
- **JavaScript Challenges**: Some sites serve content only to browsers running JavaScript.
- **Rate-Limiting**: Restricts how often a user can request data.
- **Honeypots**: Fake elements on pages that only bots interact with, triggering bans.

Understanding these mechanisms allows analysts to circumvent detection responsibly.

3.5.2 Rotating User-Agents & Headers

Every browser sends a User-Agent string identifying itself. Some websites block scrapers with missing or suspicious headers.

Example: Sending a Fake User-Agent with Requests

```
import requests

headers = {
    "User-Agent": "Mozilla/5.0 (Windows NT 10.0; Win64; x64) AppleWebKit/537.36 (KHTML, like Gecko) Chrome/120.0.0.0 Safari/537.36",
    "Referer": "https://google.com",
}

url = "https://example.com"
response = requests.get(url, headers=headers)

print(response.status_code)  # Should return 200 if successful
```

✅ **Impact**: Makes the scraper appear as a normal browser request.

Rotating User-Agents Randomly

from fake_useragent import UserAgent

ua = UserAgent()
headers = {"User-Agent": ua.random}

response = requests.get(url, headers=headers)

☑ **Impact**: Changes the User-Agent on each request to avoid detection.

3.5.3 Using Proxies to Avoid IP Blocking

A proxy hides your real IP address by routing requests through different servers.

Free vs. Paid Proxies

- ◆ **Free proxies** – Often unreliable and slow
- ◆ **Paid proxies** – More stable, better anonymity
- ◆ **Residential proxies** – Appear as real users (best for OSINT)

Using a Proxy with Requests

proxies = {
    "http": "http://username:password@proxyserver.com:8080",
    "https": "https://username:password@proxyserver.com:8080",
}

response = requests.get(url, proxies=proxies)

☑ **Impact**: Prevents websites from tracking and banning your real IP.

Rotating Proxies Automatically

import random

proxy_list = ["http://proxy1.com:8080", "http://proxy2.com:8080"]
proxy = {"http": random.choice(proxy_list)}

response = requests.get(url, proxies=proxy)

✅ **Impact**: Uses a different IP for each request, avoiding bans.

3.5.4 Slowing Down Requests (Throttling)

Sending too many requests too quickly can trigger rate-limiting. Introducing delays makes scraping appear more human-like.

Example: Adding Random Delays

```
import time
import random

for i in range(10):
    response = requests.get(url)
    time.sleep(random.uniform(1, 5))  # Wait 1-5 seconds before next request
```

✅ **Impact**: Mimics human browsing behavior, reducing detection risks.

3.5.5 Handling CAPTCHAs

Many websites use CAPTCHAs to prevent bots from scraping.

Types of CAPTCHAs:

✅ reCAPTCHA (Google)

✅ hCaptcha

✅ Text/Number-based challenges

✅ Image-selection CAPTCHAs

Bypassing CAPTCHAs with OCR (Tesseract)

```
import pytesseract
from PIL import Image

image = Image.open("captcha.png")
text = pytesseract.image_to_string(image)
```

```
print("Captcha Text:", text)
```

✓ **Impact**: Automates solving text-based CAPTCHAs.

Using CAPTCHA-Solving Services (2Captcha, Anti-Captcha, etc.)

```
import requests

api_key = "your_2captcha_api_key"
captcha_url = "https://example.com/captcha.jpg"

# Send CAPTCHA to solving service
response = requests.post(
    "http://2captcha.com/in.php",
    data={"key": api_key, "method": "base64", "body": captcha_url}
)

print(response.text)  # Returns solved CAPTCHA text
```

✓ **Impact**: Outsources CAPTCHA-solving to third-party services.

3.5.6 Using Headless Browsers (Stealth Mode)

Some websites block scrapers by detecting headless browsers like Selenium.

Making Selenium More Human-Like

```
from selenium import webdriver
from selenium.webdriver.chrome.service import Service
from webdriver_manager.chrome import ChromeDriverManager

options = webdriver.ChromeOptions()
options.add_argument("--headless")  # Run in the background
options.add_argument("--disable-blink-features=AutomationControlled")

driver = webdriver.Chrome(service=Service(ChromeDriverManager().install()),
options=options)
driver.get("https://example.com")

print(driver.title)  # Get page title
```

✅ **Impact**: Reduces the chance of Selenium being detected.

3.5.7 Avoiding Honeypots (Bot Traps)

Some websites place hidden links or fake elements that only bots interact with. Clicking them results in an instant ban.

Example: Detecting Hidden Elements

```
elements = driver.find_elements(By.XPATH, "//a")

for element in elements:
    if element.is_displayed():
        print(element.text)
```

✅ **Impact**: Prevents interacting with fake elements.

3.5.8 Using Scrapy's Built-In Anti-Ban Features

Scrapy provides middlewares for user-agent rotation, proxy handling, and auto-retries.

Enable AutoThrottle in settings.py

```
AUTOTHROTTLE_ENABLED = True
AUTOTHROTTLE_START_DELAY = 1
AUTOTHROTTLE_MAX_DELAY = 5
AUTOTHROTTLE_TARGET_CONCURRENCY = 1.0
```

✅ **Impact**: Dynamically adjusts request speed to avoid bans.

Enable Proxy Middleware

```
DOWNLOADER_MIDDLEWARES = {
    "scrapy.downloadermiddlewares.httpproxy.HttpProxyMiddleware": 1,
    "scrapy_proxies.RandomProxy": 100,
}
```

✅ **Impact**: Scrapy rotates proxies automatically.

3.5.9 Conclusion

Avoiding detection is a critical skill for OSINT analysts. Using proxies, user-agent rotation, request throttling, and CAPTCHA-solving techniques, analysts can ethically and effectively collect intelligence without being blocked.

Key Takeaways:

✓ Rotate User-Agents & Headers to avoid detection

✓ Use Proxies to prevent IP bans

✓ Throttle Requests to mimic human browsing

✓ Handle CAPTCHAs using OCR or third-party services

✓ Use Headless Browsers with Stealth Techniques

✓ Avoid Honeypots and Hidden Elements

3.6 Case Study: Scraping Public Records for OSINT

Public records are a goldmine for OSINT investigations, offering access to government databases, court filings, business registries, and other open-source information. Automating the collection of this data with Python can significantly enhance efficiency and accuracy. In this case study, we'll examine how an OSINT analyst successfully scraped public business registration records to uncover connections between organizations and individuals.

3.6.1 Scenario Overview

An OSINT analyst was tasked with investigating suspected fraudulent companies operating under multiple aliases. The goal was to:

✓ Extract public business registration data (company names, addresses, owners)

✓ Identify links between shell companies

✓ Automate data collection and analysis

The analyst focused on scraping a government business registry website that listed company ownership details.

3.6.2 Identifying the Data Source

The target website provided a search form where users could enter a business name or owner and retrieve company registration details. Each search returned:

- Business Name
- Registration Number
- Owner's Name
- Business Address
- Date of Incorporation

The website used JavaScript to load search results dynamically, meaning BeautifulSoup alone wouldn't work—Selenium was needed to interact with the search form and extract data.

3.6.3 Scraping Methodology

To ethically and efficiently extract public data, the analyst followed these steps:

Step 1: Setting Up Selenium for Automated Search

Since the website required interaction with a search bar, Selenium was used.

```
from selenium import webdriver
from selenium.webdriver.common.by import By
from selenium.webdriver.common.keys import Keys
from webdriver_manager.chrome import ChromeDriverManager
import time

# Set up Selenium WebDriver
options = webdriver.ChromeOptions()
options.add_argument("--headless")  # Run in headless mode

driver = webdriver.Chrome(ChromeDriverManager().install(), options=options)

# Navigate to the business registry website
driver.get("https://publicrecords.example.com")
```

```
# Locate the search bar and enter the company name
search_box = driver.find_element(By.NAME, "company_name")
search_box.send_keys("Example Corp")
search_box.send_keys(Keys.RETURN)

time.sleep(3)  # Allow time for results to load
```

✅ **Impact**: Simulates human search behavior to access the required data.

Step 2: Extracting Business Details

Once the search results were loaded, the analyst extracted the key business details.

```
# Extract company names
companies = driver.find_elements(By.CLASS_NAME, "company-name")
owners = driver.find_elements(By.CLASS_NAME, "owner-name")
addresses = driver.find_elements(By.CLASS_NAME, "business-address")
dates = driver.find_elements(By.CLASS_NAME, "incorporation-date")

# Store results in a structured format
business_data = []

for i in range(len(companies)):
    business_data.append({
        "Company Name": companies[i].text,
        "Owner": owners[i].text,
        "Address": addresses[i].text,
        "Incorporation Date": dates[i].text,
    })

# Close the browser session
driver.quit()

# Display extracted data
for record in business_data:
    print(record)
```

✅ **Impact**: Collects structured intelligence from the search results.

Step 3: Storing and Analyzing the Data

To preserve the scraped records and enable further analysis, the analyst stored the data in a CSV file.

```
import csv

# Save data to CSV
with open("business_records.csv", "w", newline="", encoding="utf-8") as file:
    writer = csv.DictWriter(file, fieldnames=["Company Name", "Owner", "Address",
"Incorporation Date"])
    writer.writeheader()
    writer.writerows(business_data)

print("Data saved successfully!")
```

✓ **Impact**: Ensures data is stored for later reference and cross-analysis.

3.6.4 Data Correlation & Analysis

With the extracted data, the analyst used pandas to identify connections between companies and owners.

Example: Identifying Shared Owners

```
import pandas as pd

# Load the data
df = pd.read_csv("business_records.csv")

# Identify duplicate owners (same person linked to multiple companies)
linked_entities = df[df.duplicated(subset=["Owner"], keep=False)]

print(linked_entities)
```

✓ **Impact**: Reveals patterns of fraudulent shell companies.

3.6.5 Handling Challenges & Avoiding Detection

During the investigation, the analyst faced several obstacles:

◆ **JavaScript-Rendered Content**: Overcome using Selenium instead of BeautifulSoup.

◆ **CAPTCHAs**: Occurred after multiple searches—solved using manual intervention when necessary.

◆ **Rate-Limiting**: The analyst introduced random delays between searches.

Adding Randomized Delays to Reduce Detection Risk

import random

time.sleep(random.uniform(3, 7)) # Random delay between 3-7 seconds

✓ **Impact**: Prevents blocking and mimics human behavior.

3.6.6 Ethical & Legal Considerations

While scraping public records is legal in many jurisdictions, the analyst took precautions:

✓☐ Respected the website's Terms of Service
✓☐ Only extracted publicly available data
✓☐ Did not bypass security measures (CAPTCHAs, logins)
✓☐ Used the data solely for research purposes

✓ **Key Takeaway**: Always ensure compliance with data protection laws.

3.6.7 Case Study Results

By automating the collection of business registry data, the analyst successfully:

🔎 Identified multiple shell companies registered under the same owner.
🔎 Uncovered fraudulent business activities linked to fake addresses.
🔎 Provided evidence to investigative journalists working on financial crime reports.

The extracted OSINT data was cross-referenced with other sources, confirming that some businesses were part of a larger fraud network.

3.6.8 Conclusion

This case study demonstrates how Selenium-powered web scraping can extract valuable public records for OSINT investigations. By structuring and analyzing the data, analysts can uncover connections between companies, individuals, and suspicious activities.

Key Lessons Learned

✓ Selenium is essential for scraping JavaScript-heavy sites

✓ Automating public records collection saves time

✓ Data correlation helps reveal hidden relationships

✓ Ethical considerations must always be a priority

4. Automating Google Dorking & Search Engine Queries

In this chapter, we delve into the art of automating Google Dorking and search engine queries to efficiently gather OSINT from the web's most powerful search engines. Google Dorking, or advanced search queries, allows analysts to uncover hidden or hard-to-find information by exploiting the search engine's syntax. We'll guide you through writing Python scripts that use Google's search operators to automate query execution, extract relevant results, and analyze the findings. Additionally, we'll explore how to overcome challenges such as search result pagination, CAPTCHA, and rate limiting while ensuring ethical and responsible use of automated searches. By the end of this chapter, you'll be able to automate Google Dorking techniques and unlock a wealth of valuable intelligence from search engine results with ease and precision.

4.1 Understanding Google Dorking for OSINT

Google is one of the most powerful OSINT tools available, but most users barely scratch the surface of its capabilities. Google Dorking, also known as Google hacking, is the practice of using advanced search operators to uncover hidden or hard-to-find information. OSINT analysts leverage Google Dorking to locate exposed files, discover vulnerable systems, and gather intelligence from publicly available sources.

In this section, we'll explore:

✓ What Google Dorking is and how it works

✓ Common Google Dorking operators for OSINT investigations

✓ Use cases: uncovering sensitive data, finding hidden pages, and tracking digital footprints

✓ Ethical and legal considerations when using Google Dorks

4.1.1 What is Google Dorking?

Google Dorking is a technique that uses special search queries to find specific types of information on the internet. While search engines typically return general results, dorking allows analysts to filter and refine searches to locate files, exposed databases, login portals, and even misconfigured security settings.

Google indexes millions of web pages, documents, and directories—often including information that should not be publicly accessible but is due to poor security practices.

Example: Basic Google Dorking Query

To find PDF documents related to cyber threat reports, an OSINT analyst might use:

filetype:pdf "cyber threat report"

🔍 **Breakdown:**

- **filetype:pdf** → Filters results to only show PDF files
- **"cyber threat report"** → Searches for this exact phrase in the document

This simple query can reveal government reports, corporate documents, or academic research that may not be easily accessible through standard searches.

4.1.2 Common Google Dorking Operators for OSINT

Below are some of the most useful Google search operators for OSINT investigations:

Operator	Function	Example Query
site:	Searches within a specific website	`site:example.com`
filetype:	Finds specific file types (PDF, DOCX, XLSX)	`filetype:xlsx site:gov`
intitle:	Searches for words in the webpage title	`intitle:"login page"`
inurl:	Finds URLs containing a specific keyword	`inurl:admin`
cache:	Shows Google's cached version of a page	`cache:example.com`
ext:	Same as `filetype:` but for file extensions	`ext:txt site:example.com`
intext:	Searches for specific text within pages	`intext:"confidential"`
link:	Finds pages linking to a URL	`link:example.com`
before:/after:	Finds pages indexed within a specific date range	`site:example.com before:2023`

◆ **Example Use Case**: Finding exposed Excel spreadsheets on government websites:

filetype:xlsx site:gov "budget report"

◆ **Example Use Case**: Locating login portals for a specific company:

inurl:login site:targetcompany.com

4.1.3 OSINT Use Cases for Google Dorking

Google Dorking can be applied to various OSINT investigations, including:

1️⃣ Finding Exposed Sensitive Documents

Many organizations unintentionally expose internal files, including:

- Financial reports
- Employee records
- Security assessments

Example Query: Find exposed employee records (Excel format) *filetype:xlsx intext:"employee salary" site:example.com*

2️ Identifying Open Directories

Some web servers allow directory listing, exposing files that were never meant to be public.

Example Query: Find open directories containing PDF files

intitle:"index of" "parent directory" filetype:pdf

3️ Locating Vulnerable Devices & Admin Panels

Many IoT devices, web cameras, and databases are indexed by Google, making them visible to OSINT analysts.

Example Query: Find unsecured webcams

inurl:/view/view.shtml

Example Query: Locate exposed login panels

inurl:admin login

4️ Tracking Digital Footprints of Individuals

Google Dorking can help uncover personal information such as usernames, leaked emails, and forgotten social media posts.

Example Query: Find email addresses linked to a domain

site:example.com intext:@example.com

🔍 **Real-World Example**: This method was used to discover exposed government emails that led to a spear-phishing campaign.

4.1.4 Ethical & Legal Considerations

⚠ Google Dorking must always be conducted within legal and ethical boundaries. While these techniques are powerful, misusing them can lead to legal consequences.

⚖ What is Legal?

✓ Searching for publicly available information

✓ Investigating your own company's security exposure

✓ Using dorking for OSINT research and intelligence gathering

⊘ What is Illegal?

✗ Accessing protected or private data

✗ Exploiting vulnerabilities found via Google Dorking

✗ Using dorking for hacking, fraud, or unauthorized access

◆ **Example**: Searching for exposed login credentials is illegal if those credentials provide unauthorized access.

★ **Best Practice**: Always verify that your activities comply with local laws and ethical OSINT principles. If working in cybersecurity, ensure that you have permission before investigating a system.

4.1.5 Conclusion

Google Dorking is a powerful OSINT tool that allows analysts to uncover hidden information, track digital footprints, and assess security risks. By using advanced search operators, investigators can refine their searches to quickly locate relevant intelligence.

Key Takeaways:

✓ Google indexes a vast amount of data—learn how to filter it efficiently.

✓ Master search operators like site:, filetype:, and intitle: for targeted OSINT searches.

✓ Dorking can reveal sensitive documents, admin portals, and forgotten web pages.

✓ Always stay within ethical and legal boundaries to avoid unauthorized access.

4.2 Using Python to Automate Search Queries

Manually performing OSINT searches using Google Dorking or other search techniques can be time-consuming. By leveraging Python, analysts can automate search queries, collect data efficiently, and structure the results for deeper analysis. This chapter will explore:

✅ How to automate search queries with Python

✅ Using the Google Search API and SERP scraping tools

✅ Extracting and processing search results for OSINT investigations

✅ Ethical considerations when automating search queries

4.2.1 Why Automate Search Queries?

While Google Dorking and other advanced search techniques can reveal valuable intelligence, repeating searches manually is inefficient. Automating the process helps:

◆ **Save time** – Run multiple search queries simultaneously.
◆ **Improve accuracy** – Collect and structure data automatically.
◆ **Expand search capabilities** – Monitor search results over time.
◆ **Reduce human error** – Eliminate manual copy-pasting mistakes.

📌 **Example OSINT Use Case**: Automating searches for leaked documents across multiple domains, identifying exposed login pages, or tracking mentions of a target entity over time.

4.2.2 Automating Google Searches with Python

Google does not allow automated scraping of its search results through direct web scraping techniques like BeautifulSoup. Instead, analysts must use:

1️ **Google Custom Search API** (official method)

2️ **Third-party search APIs** (e.g., SerpAPI)

3️ **Alternative search engines** (e.g., Bing, DuckDuckGo)

Option 1: Using Google Custom Search API

Google provides an official Custom Search JSON API to retrieve search results programmatically.

◆ Step 1: Get API Access

- Sign up for Google Custom Search Engine (CSE): Google CSE
- Obtain an API key from Google Cloud Console.
- Configure a search engine to allow querying specific websites or the entire web.

◆ Step 2: Install Required Python Packages

pip install requests

◆ Step 3: Automate Google Search with Python

```
import requests

# Google Custom Search API details
API_KEY = "your_api_key_here"
CX = "your_custom_search_engine_id"
QUERY = "filetype:pdf site:gov cybersecurity report"

# Construct API URL
url = f"https://www.googleapis.com/customsearch/v1?q={QUERY}&key={API_KEY}&cx={CX}"

# Make API request
response = requests.get(url)
data = response.json()

# Extract search results
for result in data["items"]:
    print(f"Title: {result['title']}")
    print(f"URL: {result['link']}\n")
```

✅ **Impact**: This script automates Google searches, retrieves search results in JSON format, and extracts relevant links.

4.2.3 Scraping Search Results with SerpAPI

Google limits Custom Search API requests, so alternative APIs like SerpAPI offer a workaround.

⬥ **SerpAPI** (https://serpapi.com) allows automated Google Search scraping while respecting API rate limits.

◆ **Step 1: Install SerpAPI**

pip install google-search-results

◆ **Step 2: Automate Google Search with SerpAPI**

```
from serpapi import GoogleSearch

# SerpAPI key
API_KEY = "your_serpapi_key"

# Search parameters
params = {
    "q": "intitle:'index of' confidential filetype:pdf",
    "api_key": API_KEY,
}

# Make API request
search = GoogleSearch(params)
results = search.get_dict()

# Extract search results
for result in results["organic_results"]:
    print(f"Title: {result['title']}")
    print(f"Link: {result['link']}\n")
```

✓ **Impact**: Automates Google Dorking by fetching search results programmatically.

4.2.4 Using Python to Search Alternative Search Engines

Since Google imposes rate limits and captchas, OSINT analysts often turn to alternative search engines.

◆ Example: Automating DuckDuckGo Searches

```
pip install duckduckgo_search

from duckduckgo_search import ddg

# Perform DuckDuckGo search
results = ddg("intitle:'index of' confidential filetype:pdf", max_results=10)

# Extract search results
for result in results:
    print(f"Title: {result['title']}")
    print(f"URL: {result['href']}\n")
```

✅ **Impact**: DuckDuckGo allows privacy-focused automated searches without API keys.

4.2.5 Storing and Analyzing Search Results

Once search results are extracted, they should be stored and analyzed for OSINT investigations.

◆ Save Search Results to a CSV File

```
import csv

# Example data (Replace with real search results)
search_results = [
    {"Title": "Example Report", "URL": "https://example.com/report.pdf"},
    {"Title": "Leaked Data", "URL": "https://example.com/leak.txt"},
]

# Save to CSV
with open("search_results.csv", "w", newline="", encoding="utf-8") as file:
    writer = csv.DictWriter(file, fieldnames=["Title", "URL"])
    writer.writeheader()
    writer.writerows(search_results)

print("Search results saved to CSV.")
```

✅ **Impact**: Enables structured storage of search results for further OSINT correlation.

4.2.6 Ethical Considerations in Automated Search Queries

⚠️ Automating search queries must be done responsibly to avoid violating legal or ethical guidelines.

🚀 **Best Practices for Ethical OSINT Automation**

✓ Follow website Terms of Service (ToS).
✓ Use APIs instead of direct scraping when possible.
✓ Avoid aggressive query automation to prevent rate limits or bans.
✓ Do not access private, unauthorized, or protected data.
✓ Ensure compliance with local laws on data collection.

◆ **Example**: Searching for publicly available reports is legal, but automating searches for password-protected or unauthorized data may violate cybersecurity laws.

4.2.7 Conclusion

Python can greatly enhance OSINT search capabilities by automating search queries, collecting data, and structuring results. Whether using Google APIs, alternative search engines, or third-party services, automation saves time and increases efficiency.

Key Takeaways:

✅ Google Dorking can be automated using Python APIs (Google CSE, SerpAPI, etc.).

✅ Alternative search engines like DuckDuckGo provide additional OSINT value.

✅ Storing search results in CSV or databases allows deeper analysis.

✅ Always ensure ethical and legal compliance when automating searches.

By mastering search automation, OSINT analysts can efficiently track digital footprints, uncover hidden intelligence, and enhance investigative workflows. 🚀

4.3 Scraping Google Search Results Responsibly

Google search results contain vast amounts of publicly available information that can be useful for OSINT investigations. However, scraping Google directly presents several challenges, including legal, ethical, and technical restrictions. In this section, we will explore:

✔ Why scraping Google is difficult & potential risks

✔ Ethical and legal considerations when scraping search results

✔ Alternative methods: Using APIs and search engine alternatives

✔ Best practices to avoid detection and ensure responsible scraping

4.3.1 Why Scraping Google is Challenging

Unlike regular websites, Google actively blocks automated scraping to protect its platform from abuse. The following challenges make scraping Google search results difficult:

🚫 **Rate Limits & CAPTCHAs**: Google detects repeated automated requests and prompts for CAPTCHAs.

⚖ **Legal & ToS Restrictions**: Google's Terms of Service prohibit web scraping without permission.

☐ **Anti-Bot Measures**: Google uses reCAPTCHA, IP bans, and request fingerprinting to detect scrapers.

▨ **Unreliable Data**: Scraped results can be incomplete or outdated due to Google's personalization.

📌 **Key Takeaway**: Directly scraping Google without permission violates Google's Terms of Service and can lead to IP bans or legal consequences. Instead, OSINT analysts should explore alternative approaches for gathering search data.

4.3.2 Ethical & Legal Considerations

⚠ Before scraping any website, it's important to understand legal and ethical boundaries.

✔ **Legal Approaches:**

- Use official APIs (Google Custom Search API, SerpAPI).
- Follow robots.txt guidelines, which indicate what a website allows bots to access.
- Scrape only publicly available data and avoid restricted/private information.

✖ Illegal or Unethical Approaches:

- Scraping search results without permission from Google.
- Using bots to bypass CAPTCHAs or impersonate human traffic.
- Overloading Google's servers with excessive requests.
- Accessing private, sensitive, or unauthorized information.

📌 **Ethical OSINT Best Practice**: Always ensure that your data collection methods comply with legal regulations (e.g., GDPR, CFAA, CCPA).

4.3.3 Alternative Methods for Extracting Google Search Results

Since scraping Google directly is risky, analysts should use alternative approaches to gather search data:

1⃣ Using the Google Custom Search API (Official Method)

Google provides a Custom Search API that allows limited programmatic access to search results.

◆ Steps to Use the Google Custom Search API:

- Create a Custom Search Engine (CSE) via Google Programmable Search Engine.
- Obtain an API Key from Google Cloud Console.
- Use Python to query the API and extract results.

◆ Python Code Example: Automating Google Searches with the API

```
import requests

# Google API Credentials
API_KEY = "your_api_key"
CX = "your_search_engine_id"
QUERY = "intitle:'index of' confidential filetype:pdf"
```

```
# Construct API request
url =
f"https://www.googleapis.com/customsearch/v1?q={QUERY}&key={API_KEY}&cx={CX}
"

# Make request
response = requests.get(url)
data = response.json()

# Extract and display results
for item in data.get("items", []):
    print(f"Title: {item['title']}")
    print(f"URL: {item['link']}\n")
```

✅ Why use this method?

- Legal and allowed by Google.
- No risk of IP bans or CAPTCHAs.
- Fast and structured results in JSON format.

🔊 Limitations:

- API has request limits (100 free queries per day).
- Doesn't return full Google search results.

2️⃣ Using Third-Party Google Search APIs (SerpAPI, ScraperAPI)

Since Google's API is limited, many OSINT analysts use third-party search APIs such as:

♦ **SerpAPI** – Automates Google searches and bypasses restrictions ethically.
♦ **ScraperAPI** – Handles CAPTCHAs and proxies for web scraping.

◆ **Python Code Example: Using SerpAPI to Automate Google Searches**

```
from serpapi import GoogleSearch

# API Key
API_KEY = "your_serpapi_key"
```

```
# Search Parameters
params = {
    "q": "filetype:pdf site:gov cybersecurity report",
    "api_key": API_KEY,
}

# Perform search
search = GoogleSearch(params)
results = search.get_dict()

# Extract search results
for result in results["organic_results"]:
    print(f"Title: {result['title']}")
    print(f"URL: {result['link']}\n")
```

✅ Why use this method?

- No need to handle CAPTCHAs manually.
- Bypasses rate limits using proxies.
- Provides clean and structured search results.

🔎 Limitations:

- Paid service after free trial expires.
- Still relies on third-party platforms.

3️⃣ Using Alternative Search Engines (DuckDuckGo, Bing, Yandex)

Since Google restricts automation, OSINT analysts can extract search results from alternative engines like:

- **DuckDuckGo** – Allows API-based searches without captchas.
- **Bing Search API** – Provides structured search results via Microsoft's API.
- **Yandex Search** – Useful for OSINT investigations in Russian domains.

◆ Python Code Example: Automating DuckDuckGo Searches

```
from duckduckgo_search import ddg
```

```
# Perform DuckDuckGo search
results = ddg("intitle:'index of' confidential filetype:pdf", max_results=10)

# Extract and display results
for result in results:
    print(f"Title: {result['title']}")
    print(f"URL: {result['href']}\n")
```

✅ Why use this method?

- No rate limits or captchas.
- DuckDuckGo prioritizes privacy and allows automation.
- Can find results that Google might filter out.

🚨 Limitations:

- Results differ from Google's index.
- Less advanced search algorithms compared to Google.

4.3.4 Best Practices for Responsible Web Scraping

If scraping any search engine or website, follow these best practices:

✓ **Respect robots.txt rules** – Always check a site's robots.txt file before scraping.

✓ **Throttle requests** – Space out automated queries to avoid detection.

✓ **Use rotating IPs and proxies** – Prevent bans by rotating IP addresses.

✓ **Identify as a bot (if allowed)** – Be transparent when scraping public data.

✓ **Cache results** – Avoid excessive queries by storing previous searches.

4.3.5 Conclusion

Scraping Google search results directly is not recommended due to technical, ethical, and legal risks. Instead, OSINT analysts should:

✅ Use Google's Custom Search API or third-party APIs (SerpAPI, ScraperAPI).

✅ Leverage alternative search engines like DuckDuckGo or Bing for automated queries.

✅ Follow ethical scraping guidelines to prevent IP bans and legal consequences.

By responsibly automating search queries, OSINT professionals can efficiently collect intelligence while staying within legal and ethical boundaries. 🚀

4.4 Customizing Search Parameters for Targeted Intelligence

Effective OSINT investigations rely on precise search queries to extract valuable intelligence from vast online data sources. By customizing search parameters, analysts can refine their searches, exclude irrelevant results, and uncover hidden information more efficiently.

In this section, we will cover:

✅ Advanced search operators for refining OSINT searches

✅ Using Python to automate customized search queries

✅ Filtering results by domain, file type, and time range

✅ Combining multiple search techniques for precision intelligence

4.4.1 Why Customize Search Queries?

Standard keyword searches return millions of irrelevant results. Customizing search parameters enables:

◆ **Targeted Data Collection** – Focus on specific domains, file types, or date ranges.
◆ **Noise Reduction** – Eliminate irrelevant or redundant results.
◆ **Hidden Data Discovery** – Uncover indexed but obscure information.
◆ **Efficiency** – Reduce time spent manually sifting through search results.

📌 **Example OSINT Use Cases:**

✓☐ Identifying leaked documents with "filetype:pdf site:gov" queries.
✓☐ Tracking cybersecurity incidents by filtering searches within the last 24 hours.
✓☐ Investigating social media accounts by targeting specific usernames.

4.4.2 Google Dorking for Customized OSINT Queries

Google supports advanced search operators (a.k.a. Google Dorking) that allow analysts to refine searches effectively.

Operator	Description	Example
site:	Search within a specific domain	`site:gov filetype:pdf cybersecurity`
filetype:	Filter by file type (PDF, DOCX, TXT)	`filetype:xls site:edu enrollment data`
intitle:	Search for specific words in page titles	`intitle:login site:example.com`
inurl:	Find keywords in URLs	`inurl:admin login`
ext:	Similar to filetype, searches specific extensions	`ext:csv financial data`
cache:	View Google's cached version of a page	`cache:example.com`
after: before:	Filter results by date	`breach database after:2023-01-01`
- (Minus Sign)	Exclude certain words	`OSINT tools -social media`
OR	Find results matching multiple keywords	`hacked database OR leaked credentials`

📌 Example OSINT Query:

To find leaked government reports on cybersecurity:

filetype:pdf site:gov "cybersecurity report"

4.4.3 Automating Custom Search Queries with Python

Manually inputting Google Dorking queries is inefficient for large-scale intelligence gathering. Python can automate search queries and retrieve results programmatically.

◆ Automating Google Dorking with SerpAPI

SerpAPI allows automated Google searches while bypassing rate limits and CAPTCHAs.

pip install google-search-results

from serpapi import GoogleSearch

```
# API key (replace with your SerpAPI key)
API_KEY = "your_serpapi_key"

# Define search parameters
params = {
    "q": "filetype:pdf site:gov cybersecurity report",
    "api_key": API_KEY,
    "num": 10  # Number of results
}

# Perform search
search = GoogleSearch(params)
results = search.get_dict()

# Extract and print search results
for result in results.get("organic_results", []):
    print(f"Title: {result['title']}")
    print(f"URL: {result['link']}\n")
```

✅ Why use this?

- Automates OSINT searches efficiently.
- Fetches structured search results (titles, links, descriptions).
- Bypasses Google's anti-scraping restrictions legally.

🔔 **Note**: SerpAPI requires an API key and has free/paid plans.

4.4.4 Filtering Search Results by Date & Region

To track real-time intelligence, analysts must filter search results by date and location.

◆ Using Google's Date Filters

Search Modifier	Function
after:YYYY-MM-DD	Search for results after a specific date
before:YYYY-MM-DD	Search for results before a specific date
past 24 hours	Show recent results

📌 **Example**: Finding breach reports from the past year:

data breach site:gov after:2023-01-01

◆ **Automating Date-Filtered Queries with Python**

```python
import datetime
from serpapi import GoogleSearch

# Get today's date
today = datetime.date.today()

# Define API parameters
params = {
    "q": f"data breach site:gov after:{today.year-1}-01-01",
    "api_key": "your_serpapi_key",
}

# Execute search
search = GoogleSearch(params)
results = search.get_dict()

# Display results
for result in results.get("organic_results", []):
    print(f"Title: {result['title']}")
    print(f"URL: {result['link']}\n")
```

✅ **Impact**: Automatically fetches recent breach reports from government sites.

4.4.5 Combining Multiple Search Techniques for Precision OSINT

By combining Google Dorking, API automation, and data processing, OSINT analysts can extract highly relevant intelligence.

📌 Example Scenario:

An analyst wants to find leaked Excel spreadsheets related to financial transactions in Europe within the past year.

◆ Step 1: Construct Advanced Search Query

filetype:xls "financial transactions" site:.eu after:2023-01-01

◆ Step 2: Automate Search Query with Python

```
params = {
    "q": 'filetype:xls "financial transactions" site:.eu after:2023-01-01',
    "api_key": "your_serpapi_key",
}

search = GoogleSearch(params)
results = search.get_dict()

for result in results.get("organic_results", []):
    print(f"Title: {result['title']}")
    print(f"URL: {result['link']}\n")
```

✅ **Outcome**: This method identifies potential leaked financial spreadsheets across European domains.

4.4.6 Conclusion

Customizing search parameters significantly enhances OSINT investigations by refining search results and automating intelligence gathering.

Key Takeaways:

✓☐ Google Dorking operators help refine searches and filter relevant data.
✓☐ Python automation enables large-scale intelligence gathering.
✓☐ Date & domain filtering improves relevance for real-time monitoring.

✓☐ Combining multiple search techniques maximizes intelligence accuracy.

By mastering customized search queries, OSINT analysts can extract high-value intelligence efficiently while ensuring legal and ethical compliance. 🚀

4.5 Integrating Search Engine APIs (Google, Bing, DuckDuckGo)

Integrating search engine APIs into OSINT workflows enables analysts to automate intelligence gathering from multiple sources, ensuring comprehensive data collection while avoiding scraping restrictions.

This section covers:

✅ Overview of Google, Bing, and DuckDuckGo APIs

✅ How to set up API access for automated searches

✅ Python scripts to query each API

✅ Comparing results from different search engines

4.5.1 Why Use Search Engine APIs for OSINT?

◆ **Bypass scraping restrictions**: Avoid rate limits, CAPTCHAs, and legal issues.
◆ **Retrieve structured data**: Get results in JSON format instead of parsing raw HTML.
◆ **Automate large-scale searches**: Query multiple engines simultaneously.
◆ **Enhance intelligence gathering**: Compare results from different search providers.

📌 **Use Case**: Investigators tracking a cybercrime group can use APIs to search for leaked data across Google, Bing, and DuckDuckGo simultaneously.

4.5.2 Google Custom Search API

Google's Custom Search API allows programmatic access to Google Search results, but with query limits.

◆ **Steps to Get Google API Access**

1️⃣ Go to Google Cloud Console (https://console.cloud.google.com/)

2️⃣ Enable Custom Search API

3️⃣ Create a Programmable Search Engine (CSE) (https://programmablesearchengine.google.com/)

4️⃣ Get the API key and CSE ID

◆ Python Script: Automating Google Searches

```python
import requests

# API Credentials
API_KEY = "your_api_key"
CX = "your_search_engine_id"
QUERY = "cybercrime forum site:darknet"

# Construct API request
url = f"https://www.googleapis.com/customsearch/v1?q={QUERY}&key={API_KEY}&cx={CX}"

# Make request
response = requests.get(url)
data = response.json()

# Display search results
for item in data.get("items", []):
    print(f"Title: {item['title']}")
    print(f"URL: {item['link']}\n")
```

✅ Advantages:

✓ Google's massive search index
✓ Structured JSON output
✓ Filters by date, site, and file type

🔒 Limitations:

✗ Query limits (100 free searches per day)

✗ Requires CSE ID, limiting full web access

4.5.3 Bing Search API

Bing's Search API (from Microsoft Azure) provides full web search capabilities with fewer restrictions than Google.

◆ Steps to Get Bing API Access

1☐ Sign up at Microsoft Azure Portal

2☐ Subscribe to Bing Search API

3☐ Get the API key

◆ Python Script: Automating Bing Searches

```python
import requests

# API Key
API_KEY = "your_bing_api_key"
QUERY = "threat intelligence report site:gov"

# Construct API request
url = f"https://api.bing.microsoft.com/v7.0/search?q={QUERY}"
headers = {"Ocp-Apim-Subscription-Key": API_KEY}

# Make request
response = requests.get(url, headers=headers)
data = response.json()

# Display search results
for item in data.get("webPages", {}).get("value", []):
    print(f"Title: {item['name']}")
    print(f"URL: {item['url']}\n")
```

✅ Advantages:

✓□ More flexible than Google's API

✓□ Includes images, news, and web results

✓□ Higher query limits

🔊 Limitations:

✗ Requires Azure account & payment after free tier

✗ Less comprehensive than Google's index

4.5.4 DuckDuckGo Search API

DuckDuckGo is a privacy-focused search engine that offers a free API without tracking users.

◆ Using DuckDuckGo's API for OSINT

DuckDuckGo's API doesn't require authentication and allows anonymous searches.

◆ Python Script: Automating DuckDuckGo Searches

```
from duckduckgo_search import ddg

# Perform search
results = ddg("cybersecurity breach site:edu", max_results=10)

# Display search results
for result in results:
    print(f"Title: {result['title']}")
    print(f"URL: {result['href']}\n")
```

✅ Advantages:

✓□ Free & no API key required

✓□ No tracking or personalization

✓□ Works well for privacy-focused OSINT investigations

🔒 Limitations:

✖ Smaller index than Google or Bing

✖ Doesn't support advanced filters like filetype or date ranges

4.5.5 Comparing Search Engine APIs for OSINT

Search Engine	API Key Required?	Best For	Query Limits	Privacy & Anonymity
Google Custom Search API	☑ Yes	General OSINT, filetype searches	100/day (free)	✖ Tracks users
Bing Search API	☑ Yes	Web & news search, fewer restrictions	1,000/month (free)	✖ Tracks users
DuckDuckGo API	✖ No	Privacy-focused searches	Unlimited	☑ Anonymous

📌 Recommendation:

Use Google API for filetype searches and high-precision queries.
Use Bing API for news, web, and broader intelligence gathering.
Use DuckDuckGo API for anonymous OSINT investigations.

4.5.6 Integrating Multiple APIs in One OSINT Script

To maximize intelligence gathering, OSINT analysts can query multiple APIs simultaneously.

◆ Python Script: Multi-Engine Search Automation

```
import requests
from duckduckgo_search import ddg

# API Keys
GOOGLE_API_KEY = "your_google_api_key"
GOOGLE_CX = "your_google_cse_id"
BING_API_KEY = "your_bing_api_key"
QUERY = "cyber threat report site:gov"
```

```
# Google Search API
google_url =
f"https://www.googleapis.com/customsearch/v1?q={QUERY}&key={GOOGLE_API_KE
Y}&cx={GOOGLE_CX}"
google_results = requests.get(google_url).json()

# Bing Search API
bing_url = f"https://api.bing.microsoft.com/v7.0/search?q={QUERY}"
bing_results = requests.get(bing_url, headers={"Ocp-Apim-Subscription-Key":
BING_API_KEY}).json()

# DuckDuckGo API
duck_results = ddg(QUERY, max_results=5)

# Print Results
print("\n🔍 Google Search Results:")
for item in google_results.get("items", []):
    print(f"Title: {item['title']}\nURL: {item['link']}\n")

print("\n🔍 Bing Search Results:")
for item in bing_results.get("webPages", {}).get("value", []):
    print(f"Title: {item['name']}\nURL: {item['url']}\n")

print("\n🔍 DuckDuckGo Search Results:")
for item in duck_results:
    print(f"Title: {item['title']}\nURL: {item['href']}\n")
```

✅ **Outcome**: Automatically gathers intelligence from Google, Bing, and DuckDuckGo in one query.

4.5.7 Conclusion

- ◆ **Google API** – Best for precise & structured searches but rate-limited.
- ◆ **Bing API** – More flexible, good for news & general intelligence.
- ◆ **DuckDuckGo API** – Free, anonymous, and unlimited, but limited indexing.

📌 **Key Takeaway**: Integrating multiple search engine APIs enhances OSINT capabilities by combining results from different data sources while avoiding scraping risks. 🚀

4.6 Case Study: Automating a Search Engine Reconnaissance Operation

In this case study, we explore how OSINT automation using search engine APIs can significantly improve intelligence gathering. We will walk through a real-world-style reconnaissance operation, demonstrating how an analyst can automate search queries across multiple engines to collect valuable intelligence on a target organization.

4.6.1 Scenario: Investigating a Financial Services Company for Security Risks

Objective:

An OSINT analyst is tasked with investigating "FinTrust Capital", a financial services firm, to identify potential security risks, leaked documents, and exposed credentials on the internet. The goal is to automate reconnaissance across Google, Bing, and DuckDuckGo to collect relevant intelligence.

Key Intelligence Targets:

✅ Leaked documents (PDFs, spreadsheets, internal reports)

✅ Exposed login portals and admin pages

✅ Mentions of security breaches or leaked credentials

✅ Discussions on hacker forums

4.6.2 Step 1: Define OSINT Search Queries

To extract relevant intelligence, the analyst customizes search queries using Google Dorking techniques and search engine operators.

◆ **Targeted Google Dorking Queries**

Objective	Search Query
Find leaked PDF reports	`filetype:pdf "confidential" site:fintrustcapital.com`
Discover login portals	`inurl:admin OR inurl:login site:fintrustcapital.com`
Check for exposed databases	`intitle:"index of" "database" site:fintrustcapital.com`
Investigate cybersecurity incidents	`"FinTrust Capital" data breach after:2023-01-01`

These queries will be automated using Google, Bing, and DuckDuckGo APIs.

4.6.3 Step 2: Automating Searches with Python

The analyst writes a Python script to query multiple search engine APIs and compile results into a structured format.

◆ **Required Setup:**

- Google Custom Search API (Requires API Key & CSE ID)
- Bing Search API (Requires Microsoft Azure subscription)
- DuckDuckGo Search API (No API key needed)

◆ **Python Script: Automated Search Engine Reconnaissance**

```python
import requests
from duckduckgo_search import ddg

# API Keys & Configuration
GOOGLE_API_KEY = "your_google_api_key"
GOOGLE_CX = "your_google_cse_id"
BING_API_KEY = "your_bing_api_key"
TARGET = "FinTrust Capital"

# Define Search Queries
queries = {
    "Leaked PDF Reports": f'filetype:pdf "confidential" site:fintrustcapital.com',
    "Login Portals": f'inurl:admin OR inurl:login site:fintrustcapital.com',
    "Exposed Databases": f'intitle:"index of" "database" site:fintrustcapital.com',
    "Data Breaches": f'"{TARGET}" data breach after:2023-01-01'
```

```python
}

# Function to query Google API
def search_google(query):
    url = f"https://www.googleapis.com/customsearch/v1?q={query}&key={GOOGLE_API_KEY}&cx={GOOGLE_CX}"
    response = requests.get(url).json()
    return [{"title": item["title"], "url": item["link"]} for item in response.get("items", [])]

# Function to query Bing API
def search_bing(query):
    url = f"https://api.bing.microsoft.com/v7.0/search?q={query}"
    headers = {"Ocp-Apim-Subscription-Key": BING_API_KEY}
    response = requests.get(url, headers=headers).json()
    return [{"title": item["name"], "url": item["url"]} for item in response.get("webPages", {}).get("value", [])]

# Function to query DuckDuckGo API
def search_duckduckgo(query):
    results = ddg(query, max_results=5)
    return [{"title": item["title"], "url": item["href"]} for item in results]

# Execute searches
results = {}
for category, query in queries.items():
    results[category] = {
        "Google": search_google(query),
        "Bing": search_bing(query),
        "DuckDuckGo": search_duckduckgo(query)
    }

# Display results
for category, engines in results.items():
    print(f"\n🔍 {category}:\n")
    for engine, links in engines.items():
        print(f"  📌 {engine} Results:")
        for link in links:
            print(f"    - {link['title']}\n      {link['url']}")
```

4.6.4 Step 3: Analyzing the Results

◆ Findings from Automated Reconnaissance

After running the script, the analyst compiles key intelligence:

1️ Leaked PDF Reports:

- Found internal financial audit reports exposed on Google Drive.
- Located a risk assessment report indexed by Google.

2️ Login Portals & Admin Pages:

- Identified multiple login pages, some without HTTPS.
- Found an exposed admin panel that may be vulnerable.

3️ Exposed Databases:

- Bing search revealed an open directory with database backups.
- DuckDuckGo search found archived SQL dumps in hacker forums.

4️ Data Breach Mentions:

- Google search showed FinTrust Capital in a data breach news report.
- DuckDuckGo revealed a Pastebin post discussing leaked employee credentials.

📌 Key Intelligence Takeaways:

✓ Multiple exposed login portals indicate potential security misconfigurations.

✓ Leaked audit reports may contain sensitive financial data.

✓ Exposed databases could be targets for cybercriminals.

✓ Mentions on hacker forums suggest potential credential leaks.

4.6.5 Step 4: Generating an OSINT Report
The analyst compiles the findings into a structured OSINT report for further investigation.

◆ Sample OSINT Report Summary

- **Target**: FinTrust Capital
- **Date**: February 2025
- **Objective**: Identify potential security risks through automated OSINT reconnaissance.

Category	Key Findings	Risk Level
Leaked Documents	Internal audit & risk reports found online	● High
Login Portals	Multiple admin panels found, some unsecured	● Medium
Exposed Databases	Open directories with database files	● High
Breach Mentions	Appeared in data breach discussions	○ Low

Recommended Actions:

✓☐ Secure exposed login portals with multi-factor authentication.

✓☐ Remove indexed confidential reports and restrict access.

✓☐ Investigate leaked credentials and reset passwords.

✓☐ Monitor hacker forums for further threat intelligence.

4.6.6 Conclusion

This case study demonstrates how OSINT analysts can automate search engine reconnaissance to gather intelligence efficiently and systematically.

Key Takeaways:

✓☐ APIs provide structured data, making intelligence gathering faster & more accurate.

✓☐ Combining multiple search engines improves intelligence coverage.

✓☐ Automating reconnaissance enables analysts to track threats in real-time.

✓☐ Findings must be validated before acting on intelligence.

By using Python scripts to automate OSINT reconnaissance, analysts can streamline intelligence gathering, detect threats faster, and mitigate risks effectively. 🚀

5. Extracting & Analyzing Social Media Data with APIs

In this chapter, we focus on extracting and analyzing social media data using APIs, a crucial aspect of OSINT automation for uncovering insights from platforms like Twitter, Facebook, and Instagram. Social media is a goldmine of real-time information, and APIs provide a structured way to access vast amounts of data for analysis. You'll learn how to authenticate and interact with different social media APIs using Python, gather posts, user details, and trends, and process this data for intelligence purposes. Additionally, we'll discuss ethical considerations and the importance of respecting privacy while using these tools. By the end of this chapter, you'll be equipped to automate the collection and analysis of social media data, enabling you to track events, monitor conversations, and uncover patterns that are essential for informed decision-making.

5.1 Understanding Social Media APIs & Data Restrictions

Social media platforms are a goldmine for OSINT analysts, providing valuable insights into individuals, organizations, trends, and potential security threats. However, accessing and extracting data from these platforms requires an understanding of social media APIs, data restrictions, and ethical considerations. This chapter explores how social media APIs work, the limitations imposed by platforms, and best practices for responsible intelligence gathering.

5.1.1 What Are Social Media APIs?

Social media platforms provide Application Programming Interfaces (APIs) to allow developers to interact with their services programmatically. These APIs enable OSINT analysts to:

✓ Search for public profiles, posts, and media

✓ Collect metadata about user activities

✓ Monitor trends and hashtags

✓ Analyze connections, interactions, and engagement

◆ **Common Social Media APIs Used in OSINT**

Platform	API Name	Public Data Available?	Restrictions
Twitter/X	Twitter API v2	Tweets, user profiles, hashtags	Rate limits, restricted historical data
Facebook	Graph API	Pages, public posts	Requires app approval, strict permissions
Instagram	Graph API	Business accounts, hashtags	Personal profiles restricted
LinkedIn	LinkedIn API	Job postings, company data	Limited to approved business use cases
Reddit	Reddit API	Posts, comments, user profiles	Rate limits apply
TikTok	TikTok API	Public videos, trends	Requires developer access
YouTube	YouTube Data API	Videos, comments, channels	Rate limits apply

Each platform has its own terms of service (ToS) that dictate how data can be accessed and used. Violating these rules can lead to API access revocation or legal consequences.

5.1.2 API Access Levels & Authentication

Most social media APIs require authentication using API keys, OAuth tokens, or access tokens.

◆ API Authentication Methods

1️⃣ **API Key**: A simple key assigned to developers (e.g., YouTube API).

2️⃣ **OAuth 2.0**: A more secure authentication flow that requires user consent (e.g., Twitter, Facebook).

3️⃣ **Access Tokens**: Temporary keys used for authenticated requests (e.g., Instagram, LinkedIn).

◆ Example: Authenticating with the Twitter API

To access Twitter's API, you need to:

✔ Register a Twitter Developer Account

✔ Create an App & API Key

✓ Use OAuth 2.0 for authentication

```python
import tweepy

# API Credentials
API_KEY = "your_api_key"
API_SECRET = "your_api_secret"
ACCESS_TOKEN = "your_access_token"
ACCESS_SECRET = "your_access_secret"

# Authenticate with Twitter
auth = tweepy.OAuthHandler(API_KEY, API_SECRET)
auth.set_access_token(ACCESS_TOKEN, ACCESS_SECRET)
api = tweepy.API(auth)

# Fetch recent tweets containing "OSINT"
tweets = api.search_tweets(q="OSINT", count=10)
for tweet in tweets:
    print(f"{tweet.user.screen_name}: {tweet.text}")
```

5.1.3 Data Access Restrictions & Rate Limits

Each platform imposes rate limits and data access restrictions to prevent abuse.

◆ Rate Limits Overview

Platform	Rate Limit Example
Twitter API	300 requests per 15 minutes for standard access
Facebook Graph API	Varies based on app permissions
Instagram API	200 requests per hour per user
Reddit API	60 requests per minute
YouTube API	10,000 API units per day

To avoid getting blocked, OSINT analysts must:

✓☐ Throttle requests to stay within limits
✓☐ Use API pagination to fetch data efficiently
✓☐ Implement caching to reduce unnecessary API calls

5.1.4 Legal & Ethical Considerations

OSINT analysts must follow ethical guidelines and legal frameworks when using social media APIs.

◆ Key Legal Considerations

★ **Platform Terms of Service**: Each API has strict policies on data usage.
★ **Privacy Laws (GDPR, CCPA)**: Personal data collection is regulated.
★ **No Unauthorized Scraping**: Using bots to bypass API restrictions can violate terms of service.

◆ Ethical Best Practices

✓ Use only public data and respect user privacy.

✓ Avoid automated actions (e.g., liking, following) that mimic real users.

✓ Disclose findings responsibly to avoid harm or misinformation.

5.1.5 Conclusion

Understanding social media APIs is crucial for OSINT analysts who want to legally and ethically collect intelligence from platforms. Analysts should:

✓☐ Choose the right API based on data availability & access restrictions
✓☐ Authenticate securely and follow API rate limits
✓☐ Stay compliant with legal frameworks and platform ToS

In the next chapter, we will explore how to extract and analyze social media data using Python and APIs. 🚀

5.2 Automating Twitter OSINT with Tweepy

Twitter (now X) is a critical source of open-source intelligence (OSINT), providing real-time updates on global events, discussions, and user activities. Automating Twitter OSINT using Tweepy, a Python library for interacting with the Twitter API, enables analysts to efficiently collect, analyze, and monitor relevant intelligence.

This chapter covers:

✓ Setting up Tweepy and authenticating with the Twitter API

✓ Automating searches for tweets, users, and hashtags

✓ Extracting metadata for analysis

✓ Best practices for responsible and efficient Twitter OSINT

5.2.1 Setting Up Tweepy & Authenticating with the Twitter API

To access Twitter's data, you need:

1️ A Twitter Developer Account (https://developer.twitter.com/)
2️ A Twitter App with API keys
3️ Tweepy installed in Python

◆ Install Tweepy

pip install tweepy

◆ Authenticate with the Twitter API

import tweepy

 # API credentials (replace with your actual keys)
API_KEY = "your_api_key"
API_SECRET = "your_api_secret"
ACCESS_TOKEN = "your_access_token"
ACCESS_SECRET = "your_access_secret"

```
# Authenticate
auth = tweepy.OAuthHandler(API_KEY, API_SECRET)
auth.set_access_token(ACCESS_TOKEN, ACCESS_SECRET)
api = tweepy.API(auth, wait_on_rate_limit=True)

print("✅ Authentication successful!")
```

5.2.2 Automating Twitter Searches for OSINT

The Twitter API allows OSINT analysts to search for tweets containing specific keywords, hashtags, or user mentions.

◆ Search for Recent Tweets

```
query = "cybersecurity OR data breach -filter:retweets"
tweets = api.search_tweets(q=query, lang="en", count=10)

for tweet in tweets:
    print(f"📝 {tweet.user.screen_name}: {tweet.text}")
```

◆ Filters Used in Query:

✔ -filter:retweets → Excludes retweets

✔ lang="en" → Fetches only English tweets

5.2.3 Extracting Metadata for Analysis

Each tweet contains valuable metadata, including:

- **Username** (tweet.user.screen_name)
- **Timestamp** (tweet.created_at)
- **Geolocation** (tweet.coordinates)
- **Engagement Metrics** (tweet.favorite_count, tweet.retweet_count)

◆ Extracting & Structuring Tweet Data

```
import pandas as pd
```

```
data = []
for tweet in tweets:
    data.append({
        "Username": tweet.user.screen_name,
        "Tweet": tweet.text,
        "Date": tweet.created_at,
        "Likes": tweet.favorite_count,
        "Retweets": tweet.retweet_count,
        "Location": tweet.user.location
    })

df = pd.DataFrame(data)
print(df.head())
```

✅ The extracted data can be exported to CSV for further analysis:

```
df.to_csv("twitter_osint_results.csv", index=False)
```

5.2.4 Monitoring Hashtags & Trends

Tracking hashtags allows analysts to monitor viral content and events in real time.

◆ Fetching Trending Topics by Location

```
WOEID_USA = 23424977  # Yahoo! Where On Earth ID for USA
trends = api.get_place_trends(WOEID_USA)

for trend in trends[0]["trends"][:10]:  # Top 10 trends
    print(f" 🔥 {trend['name']} - {trend['tweet_volume']} tweets")
```

5.2.5 Automating Twitter Intelligence Reports

An OSINT analyst can schedule automated intelligence reports using Python's schedule library.

◆ Automating Twitter Data Collection Every Hour

```
import schedule
import time
```

```
def fetch_twitter_osint():
    print("Q Fetching latest OSINT tweets...")
    tweets = api.search_tweets(q="OSINT OR cybersecurity", count=5)
    for tweet in tweets:
        print(f"{tweet.user.screen_name}: {tweet.text}")

# Schedule task
schedule.every(1).hours.do(fetch_twitter_osint)

while True:
    schedule.run_pending()
    time.sleep(60)  # Check every minute
```

5.2.6 Best Practices for Responsible Twitter OSINT

✓ **Respect Rate Limits**: The free-tier API limits searches to 300 requests per 15 minutes.

✓ **Comply with Twitter's API Policies**: Do not store or share private user data.

✓ **Avoid Excessive Scraping**: Overuse can result in account suspension.

✓ **Use Geolocation Filters**: If tracking regional events, use geocode.

5.2.7 Conclusion

Automating Twitter OSINT with Tweepy allows analysts to quickly collect and analyze intelligence from the platform. By combining keyword searches, metadata extraction, and automation, OSINT analysts can enhance their ability to track emerging threats, breaking news, and cybersecurity risks. 🚀

5.3 Extracting Facebook & Instagram Data via APIs & Scraping

Facebook and Instagram contain vast amounts of publicly available data, making them valuable sources for OSINT investigations. However, these platforms have strict API limitations and anti-scraping measures, making data extraction more challenging compared to Twitter. This chapter explores:

✅ How to use the Facebook Graph API and Instagram Graph API

✅ Techniques for extracting public posts, profiles, and metadata

✅ Ethical and legal considerations when scraping Facebook and Instagram

✅ Alternative OSINT methods when API access is restricted

5.3.1 Understanding Facebook & Instagram APIs

Both Facebook and Instagram offer APIs that allow access to public data. However, Facebook owns Instagram, and its API policies apply to both platforms.

API	Purpose	Key Limitations
Facebook Graph API	Access public pages, posts, comments, and events	Requires app approval & user permissions
Instagram Graph API	Fetch posts, comments, and user data (for business accounts)	Personal accounts are restricted
Instagram Basic Display API	Provides basic profile and media data	Only works for **your** own account

Since these APIs are heavily restricted, analysts often rely on web scraping when API access is denied.

5.3.2 Setting Up the Facebook Graph API

◆ Steps to Get API Access

1☐ **Create a Facebook Developer Account** → developers.facebook.com

2☐ **Create an App** → Generate an App ID and secret key

3☐ **Request Permissions** → Example: pages_read_engagement, pages_read_user_content

4☐ **Get an Access Token** → Needed for API requests

◆ Authenticating and Fetching Public Data

```python
import requests

ACCESS_TOKEN = "your_facebook_access_token"
BASE_URL = "https://graph.facebook.com/v18.0"

# Fetch public posts from a Facebook Page
PAGE_ID = "cnn"
url = f"{BASE_URL}/{PAGE_ID}/posts?access_token={ACCESS_TOKEN}"

response = requests.get(url)
data = response.json()

for post in data["data"]:
    print(f"📝 {post['message']} - {post['created_time']}")
```

✅ **Use Case**: Extract posts from public pages (e.g., news pages, official company accounts).

✖ **Limitation**: Personal accounts and private groups cannot be accessed via API.

5.3.3 Extracting Instagram Data via API

The Instagram Graph API is only available for business accounts. To use it:

✓ Convert a personal account into a business account

✓ Connect it to a Facebook Page

✓ Use the Instagram Graph API with authentication

◆ **Fetching Instagram Posts from a Business Account**

```python
INSTAGRAM_ACCOUNT_ID = "your_instagram_business_id"
url =
f"{BASE_URL}/{INSTAGRAM_ACCOUNT_ID}/media?access_token={ACCESS_TOKE
N}"

response = requests.get(url)
data = response.json()

for post in data["data"]:
```

print(f"□ Post ID: {post['id']} - {post['caption']}")

✗ Limitation: The API does not work for private users.

5.3.4 Scraping Public Facebook & Instagram Data

Since API access is restricted, analysts often scrape public data. However, scraping Facebook and Instagram comes with legal and ethical risks, as both platforms actively block scrapers.

◆ Using BeautifulSoup to Extract Facebook Public Posts

```
import requests
from bs4 import BeautifulSoup

URL = "https://www.facebook.com/cnn/posts"
headers = {"User-Agent": "Mozilla/5.0"}

response = requests.get(URL, headers=headers)
soup = BeautifulSoup(response.text, "html.parser")

# Extract post text
posts = soup.find_all("div", class_="userContent")
for post in posts[:5]:
    print(f"📝 {post.text.strip()}")
```

◆ Challenges in Scraping Facebook:

✓ JavaScript rendering: Facebook loads content dynamically, requiring Selenium.

✓ IP blocking: Frequent requests can trigger rate limits.

✓ CAPTCHAs: May appear if scraping is detected.

5.3.5 Scraping Instagram Profiles with Selenium

Instagram's data is heavily JavaScript-based, requiring Selenium to extract content dynamically.

◆ Install Selenium & WebDriver

pip install selenium

◆ Automating Instagram Profile Extraction

```
from selenium import webdriver
from selenium.webdriver.common.by import By
import time

# Setup WebDriver (Ensure you have ChromeDriver installed)
driver = webdriver.Chrome()
driver.get("https://www.instagram.com/instagram/")

time.sleep(5)  # Wait for page to load

# Extract post captions
posts = driver.find_elements(By.XPATH, "//div[contains(@class,'_aacl')]")
for post in posts[:5]:
    print(f"□ {post.text}")

driver.quit()
```

✓ **Use Case**: Extracting Instagram captions, follower counts, and hashtags.

✗ **Limitation**: Requires frequent updates as Instagram changes its layout.

5.3.6 Ethical & Legal Considerations

🔏 Important Notes on Scraping & API Use

✓ **Follow Facebook & Instagram's Terms of Service** – Unauthorized scraping can lead to account bans.

✓ **Avoid collecting private data** – Focus on public content only.

✓ **Use APIs where possible** – Only resort to scraping when APIs fail.

✓ **Rate-limit requests** – To prevent detection and blocking.

◆ Alternative OSINT Methods:

✓ Use Google Dorking: site:facebook.com "keyword"

✓ Monitor public accounts manually

✓ Leverage third-party tools like Maltego & Social Searcher

5.3.7 Conclusion

Extracting OSINT data from Facebook & Instagram is challenging due to strict API limitations and anti-scraping measures. This chapter covered:

✓ Using the Facebook & Instagram APIs for business and public data

✓ Scraping public Facebook and Instagram content responsibly

✓ Ethical considerations for using automation tools

Next, we will explore how to analyze and visualize social media OSINT data using Python! 🚀

5.4 LinkedIn & Reddit OSINT Automation Techniques

LinkedIn and Reddit are valuable platforms for OSINT investigations. LinkedIn provides insights into professional networks, job histories, and corporate intelligence, while Reddit serves as a hub for discussions, leaks, and underground communities. However, both platforms have strict API restrictions and anti-scraping measures, requiring analysts to use alternative automation techniques.

This chapter covers:

✓ LinkedIn OSINT techniques (API access, scraping, alternative methods)

✓ Extracting discussions and user insights from Reddit using PRAW & web scraping

✓ Ethical & legal considerations when automating OSINT from these platforms

5.4.1 Extracting OSINT from LinkedIn

◆ **Why LinkedIn for OSINT?**

✓ **Corporate Intelligence** → Identify employees, company structure, and industry trends

✓ **Threat Actor Tracking** → Detect fake accounts and suspicious job postings

✓ **Resume Analysis** → Track career movements and expertise

✓ **Connection Mapping** → Understand relationships between individuals and organizations

◆ **Challenges with LinkedIn OSINT:**

✗ **No Official API Access** → LinkedIn's API is restricted to approved partners only

✗ **Strict Anti-Scraping Measures** → Frequent requests can lead to account bans

✗ **Login Required** → Public profile data is limited

5.4.2 Automating LinkedIn OSINT with Scraping

Since LinkedIn's API is closed, analysts often rely on Selenium-based web scraping to extract public profile data.

◆ **Scraping LinkedIn Public Profiles with Selenium**

```
from selenium import webdriver
from selenium.webdriver.common.by import By
import time

# Setup WebDriver (Ensure you have ChromeDriver installed)
driver = webdriver.Chrome()

# Open a public LinkedIn profile
driver.get("https://www.linkedin.com/in/satyanadella/")

time.sleep(5)  # Wait for page to load

# Extract Name
name = driver.find_element(By.TAG_NAME, "h1").text
print(f" Name: {name}")

# Extract Headline
```

```
headline = driver.find_element(By.XPATH, "//div[contains(@class, 'text-body-medium')]").text
print(f"🗎 Headline: {headline}")

driver.quit()
```

☑ **Use Case**: Extracting names, job titles, locations, and companies

✗ **Limitations:**

- Requires LinkedIn login for more detailed information
- Risk of detection (use rotating proxies & delays)

5.4.3 Alternative LinkedIn OSINT Techniques

Since scraping LinkedIn directly is risky, analysts can use:

✓ **Google Dorking:**

```
site:linkedin.com/in "cybersecurity analyst"
```

✓ Third-Party OSINT Tools: Maltego, Hunter.io, and People Data Labs

✓ Monitoring Job Listings: To track hiring trends and internal shifts

5.4.4 Extracting OSINT from Reddit

◆ **Why Reddit for OSINT?**

✓ **Threat Intelligence** → Monitor hacking forums, data leaks, and underground groups

✓ **Keyword Monitoring** → Track discussions about specific topics (e.g., "zero-day exploit")

✓ **User Activity Analysis** → Identify influencers in niche communities

✓ **Sentiment Analysis** → Analyze public perception of events and organizations

5.4.5 Automating Reddit OSINT with PRAW (Python Reddit API Wrapper)

Reddit provides a public API that allows analysts to fetch posts, comments, and user data without scraping.

◆ Install PRAW

pip install praw

◆ Authenticate with the Reddit API

import praw

```
# Reddit API Credentials
reddit = praw.Reddit(
    client_id="your_client_id",
    client_secret="your_client_secret",
    user_agent="osint_scraper"
)

print("✅ Reddit API authentication successful!")
```

5.4.6 Fetching Subreddit Discussions for OSINT

Reddit's API allows searching for discussions based on keywords and subreddits.

◆ **Example**: Searching for Cybersecurity Discussions

```
subreddit = reddit.subreddit("cybersecurity")

for post in subreddit.search("data breach", limit=5):
    print(f"🔥 {post.title} ({post.score} upvotes)")
    print(f"🔗 {post.url}\n")
```

✅ **Use Case**: Monitor breach discussions, hacking forums, and emerging threats

5.4.7 Extracting User Comments & Metadata

Each Reddit post contains valuable metadata, including comments, timestamps, and user details.

◆ Fetching Comments from a Reddit Post

*submission =
reddit.submission(url="https://www.reddit.com/r/cybersecurity/comments/xyz123")*

*for comment in submission.comments[:5]: # Limit to first 5 comments
    print(f"💬 {comment.body} (by {comment.author})")*

✅ **Use Case**: Extract insights from discussions related to hacking, cybercrime, and OSINT techniques

5.4.8 Scraping Reddit for Additional Insights

If API access is restricted, BeautifulSoup can be used for basic web scraping.

◆ Scraping Reddit Discussions

*import requests
from bs4 import BeautifulSoup*

*URL = "https://www.reddit.com/r/cybersecurity/"
headers = {"User-Agent": "Mozilla/5.0"}*

*response = requests.get(URL, headers=headers)
soup = BeautifulSoup(response.text, "html.parser")*

*posts = soup.find_all("h3") # Extract post titles
for post in posts[:5]:
    print(f"📌 {post.text}")*

✅ **Use Case**: Monitoring public discussions without API authentication
✖ **Limitations**: Reddit's dynamic content may require Selenium

5.4.9 Ethical & Legal Considerations

🔟 Key Guidelines for Automating LinkedIn & Reddit OSINT

✔ **Do not scrape private data** → Stick to publicly available content

✓ **Respect platform policies** → Repeated scraping may lead to IP bans

✓ **Use official APIs when possible** → Reduces legal risks

✓ **Avoid automated login bypass techniques** → This violates LinkedIn's ToS

5.4.10 Conclusion

✓ LinkedIn is a valuable source for corporate intelligence, but API restrictions and anti-scraping measures require alternative OSINT techniques.

✓ Reddit provides public discussion data, making it ideal for threat intelligence and sentiment analysis.

5.5 Analyzing Hashtags, Mentions & Social Network Trends

Social media platforms generate vast amounts of data that can provide valuable intelligence when analyzed correctly. Hashtags, mentions, and trending topics help OSINT analysts track emerging discussions, identify influential users, and map social networks. This chapter covers:

✓ Extracting and analyzing hashtags from platforms like Twitter, Instagram, and Reddit

✓ Identifying mentions and their role in network analysis

✓ Tracking trending topics using APIs and automated monitoring scripts

✓ Ethical considerations in social media data analysis

5.5.1 Understanding the Importance of Hashtags & Mentions

◆ **Why Track Hashtags?**

✓ **Event Monitoring** – Track real-time discussions on global incidents

✓ **Disinformation Tracking** – Detect coordinated campaigns

✓ **Influencer Analysis** – Identify key players in a topic

✓ **Sentiment Analysis** – Understand public opinion on a subject

◆ Why Track Mentions?

✓ **Threat Intelligence** – Detect when a brand, person, or topic is being discussed

✓ **Network Mapping** – Analyze relationships between users

✓ **Trend Prediction** – Forecast emerging discussions before they go viral

5.5.2 Extracting Hashtag Data from Twitter with Tweepy

Twitter is one of the most powerful platforms for OSINT due to its open API.

◆ Install Tweepy (Python Twitter API wrapper)

```
pip install tweepy
```

◆ Authenticate with the Twitter API

```
import tweepy

# Twitter API Credentials
api_key = "your_api_key"
api_secret = "your_api_secret"
access_token = "your_access_token"
access_secret = "your_access_secret"

auth = tweepy.OAuth1UserHandler(api_key, api_secret, access_token, access_secret)
api = tweepy.API(auth)

print("✅ Twitter API authentication successful!")
```

5.5.3 Searching for Hashtags on Twitter

◆ Example: Tracking #CyberSecurity Discussions

```
hashtag = "#CyberSecurity"

tweets = tweepy.Cursor(api.search_tweets, q=hashtag, lang="en").items(10)
```

```
for tweet in tweets:
    print(f"◀» {tweet.user.screen_name}: {tweet.text}\n")
```

✅ **Use Case**: Track discussions on cybersecurity threats, data breaches, and global events.

5.5.4 Extracting Mentions from Tweets

Mentions (@username) indicate engagement and influence.

◆ **Example: Extracting Mentions from Tweets**

```
query = "data breach -filter:retweets"  # Exclude retweets for better accuracy
tweets = tweepy.Cursor(api.search_tweets, q=query, lang="en").items(10)
```

```
for tweet in tweets:
    mentions = [mention['screen_name'] for mention in tweet.entities['user_mentions']]
    if mentions:
        print(f"🔗 {tweet.user.screen_name} mentioned: {', '.join(mentions)}")
```

✅ **Use Case**: Identify who is being talked about in major cybersecurity incidents.

5.5.5 Extracting Trending Hashtags with Twitter API

◆ **Get Top Trending Topics by Location (e.g., Worldwide)**

```
# Fetch worldwide trends (WOEID 1 = Global)
trends = api.get_place_trends(id=1)
```

```
for trend in trends[0]["trends"][:10]:
    print(f"🔥 Trending: {trend['name']} - {trend['tweet_volume']} tweets")
```

✅ **Use Case**: Track global discussions, emerging threats, or viral misinformation campaigns.

5.5.6 Instagram Hashtag & Mention Tracking

◆ **Instagram Hashtag Search via API**
```
```

Unlike Twitter, Instagram restricts public API access. However, business accounts can retrieve hashtag data.

◆ **Example: Fetching Instagram Hashtag Data**

```
import requests

ACCESS_TOKEN = "your_instagram_access_token"
HASHTAG_ID = "17841593644060714"  # Example hashtag ID for #CyberSecurity

url = f"https://graph.facebook.com/v18.0/{HASHTAG_ID}/recent_media?user_id=your_user_id&access_token={ACCESS_TOKEN}"

response = requests.get(url)
data = response.json()

for post in data["data"]:
    print(f"□ {post['caption']}")
```

✓ **Use Case**: Identify trending cybersecurity-related Instagram discussions.
✗ **Limitation**: Instagram restricts data collection to business accounts only.

5.5.7 Reddit Hashtag & Mention Analysis

Reddit does not use hashtags like Twitter or Instagram, but subreddit keywords function similarly.

◆ **Fetch Posts Containing a Keyword (e.g., "hacking")**

```
import praw

reddit = praw.Reddit(client_id="your_client_id", client_secret="your_client_secret", user_agent="osint_scraper")

subreddit = reddit.subreddit("hacking")

for post in subreddit.search("hacking", limit=5):
    print(f"∞ {post.title} ({post.score} upvotes)\n{post.url}\n")
```

✅ **Use Case**: Identify trending hacking discussions, data leaks, or cyber threats.

5.5.8 Network Analysis of Hashtags & Mentions

Visualizing social media trends helps detect coordinated campaigns and disinformation efforts.

◆ Use NetworkX to Build a Graph of Hashtag Usage

```
import networkx as nx
import matplotlib.pyplot as plt

G = nx.Graph()

# Example hashtag connections
G.add_edges_from([("#CyberSecurity", "#InfoSec"), ("#Hacking", "#ThreatIntel"),
("#OSINT", "#SpyTech")])

plt.figure(figsize=(8,6))
nx.draw(G, with_labels=True, node_color="lightblue", edge_color="gray", font_size=12)
plt.show()
```

✅ **Use Case**: Identify connections between hashtags & coordinated influence campaigns.

5.5.9 Ethical & Legal Considerations

📖 Key Guidelines for Social Media OSINT

✔ **Respect Platform ToS** → Avoid automated scraping where APIs exist

✔ **Do Not Engage with Monitored Content** → Stay passive in investigations

✔ **Be Aware of Bias & Disinformation** → Verify sources before reporting intelligence

✔ **Consider Anonymization** → Protect your identity while collecting data

5.5.10 Conclusion

This chapter explored how hashtags, mentions, and trends provide critical intelligence for OSINT investigations. APIs and scraping techniques help analysts track discussions in real time, uncover disinformation campaigns, and visualize social networks.

5.6 Case Study: Tracking a Viral Social Media Campaign with Python

Social media platforms play a crucial role in shaping public opinion, spreading information, and influencing trends. Tracking a viral campaign can provide insights into how information spreads, who the key influencers are, and whether a campaign is organic or manipulated. This case study demonstrates how OSINT analysts can use Python and APIs to monitor and analyze a viral social media campaign in real-time.

5.6.1 Defining the Case Study

For this case study, we'll track a hypothetical viral campaign:

📌 **Campaign Name:** #CyberSecurityAwareness
📌 **Objective**: Raising awareness about cybersecurity threats
📌 **Platforms Analyzed**: Twitter, Instagram, and Reddit

📌 **Analysis Goals:**

✓ Identify key influencers & engagement levels

✓ Track the spread of the hashtag over time

✓ Analyze sentiment and detect potential disinformation

5.6.2 Step 1 – Tracking Twitter Hashtag Popularity

Extracting Tweets with Tweepy

First, we'll use the Twitter API to extract tweets containing #CyberSecurityAwareness.

◆ **Install Tweepy (if not installed):**

pip install tweepy

◆ **Python Script to Fetch Tweets by Hashtag:**

```
import tweepy

# Twitter API Credentials
api_key = "your_api_key"
api_secret = "your_api_secret"
access_token = "your_access_token"
access_secret = "your_access_secret"

# Authenticate with Twitter API
auth = tweepy.OAuth1UserHandler(api_key, api_secret, access_token, access_secret)
api = tweepy.API(auth)

# Search for tweets containing the hashtag
hashtag = "#CyberSecurityAwareness"
tweets = tweepy.Cursor(api.search_tweets, q=hashtag, lang="en",
tweet_mode="extended").items(20)

for tweet in tweets:
    print(f"🔊 {tweet.user.screen_name}: {tweet.full_text}\n")
```

✅ Insights Gained:

- Real-time tweets mentioning the campaign
- Identifies users discussing the topic
- Helps track how often the hashtag appears

5.6.3 Step 2 – Identifying Key Influencers

◆ **Extracting Most Retweeted & Liked Tweets:**

```
top_tweets = sorted(tweets, key=lambda tweet: tweet.retweet_count, reverse=True)

for tweet in top_tweets[:5]:  # Top 5 most retweeted
    print(f"🔥 {tweet.user.screen_name}: {tweet.full_text} (Retweets:
{tweet.retweet_count})")
```

✅ Insights Gained:

- Identifies top influencers spreading the campaign

- Shows how much engagement the campaign has

5.6.4 Step 3 – Analyzing Instagram Hashtag Popularity

Unlike Twitter, Instagram's API restricts public data collection. However, business accounts can access hashtag insights.

◆ Fetching Instagram Posts with the Hashtag

```
import requests

ACCESS_TOKEN = "your_instagram_access_token"
HASHTAG_ID = "17841593644060714"  # Example hashtag ID for
#CyberSecurityAwareness

url =
f"https://graph.facebook.com/v18.0/{HASHTAG_ID}/recent_media?user_id=your_user_i
d&access_token={ACCESS_TOKEN}"
response = requests.get(url)
data = response.json()

for post in data["data"]:
    print(f"□ {post['caption']}")
```

✅ Insights Gained:

- Number of Instagram posts using the hashtag
- Tracks campaign engagement across platforms

5.6.5 Step 4 – Extracting Reddit Mentions of the Campaign

Reddit is useful for tracking discussions about campaigns in tech and security-related subreddits.

◆ Fetch Recent Posts Mentioning the Campaign on Reddit

```
import praw

reddit = praw.Reddit(client_id="your_client_id", client_secret="your_client_secret",
user_agent="osint_scraper")
```

```
subreddit = reddit.subreddit("cybersecurity")

for post in subreddit.search("CyberSecurityAwareness", limit=5):
    print(f"🔗 {post.title} ({post.score} upvotes)\n{post.url}\n")
```

✅ Insights Gained:

- Measures public interest in the campaign
- Identifies potential concerns or criticisms

5.6.6 Step 5 – Sentiment Analysis on Social Media Data

To determine whether the campaign is positively or negatively received, we'll perform sentiment analysis using TextBlob.

◆ **Install TextBlob:**

```
pip install textblob
```

◆ **Analyze Sentiment of Tweets:**

```
from textblob import TextBlob

for tweet in tweets:
    sentiment = TextBlob(tweet.full_text).sentiment.polarity
    sentiment_label = "Positive" if sentiment > 0 else "Negative" if sentiment < 0 else "Neutral"
    print(f"📝 {tweet.user.screen_name}: {tweet.full_text} → Sentiment: {sentiment_label}")
```

✅ Insights Gained:

- Determines whether the campaign is well-received
- Flags potential negative sentiment or disinformation

5.6.7 Step 6 – Visualizing Campaign Data

Visualizing hashtag trends over time helps identify spikes in engagement.

◆ Install Matplotlib & Pandas:

pip install matplotlib pandas

◆ Plot Hashtag Popularity Over Time:

```
import matplotlib.pyplot as plt
import pandas as pd

# Example hashtag data over days
dates = ["Feb 1", "Feb 2", "Feb 3", "Feb 4", "Feb 5"]
tweet_counts = [50, 120, 300, 800, 1500]

plt.figure(figsize=(8,5))
plt.plot(dates, tweet_counts, marker="o", linestyle="-", color="b")
plt.xlabel("Date")
plt.ylabel("Number of Tweets")
plt.title("Hashtag Popularity Over Time")
plt.grid()
plt.show()
```

✅ **Insights Gained:**

- Detects when the campaign gained traction
- Shows potential bot-driven spikes

5.6.8 Key Findings from the Case Study

◆ How fast did the campaign spread?

✔ Our analysis shows that #CyberSecurityAwareness started with low engagement but grew rapidly on Day 3.

◆ Who were the biggest influencers?

✓ A few key Twitter accounts generated thousands of retweets, significantly amplifying the message.

◆ **Was there negative sentiment or disinformation?**

✓ Sentiment analysis revealed 90% positive mentions but also identified a small wave of disinformation linking the campaign to fake cybersecurity alerts.

◆ **Which platform drove the most engagement?**

✓ Twitter and Reddit outperformed Instagram, suggesting that OSINT analysts should focus on Twitter for similar campaigns.

5.6.9 Ethical Considerations in Campaign Monitoring

⚠ **Key Considerations:**

✓ **Do not engage with monitored content** → Passive analysis only
✓ **Respect platform ToS** → Avoid scraping where APIs exist
✓ **Verify disinformation before reporting** → Cross-check sources

5.6.10 Conclusion

✓ Social media OSINT can track viral trends, identify influencers, and detect disinformation.

✓ Automating data collection across platforms (Twitter, Instagram, Reddit) improves intelligence gathering.

✓ Sentiment analysis and network visualization provide deeper insights into the campaign's impact.

6. Automating Email & Domain Investigations

In this chapter, we explore how to automate email and domain investigations to enhance your OSINT capabilities in tracking online identities, uncovering connections, and identifying potential threats. Using Python, we'll guide you through automating the process of querying WHOIS databases, checking domain registrants, and examining email metadata to gain deeper insights into the ownership and history of domains and email addresses. You'll also learn how to use APIs to retrieve information about email addresses, detect potential fraud, and correlate data across multiple sources. By the end of this chapter, you will have the tools to automate investigations into domains and emails, allowing you to uncover crucial intelligence that can support cybersecurity, threat analysis, and other investigative work.

6.1 Extracting Email Data from Public Breach Databases

Email addresses are a valuable OSINT asset, often leading to deeper intelligence on individuals, organizations, and potential security risks. Public breach databases contain leaked email credentials from past data breaches, helping analysts assess account compromises, phishing risks, and threat actor activities.

This chapter covers:

✓ Using public breach lookup services (Have I Been Pwned, Dehashed, LeakCheck)

✓ Automating email search with Python APIs

✓ Extracting and analyzing compromised credentials

✓ Ethical & legal considerations in email investigations

6.1.1 Understanding Public Breach Databases

A data breach occurs when hackers expose sensitive information from compromised systems. These breaches often contain:

📌 Email addresses (user credentials)
📌 Passwords (sometimes hashed or plaintext)
📌 Phone numbers & personal details

◆ Sources of Public Breach Data

- **Have I Been Pwned (HIBP)** → https://haveibeenpwned.com
- **Dehashed** → https://www.dehashed.com
- **LeakCheck** → https://leakcheck.io

Hacked databases on forums/dark web (⚠ requires caution)

! Note: Some services require API keys for automation.

6.1.2 Using Have I Been Pwned API to Check Email Breaches

Have I Been Pwned (HIBP) is one of the most widely used public breach search tools. It allows users to check if an email has been exposed in known data breaches.

◆ Step 1: Get API Key

Sign up for an API key at: HIBP API Key

◆ Install Required Python Libraries

pip install requests

◆ Python Script to Check Email in Data Breaches

```
import requests

API_KEY = "your_hibp_api_key"
email = "target@example.com"

headers = {
    "hibp-api-key": API_KEY,
    "User-Agent": "OSINT-Script"
}

url = f"https://haveibeenpwned.com/api/v3/breachedaccount/{email}"
```

```
response = requests.get(url, headers=headers)

if response.status_code == 200:
    breaches = response.json()
    for breach in breaches:
        print(f"● Breach: {breach['Name']} | Date: {breach['BreachDate']} | Exposed Data:
{', '.join(breach['DataClasses'])}")
else:
    print("✅ No breaches found for this email.")
```

✅ Insights Gained:

- Shows which breaches exposed the email
- Identifies what data (passwords, phone numbers, etc.) was leaked
- Helps analysts assess risk levels

6.1.3 Searching Leaked Emails & Passwords with Dehashed API

Dehashed provides email and password leak searches for OSINT analysts.

◆ Python Script to Search for Emails in Dehashed

```
import requests

DEHASHED_USERNAME = "your_email"
DEHASHED_PASSWORD = "your_password"
email = "target@example.com"

response = requests.get(
    f"https://api.dehashed.com/search?query={email}",
    auth=(DEHASHED_USERNAME, DEHASHED_PASSWORD)
)

if response.status_code == 200:
    print(response.json())
else:
    print("✗ No results found or API access denied.")
```

✅ Insights Gained:

- Extracts passwords, IPs, and other associated data
- Finds historical breaches related to an email

6.1.4 Checking Email Breaches with LeakCheck API

LeakCheck offers paid breach lookups with API access.

◆ Python Script to Automate LeakCheck API Searches

```python
import requests

LEAKCHECK_API_KEY = "your_leakcheck_api_key"
email = "target@example.com"

url = f"https://leakcheck.io/api/public?key={LEAKCHECK_API_KEY}&query={email}"

response = requests.get(url)
data = response.json()

if data["success"]:
    for leak in data["result"]:
        print(f"● Breach: {leak['database']} | Password: {leak['password']}")
else:
    print("✅ No breaches found.")
```

✅ Insights Gained:

- Retrieves plaintext passwords (if available)
- Helps analysts verify credential leaks

6.1.5 Analyzing Breach Data for OSINT Investigations

Once an email is found in breach databases, analysts can:

✔ Correlate breaches across multiple sources

✔ Check password reuse across platforms

✓ Identify linked accounts using usernames/IPs

◆ **Example Data Analysis: Grouping Breach Info**

```
breach_data = [
    {"email": "target@example.com", "source": "LinkedIn", "password": "123456"},
    {"email": "target@example.com", "source": "Dropbox", "password": "password123"}
]

for entry in breach_data:
    print(f"● {entry['email']} found in {entry['source']} breach with password:
{entry['password']}")
```

✅ **Use Case**: Detecting password reuse across breaches.

6.1.6 Ethical & Legal Considerations in Email OSINT

🔒 **Key Legal & Ethical Guidelines:**

✓ Use only publicly available databases (HIBP, Dehashed)

✓ Do not attempt unauthorized access to leaked credentials

✓ Obtain proper consent for investigations involving personal data

✓ Report compromised credentials responsibly (to companies or individuals)

6.1.7 Conclusion

✅ Public breach databases help OSINT analysts identify compromised emails and passwords.

✅ Python automation with APIs (HIBP, Dehashed, LeakCheck) improves efficiency in breach investigations.

✅ Analysts must follow strict ethical & legal standards when handling breached data.

6.2 Verifying Email Addresses & Identifying Associated Accounts

Verifying an email address and uncovering associated accounts is a critical step in OSINT investigations. This process helps determine whether an email is active, who it belongs to, and what social media, breached databases, and online services are linked to it.

This chapter covers:

✅ Email verification techniques (SMTP, API-based checks)

✅ Finding social media accounts linked to an email

✅ Using OSINT tools & Python scripts to automate lookups

✅ Ethical considerations in email investigations

6.2.1 Why Verify Email Addresses?

Verifying an email can:

✓ Confirm if an email is valid & active

✓ Identify associated social media profiles

✓ Detect potential fraud, phishing, or impersonation

✓ Improve accuracy in OSINT investigations

Common Ways to Verify an Email:

◆ **SMTP Verification** → Check if an email server accepts messages

◆ **OSINT APIs** → Services like Hunter.io & EmailRep fetch email reputation

◆ **Social Media Lookups** → Search for linked profiles

◆ **Leaked Data Searches** → Check if the email appears in breaches

6.2.2 Email Verification via SMTP Check

SMTP (Simple Mail Transfer Protocol) verification checks whether an email exists on the recipient's mail server.

◆ Python Script to Verify an Email via SMTP

```python
import smtplib

def verify_email(email):
    try:
        domain = email.split("@")[1]
        mx_record = f"mx.{domain}"  # Assume standard MX record format

        server = smtplib.SMTP(mx_record)
        server.set_debuglevel(0)
        server.helo()
        server.mail("test@example.com")
        code, message = server.rcpt(email)

        if code == 250:
            return f"✓ Email {email} is valid!"
        else:
            return f"✗ Email {email} does not exist!"
    except Exception as e:
        return f"⚠ Error verifying email: {e}"

email = "target@example.com"
print(verify_email(email))
```

✓ Insights Gained:

- Confirms if an email exists
- Helps detect disposable or fake emails

⚠ Limitations:

- Some mail servers block SMTP lookups
- Doesn't confirm if the user actively checks the email

6.2.3 Checking Email Reputation with EmailRep API

EmailRep.io provides email reputation & OSINT intelligence.

◆ Install Required Library:

pip install requests

◆ Python Script to Check Email Reputation with EmailRep

```
import requests

email = "target@example.com"
url = f"https://emailrep.io/{email}"

response = requests.get(url)
data = response.json()

if response.status_code == 200:
    print(f"✉ Email: {email}")
    print(f"☐ Reputation: {data['reputation']}")
    print(f"☐ Associated Domains: {data['details']['profiles']}")
else:
    print("✗ Unable to retrieve email reputation.")
```

✅ Insights Gained:

- Checks if an email is flagged as suspicious or spammy
- Finds associated domains & accounts
- Detects if the email is disposable, temporary, or known for fraud

6.2.4 Searching for Social Media Accounts Linked to an Email

1☐ Manual Lookups

Many social media platforms allow password reset lookups to check if an email is registered:

- **Twitter** → Enter email on the forgot password page

- **Facebook** → Check account recovery page

- **LinkedIn** → Try signing up, and LinkedIn will show if the email is taken

2️ Automating Social Media Lookups with Python

◆ Python Script to Search for Email on HaveIBeenPwned & Dehashed

```
import requests

HIBP_API_KEY = "your_hibp_api_key"
email = "target@example.com"

headers = {"hibp-api-key": HIBP_API_KEY}
url = f"https://haveibeenpwned.com/api/v3/breachedaccount/{email}"

response = requests.get(url, headers=headers)

if response.status_code == 200:
    breaches = response.json()
    for breach in breaches:
        print(f"● Found in breach: {breach['Name']} (Date: {breach['BreachDate']})")
else:
    print("✔ No breaches found for this email.")
```


✔ Insights Gained:

- Finds leaked email-password combos
- Identifies potential hacked social media accounts

6.2.5 Checking If an Email is Associated with a Domain

If an email is corporate (e.g., john@company.com), checking the domain's WHOIS data can reveal:

✔ The company's domain registration details

✓ If the email belongs to a legitimate organization

◆ Python Script to Extract WHOIS Data

```python
import whois

email_domain = "example.com"

try:
    domain_info = whois.whois(email_domain)
    print(f"□ Domain: {email_domain}")
    print(f"▦ Registered On: {domain_info.creation_date}")
    print(f"🔎 Registrar: {domain_info.registrar}")
except Exception as e:
    print(f"⚠ Error fetching WHOIS: {e}")
```

✅ Insights Gained:

- Checks if the email domain is legitimate
- Helps find company details & registration dates

6.2.6 Ethical & Legal Considerations

🏛 Important OSINT Rules:

✓ Only use public APIs & legal lookup services

✓ Do not engage in unauthorized access to email accounts

✓ Respect user privacy when handling leaked data

◆ Legally Acceptable OSINT Sources:

✅ **HavelBeenPwned API** → Publicly available breach data

✅ **EmailRep API** → OSINT-based reputation lookup

✅ **WHOIS data** → Public domain registration info

✗ Avoid unauthorized hacking methods like brute-force login attempts or phishing.

6.2.7 Conclusion

✓ Email verification helps confirm legitimacy & associated accounts

✓ APIs like EmailRep & HavelBeenPwned automate OSINT email lookups

✓ Social media & WHOIS checks provide deeper insights into email ownership

✓ Ethical email investigations ensure compliance with legal frameworks

6.3 Using Python to Automate WHOIS & Domain Lookups

Domain intelligence is a crucial aspect of OSINT investigations. By analyzing WHOIS records, DNS information, and IP history, analysts can uncover valuable insights about a website's owner, infrastructure, and potential connections to other entities. Automating these lookups with Python streamlines the process, making it faster and more efficient.

📌 **What You'll Learn in This Chapter**

✓ Understanding WHOIS records and domain registration data

✓ Using Python to automate WHOIS lookups

✓ Extracting DNS records for deeper intelligence

✓ Identifying historical WHOIS changes & domain ownership patterns

✓ Ethical and legal considerations in domain investigations

6.3.1 Understanding WHOIS & Domain Intelligence

WHOIS is a protocol that allows users to query domain registration details. These records typically include:

📌 Registrant Name & Contact Info (unless privacy-protected)
📌 Registrar Information (GoDaddy, Namecheap, etc.)
📌 Creation & Expiration Dates
📌 Name Servers (Which servers the domain is hosted on)

📌 Associated Domains (Reverse WHOIS can reveal linked domains)

◆ **Use Cases in OSINT:**

✔ Identifying who owns a domain

✔ Tracking threat actor infrastructure (e.g., phishing domains)

✔ Discovering related domains & subdomains

✔ Detecting domain expiration & takeovers

6.3.2 Automating WHOIS Lookups with Python

Python makes it easy to retrieve WHOIS data using the whois library.

◆ **Install Required Package:**

pip install python-whois

◆ **Python Script for WHOIS Lookups**

```
import whois

def get_whois_info(domain):
    try:
        domain_info = whois.whois(domain)
        print(f"□ Domain: {domain}")
        print(f"🎞 Created On: {domain_info.creation_date}")
        print(f"🔎 Registrar: {domain_info.registrar}")
        print(f"📌 Name Servers: {', '.join(domain_info.name_servers)}")
        print(f"🔗 Status: {domain_info.status}")
    except Exception as e:
        print(f"⚠ Error fetching WHOIS data: {e}")

domain = "example.com"
get_whois_info(domain)
```

✅ Insights Gained:

- Identifies domain ownership & creation details
- Detects potential domain privacy protection
- Helps link multiple domains under the same registrar

⚠ Limitations:

- Many domains use privacy protection services (e.g., Cloudflare, WhoisGuard)
- Some registrars limit WHOIS queries to prevent abuse

6.3.3 Extracting DNS Records for OSINT Investigations

DNS (Domain Name System) records provide additional intelligence, including:

- **A Records** → Maps a domain to an IP address

- **MX Records** → Shows mail servers handling email for the domain

- **TXT Records** → Contains SPF, DKIM, or verification data

◆ **Python Script to Fetch DNS Records**

```python
import dns.resolver

def get_dns_records(domain):
    try:
        print(f"🔎 DNS Records for {domain}:")

        # Get A Record (IP Address)
        a_records = dns.resolver.resolve(domain, 'A')
        print(f"□ A Record: {[ip.to_text() for ip in a_records]}")

        # Get MX Records (Mail Servers)
        mx_records = dns.resolver.resolve(domain, 'MX')
        print(f"✉@ MX Record: {[mx.exchange.to_text() for mx in mx_records]}")

        # Get TXT Records
        txt_records = dns.resolver.resolve(domain, 'TXT')
        print(f"📌 TXT Record: {[txt.to_text() for txt in txt_records]}")
```

```
    except Exception as e:
        print(f"⚠ Error fetching DNS records: {e}")

domain = "example.com"
get_dns_records(domain)
```

✅ Insights Gained:

- Identifies website hosting infrastructure
- Extracts email security settings (SPF, DKIM, DMARC)
- Helps detect malicious domains (typosquatting, phishing sites)

6.3.4 Tracking Historical WHOIS & Domain Ownership Changes

Tracking past WHOIS records can reveal:

✓ Ownership changes over time (linked to fraud or criminal activity)

✓ Expired domains & takeovers

✓ Pattern analysis for threat intelligence

◆ Services for Historical WHOIS Lookups:

- **WhoisXML API** → Paid service for historical WHOIS

- **SecurityTrails** → Offers domain history data

- **Wayback Machine (Archive.org)** → Screenshots of old domains

◆ Python Script to Automate WhoisXML API Queries

```
import requests

API_KEY = "your_whoisxml_api_key"
domain = "example.com"

url =
f"https://www.whoisxmlapi.com/whoisserver/WhoisService?apiKey={API_KEY}&domain
Name={domain}&outputFormat=json"
```

```
response = requests.get(url)
data = response.json()

if "WhoisRecord" in data:
    print(f"▦ Previous Owner: {data['WhoisRecord']['registrant']['name']}")
    print(f"🔎 Previous Country: {data['WhoisRecord']['registrant']['country']}")
    print(f"🕐 Last Updated: {data['WhoisRecord']['updatedDate']}")
else:
    print("✗ No historical data found.")
```

✅ Insights Gained:

- Tracks changes in ownership
- Detects registrar transfers
- Helps uncover hidden connections between domains

6.3.5 Identifying Associated Domains (Reverse WHOIS)

Reverse WHOIS helps find other domains registered by the same entity. This is useful for:

✓ Linking phishing domains to common owners

✓ Investigating cybercriminal infrastructure

✓ Tracking threat actors across multiple domains

◆ **Python Script to Automate Reverse WHOIS (SecurityTrails API)**

```
import requests

API_KEY = "your_securitytrails_api_key"
search_term = "target@example.com"

url = f"https://api.securitytrails.com/v1/search/registrant?apikey={API_KEY}&q={search_term}"

response = requests.get(url)
data = response.json()
```

```
if "records" in data:
    print("🔎 Domains registered by this email:")
    for record in data["records"]:
        print(f"□ {record['hostname']}")
else:
    print("✗ No associated domains found.")
```

✅ **Insights Gained:**

- Finds multiple domains registered by the same email/IP
- Tracks potentially fraudulent networks

6.3.6 Ethical & Legal Considerations in Domain Lookups

🔒 **Important OSINT Guidelines:**

✓ Use only legal & public WHOIS services

✓ Respect privacy laws (GDPR restricts some WHOIS data)

✓ Do not engage in unauthorized access

◆ **Legally Acceptable OSINT Sources:**

✅ **WHOIS databases** → Public domain records

✅ **SecurityTrails API** → Historical WHOIS data

✅ **DNS lookups** → Publicly available information

✗ Avoid using illegal methods like brute-force queries or unauthorized hacking.

6.3.7 Conclusion

✅ WHOIS & domain lookups provide critical OSINT intelligence

✅ Python automation simplifies DNS, WHOIS, and historical record analysis

✅ Reverse WHOIS & IP tracking help uncover hidden connections

✅ Ethical OSINT practices ensure compliance with data privacy laws

6.4 Extracting DNS, IP & Hosting Information Programmatically

In OSINT investigations, DNS records, IP addresses, and hosting details provide valuable intelligence about a domain's infrastructure, ownership, and potential links to other online entities. Automating these lookups with Python allows analysts to gather this information efficiently, aiding in threat intelligence, cybersecurity investigations, and attribution efforts.

📌 **What You'll Learn in This Chapter**

✅ Extracting DNS records (A, MX, TXT, NS) with Python

✅ Finding IP addresses and geolocation data

✅ Identifying web hosting providers & ASNs

✅ Detecting shared hosting & related domains

✅ Automating lookups with OSINT APIs

6.4.1 Understanding DNS & Hosting Data for OSINT

◆ DNS (Domain Name System) translates domain names into IP addresses. Key DNS records include:

✔ **A Record** → Maps domain to an IPv4 address

✔ **AAAA Record** → Maps domain to an IPv6 address

✔ **MX Record** → Specifies mail servers for the domain

✔ **NS Record** → Lists authoritative name servers

✔ **TXT Record** → Stores SPF/DKIM/DMARC authentication data

◆ **Hosting Information reveals:**

✔ Server locations & ISPs

✓ Web hosting providers (Cloudflare, AWS, DigitalOcean, etc.)

✓ Shared hosting (multiple domains on the same server)

◆ **IP Address Intelligence helps:**

✓ Identify the domain's physical location

✓ Uncover related infrastructure (subdomains, aliases, etc.)

✓ Detect malicious or suspicious hosting patterns

6.4.2 Extracting DNS Records with Python

Python's dnspython library allows querying DNS records efficiently.

◆ **Install Required Package:**

pip install dnspython

◆ **Python Script to Fetch DNS Records:**

```
import dns.resolver

def get_dns_records(domain):
    try:
        print(f"🔎 DNS Records for {domain}:")

        # Get A Record (IPv4 Address)
        a_records = dns.resolver.resolve(domain, 'A')
        print(f"□ A Record: {[ip.to_text() for ip in a_records]}")

        # Get MX Records (Mail Servers)
        mx_records = dns.resolver.resolve(domain, 'MX')
        print(f"📧 MX Record: {[mx.exchange.to_text() for mx in mx_records]}")

        # Get NS Records (Name Servers)
        ns_records = dns.resolver.resolve(domain, 'NS')
        print(f"📌 Name Servers: {[ns.to_text() for ns in ns_records]}")
```

```
# Get TXT Records (SPF, DKIM, DMARC)
txt_records = dns.resolver.resolve(domain, 'TXT')
print(f"📜 TXT Record: {[txt.to_text() for txt in txt_records]}")

except Exception as e:
    print(f"⚠ Error fetching DNS records: {e}")

domain = "example.com"
get_dns_records(domain)
```

✅ Insights Gained:

✔ Identifies web server & email infrastructure

✔ Reveals DNS security settings (SPF, DKIM, DMARC)

✔ Helps in detecting phishing or fake domains

6.4.3 Finding IP Addresses & Hosting Information

Finding IP addresses & hosting details can help uncover:

✔ The physical location of a website

✔ Whether the domain is hosted on a shared or dedicated server

✔ The ISP & hosting provider for the website

◆ Python Script to Extract IP Address of a Domain:

```
import socket

def get_ip(domain):
    try:
        ip_address = socket.gethostbyname(domain)
        print(f"□ Domain: {domain}")
        print(f"📌 IP Address: {ip_address}")
    except Exception as e:
        print(f"⚠ Error retrieving IP: {e}")
```

```
domain = "example.com"
get_ip(domain)
```

✅ Insights Gained:

✔ Determines the real server behind a website

✔ Helps in bypassing Cloudflare protection (if a direct IP is exposed)

6.4.4 Geolocating IP Addresses for OSINT

IP geolocation helps determine where a website or server is physically hosted.

◆ Using the IPinfo API to Get Geolocation Data:

1️⃣ Sign up for a free API key at ipinfo.io
2️⃣ Install the Requests Library:

pip install requests

3️⃣ Python Script to Fetch IP Geolocation Data:

```
import requests

API_KEY = "your_ipinfo_api_key"
ip_address = "8.8.8.8"  # Example IP

url = f"https://ipinfo.io/{ip_address}/json?token={API_KEY}"
response = requests.get(url)
data = response.json()

if "country" in data:
    print(f"□ IP Address: {ip_address}")
    print(f"📍 Location: {data['city']}, {data['region']}, {data['country']}")
    print(f"🏢 ISP: {data['org']}")
else:
    print("✖ Unable to retrieve geolocation data.")
```

✅ **Insights Gained:**

✔ Physical location of a web server

✔ ISP details & hosting provider

✔ Potential threat actor locations

6.4.5 Identifying Shared Hosting & Associated Domains

If a website is on shared hosting, it may be linked to other suspicious domains.

◆ **Using SecurityTrails API to Find Associated Domains:**

```
import requests

API_KEY = "your_securitytrails_api_key"
ip_address = "192.168.1.1"

url =
f"https://api.securitytrails.com/v1/domain/{ip_address}/associated?apikey={API_KEY}"
response = requests.get(url)
data = response.json()

if "records" in data:
    print("🔎 Domains sharing this IP:")
    for record in data["records"]:
        print(f"□ {record['hostname']}")
else:
    print("✘ No associated domains found.")
```

✅ **Insights Gained:**

✔ Detects multiple websites on the same server

✔ Helps track down malicious networks

✔ Uncovers links between cybercrime operations

6.4.6 Automating Hosting & ASN Lookups

Autonomous System Number (ASN) lookups provide insights into:

✓ Who owns an IP range

✓ What other websites they control

✓ Hosting patterns & potential infrastructure overlap

◆ **Using the IPinfo API to Get ASN Data:**

```
url = f"https://ipinfo.io/{ip_address}/json?token={API_KEY}"
response = requests.get(url)
data = response.json()

if "asn" in data:
    print(f"🎫 ASN: {data['asn']}")
    print(f"□ ISP: {data['org']}")
else:
    print("✗ No ASN data found.")
```

✅ Insights Gained:

✓ Tracks who is behind a hosting service

✓ Detects suspicious hosting patterns

✓ Uncovers infrastructure used in cyberattacks

6.4.7 Ethical & Legal Considerations

🚨 **Key OSINT Rules:**

✓ Use public APIs & legal lookup services

✓ Do not engage in unauthorized access

✓ Respect GDPR & privacy laws when handling IP data

◆ **Legally Acceptable OSINT Sources:**

✓ **IPinfo.io & SecurityTrails API** → Publicly available hosting & ASN data

✓ **WHOIS databases** → Public domain records

✓ **Passive DNS services** → Monitor changes in domain infrastructure

✗ Avoid unauthorized scanning or hacking techniques.

6.4.8 Conclusion

✓ DNS & IP lookups provide deep OSINT intelligence

✓ Python automation simplifies domain investigations

✓ IP geolocation & ASN data help track online infrastructure

✓ Ethical OSINT practices ensure compliance with legal standards

6.5 Monitoring Domain & Email Reputation with Automation

In OSINT and cybersecurity investigations, domain and email reputation monitoring helps analysts detect phishing sites, spam campaigns, and malicious infrastructure. Automating this process with Python allows real-time tracking of blacklisted domains, compromised email accounts, and suspicious IP addresses.

📌 **What You'll Learn in This Chapter**

✓ Checking domain reputation using OSINT APIs

✓ Automating email breach & blacklist lookups

✓ Detecting malicious domains linked to cyber threats

✓ Monitoring changes in domain reputation over time

✓ Ethical considerations in domain & email tracking

6.5.1 Why Monitor Domain & Email Reputation?

- **For Cyber Threat Intelligence (CTI)** → Detect phishing, malware, and scam websites
- **For Brand Protection** → Identify impersonation domains targeting organizations
- **For SOC Analysts & Blue Teams** → Monitor corporate emails for leaks & breaches
- **For OSINT Investigators** → Track malicious domains used by threat actors

6.5.2 Checking Domain Reputation with Python

Domain reputation scoring helps determine if a website is flagged for phishing, malware, or spam. Various OSINT APIs provide this data, including VirusTotal, AbuseIPDB, and URLVoid.

◆ Using VirusTotal API to Check Domain Reputation

1️⃣ Sign up at VirusTotal and get an API key

2️⃣ Install Requests Library:

pip install requests

3️⃣ Python Script to Check Domain Reputation:

```
import requests

API_KEY = "your_virustotal_api_key"
domain = "example.com"

url = f"https://www.virustotal.com/api/v3/domains/{domain}"
headers = {"x-apikey": API_KEY}

response = requests.get(url, headers=headers)
data = response.json()

if "data" in data:
    stats = data["data"]["attributes"]["last_analysis_stats"]
    print(f"🔍 Domain Reputation for {domain}:")
    print(f"✅ Harmless: {stats['harmless']}")
```

```
    print(f"⚠ Suspicious: {stats['suspicious']}")
    print(f"✗ Malicious: {stats['malicious']}")
else:
    print("✗ No reputation data found.")
```

✅ Insights Gained:

✓ Detects malware-infected & phishing websites

✓ Identifies domains linked to cybercrime

✓ Helps security teams blocklist dangerous sites

6.5.3 Monitoring Email Breaches & Blacklists

Monitoring email reputation can reveal compromised credentials, spam listings, and phishing indicators.

Checking Email Breach Data via Have I Been Pwned (HIBP)

1️ Get an API Key from HIBP

2️ Python Script to Check Email Breaches:

```
import requests

API_KEY = "your_hibp_api_key"
email = "example@example.com"

url = f"https://haveibeenpwned.com/api/v3/breachedaccount/{email}"
headers = {"hibp-api-key": API_KEY, "User-Agent": "OSINT-Script"}

response = requests.get(url, headers=headers)
if response.status_code == 200:
    breaches = response.json()
    print(f"✉ Email {email} found in {len(breaches)} breaches:")
    for breach in breaches:
        print(f"⚠ Breach: {breach['Name']} - {breach['BreachDate']}")
else:
```

print("✅ No breaches found for this email.")

✅ Insights Gained:

✔ Identifies compromised emails

✔ Helps in preventing account takeovers

✔ Assists OSINT analysts in profiling threat actors

6.5.4 Checking IP & Domain Blacklists

If an IP or domain is blacklisted, it may be flagged for spam, malware, or hacking activity.

◆ Using AbuseIPDB API to Check for Blacklisted IPs

1️⃣ Get an API key from AbuseIPDB

2️⃣ Python Script to Check an IP Reputation:

```python
import requests

API_KEY = "your_abuseipdb_api_key"
ip_address = "8.8.8.8"

url = f"https://api.abuseipdb.com/api/v2/check?ipAddress={ip_address}"
headers = {"Key": API_KEY, "Accept": "application/json"}

response = requests.get(url, headers=headers)
data = response.json()

if "data" in data:
    print(f"🔎 IP Reputation for {ip_address}:")
    print(f"⚠ Abuse Score: {data['data']['abuseConfidenceScore']}")
    print(f"📅 Last Reported: {data['data']['lastReportedAt']}")
else:
    print("✅ No blacklisting found.")
```

✅ Insights Gained:

✓ Detects spam servers & botnet activity

✓ Helps in blocking malicious IPs in firewalls

✓ Supports threat hunting & forensic investigations

6.5.5 Automating Domain Reputation Monitoring

To track domain reputation over time, set up an automated monitoring script that runs daily.

◆ **Example**: Automating Domain Reputation Checks with a Scheduler

```
import time
import requests

API_KEY = "your_virustotal_api_key"
domains = ["example.com", "suspicious-site.com"]

def check_domain_reputation(domain):
    url = f"https://www.virustotal.com/api/v3/domains/{domain}"
    headers = {"x-apikey": API_KEY}
    response = requests.get(url, headers=headers)
    data = response.json()

    if "data" in data:
        stats = data["data"]["attributes"]["last_analysis_stats"]
        return {
            "domain": domain,
            "harmless": stats["harmless"],
            "suspicious": stats["suspicious"],
            "malicious": stats["malicious"]
        }
    return None

while True:
    print("🔍 Running daily domain reputation check...")
    for domain in domains:
```

```
    result = check_domain_reputation(domain)
    if result:
        print(result)
    time.sleep(86400)  # Run every 24 hours
```

✅ Automated Monitoring Benefits:

✓ Detects newly flagged phishing sites

✓ Tracks domain reputation changes

✓ Alerts security teams about emerging threats

6.5.6 Ethical & Legal Considerations

🔏 Key Ethical Rules:

✓ Do not monitor private emails without consent

✓ Use only authorized OSINT APIs

✓ Do not engage in unauthorized domain scanning

◆ Legally Acceptable OSINT Sources:

✅ **VirusTotal & AbuseIPDB** → Publicly available blacklists

✅ **Have I Been Pwned (HIBP)** → Publicly reported breaches

✅ **WHOIS & Passive DNS Services** → Openly available domain data

✗ Avoid using illegal hacking tools to access private accounts or systems.

6.5.7 Conclusion

✅ Automated monitoring helps track phishing, spam, and hacked accounts

✅ Python scripts enable real-time OSINT intelligence

✅ Reputation tracking improves cybersecurity defenses

✅ Ethical OSINT ensures compliance with laws & regulations

6.6 Case Study: Tracking Phishing Emails Using OSINT Automation

Phishing remains one of the most effective attack vectors for cybercriminals, often leading to credential theft, financial fraud, and malware infections. In this case study, we will explore how OSINT automation can help track phishing emails, identify their origins, and detect associated malicious domains. By leveraging Python and various OSINT tools, we can automate the investigation of phishing attempts and enhance cyber threat intelligence.

6.6.1 Case Background: A Surge in Phishing Emails

A financial institution noticed a surge in phishing emails targeting its customers. These emails impersonated the bank and included links to fake login pages designed to steal user credentials. The security team needed an automated approach to:

- Extract email metadata (headers, sender information)
- Analyze links for malicious domains
- Check domain reputation & blacklist status
- Identify associated infrastructure (IPs, WHOIS data)
- Monitor similar phishing campaigns over time

6.6.2 Step 1: Extracting Email Headers & Analyzing Metadata

Email headers contain vital forensic details, including sender information, mail server IPs, and relay points. Python can automate the extraction of these details.

Python Script to Parse Email Headers

```
import email
from email import policy
from email.parser import BytesParser

def extract_email_metadata(email_file):
    with open(email_file, "rb") as f:
        msg = BytesParser(policy=policy.default).parse(f)
```

```python
    metadata = {
        "From": msg["From"],
        "To": msg["To"],
        "Subject": msg["Subject"],
        "Received": msg["Received"],
        "Return-Path": msg["Return-Path"]
    }

    return metadata

email_file = "phishing_email.eml"  # Replace with actual email file
metadata = extract_email_metadata(email_file)

for key, value in metadata.items():
    print(f"{key}: {value}")
```

Key Insights from Email Headers:

- Identifies spoofed senders
- Reveals IP addresses used to send phishing emails
- Helps trace back to compromised mail servers

6.6.3 Step 2: Extracting & Analyzing Suspicious URLs

Phishing emails often contain malicious URLs that lead to fake login pages. Python can extract links from email bodies and check their reputation.

Extracting URLs from Email Content

```python
import re

def extract_urls_from_email(email_body):
    urls = re.findall(r'https?://[^\s]+', email_body)
    return urls

email_body = """Click here to verify your account: https://malicious-site.com/login"""
urls = extract_urls_from_email(email_body)

print(" Extracted URLs:", urls)
```

Why Does This Matters?

- Identifies malicious links used in phishing emails
- Helps security teams block dangerous URLs

Checking Domain Reputation with VirusTotal API

```
import requests

API_KEY = "your_virustotal_api_key"
url_to_check = "malicious-site.com"

vt_url = f"https://www.virustotal.com/api/v3/domains/{url_to_check}"
headers = {"x-apikey": API_KEY}

response = requests.get(vt_url, headers=headers)
data = response.json()

if "data" in data:
    stats = data["data"]["attributes"]["last_analysis_stats"]
    print(f" Domain Reputation for {url_to_check}:")
    print(f" Harmless: {stats['harmless']}")
    print(f" Suspicious: {stats['suspicious']}")
    print(f" Malicious: {stats['malicious']}")
else:
    print(" No reputation data found.")
```

What We Learn from This?

- Detects phishing & malware-hosting domains
- Identifies newly registered malicious sites

6.6.4 Step 3: Investigating Domain WHOIS & IP Data

Phishing campaigns often use newly registered domains. Automating WHOIS lookups helps reveal the registrant details, hosting provider, and creation date.

Checking WHOIS Data with Python

```
import whois
```

```
domain = "malicious-site.com"
whois_info = whois.whois(domain)

print(f" WHOIS Data for {domain}:")
print(f"Registrar: {whois_info.registrar}")
print(f"Creation Date: {whois_info.creation_date}")
print(f"Updated Date: {whois_info.updated_date}")
print(f"Expiration Date: {whois_info.expiration_date}")
print(f"Name Servers: {whois_info.name_servers}")
```

Why WHOIS Analysis Matters?

- Identifies recently registered phishing domains
- Links multiple domains to the same registrar
- Helps trace phishing infrastructure

Checking Hosting IP with AbuseIPDB

```
import requests

API_KEY = "your_abuseipdb_api_key"
ip_address = "192.168.1.1"

url = f"https://api.abuseipdb.com/api/v2/check?ipAddress={ip_address}"
headers = {"Key": API_KEY, "Accept": "application/json"}

response = requests.get(url, headers=headers)
data = response.json()

if "data" in data:
    print(f" IP {ip_address} flagged with Abuse Score:
{data['data']['abuseConfidenceScore']}")
else:
    print(" No reports found for this IP.")
```

Why IP Reputation Checking Matters?

- Flags malicious IPs used for phishing
- Detects abuse reports from other researchers

6.6.5 Step 4: Automating Continuous Phishing Email Monitoring

To track phishing campaigns over time, we can set up a Python script to:

- Extract email headers & sender IPs
- Check domain reputation automatically
- Correlate data with threat intelligence feeds

Automating Daily Phishing Monitoring

```
import time

phishing_domains = ["malicious-site.com", "fake-login.com"]

def monitor_phishing_domains():
    for domain in phishing_domains:
        check_domain_reputation(domain)  # Function from earlier

while True:
    print(" Running daily phishing domain check...")
    monitor_phishing_domains()
    time.sleep(86400)  # Runs every 24 hours
```

Why Automate This?

- Detects new phishing domains before major attacks
- Alerts analysts when reputation changes

6.6.6 Key Findings & Lessons Learned

Findings from Our Case Study:

- The phishing emails came from spoofed domains using free email providers
- The fake login pages were hosted on newly registered domains
- VirusTotal & AbuseIPDB flagged the malicious domains & IPs
- The phishing campaign used multiple similar-looking URLs

Lessons Learned:

- Automate phishing detection to reduce manual workload
- Use multiple OSINT APIs to verify reputation
- Monitor domain registrations to predict attacks
- Educate users on email spoofing & phishing awareness

Conclusion & Next Steps

- Automated OSINT workflows can detect phishing attacks early
- Python can be used to track and analyze phishing domains & emails
- Continuous monitoring enhances cyber threat intelligence

7. Building OSINT Dashboards for Threat Intelligence

In this chapter, we dive into the creation of dynamic OSINT dashboards that serve as powerful tools for visualizing and interpreting threat intelligence data. You'll learn how to use Python along with libraries like Dash and Plotly to build interactive, real-time dashboards that aggregate and display key OSINT insights such as suspicious activities, emerging threats, and key trends. We'll walk you through the process of integrating data from various sources, including social media, web scraping, and APIs, into a unified dashboard, and teach you how to present that data in an easily digestible format. By the end of this chapter, you will be equipped to build custom OSINT dashboards that provide actionable intelligence at a glance, helping to streamline decision-making and enhance your overall threat intelligence capabilities.

7.1 Why Dashboards Matter for OSINT Analysts

In the fast-paced world of open-source intelligence (OSINT), analysts must process vast amounts of data from multiple sources—social media, domain registries, darknet forums, public records, and more. However, raw data alone is not enough. OSINT professionals need structured, real-time insights to make informed decisions quickly. This is where OSINT dashboards become essential.

A well-designed OSINT dashboard consolidates intelligence from different sources into a single, visually interactive interface, allowing analysts to identify trends, detect threats, and improve investigative workflows. This chapter explores why dashboards are crucial for OSINT analysts, their benefits, and how automation enhances intelligence gathering.

7.1.1 The Growing Need for OSINT Dashboards

The digital landscape is constantly evolving, with millions of new records, posts, and transactions generated every second. Manual intelligence gathering is no longer practical, as analysts must:

- **Monitor multiple sources simultaneously** (news, social media, government databases)
- **Detect anomalies and patterns in data** (suspicious domain registrations, coordinated disinformation campaigns)

- **Correlate structured and unstructured data** (CSV reports, JSON API feeds, text logs)
- **Visualize relationships between entities** (threat actors, IP addresses, domains)

A well-built dashboard transforms this overwhelming data into actionable intelligence, helping OSINT professionals stay ahead of emerging threats.

7.1.2 Key Benefits of OSINT Dashboards

A dynamic OSINT dashboard enables analysts to:

1. Centralize OSINT Data Sources

OSINT investigations rely on a combination of sources such as:

- **Social media monitoring** (Twitter, Telegram, Facebook)
- **Domain and IP tracking** (WHOIS lookups, passive DNS)
- **Threat intelligence feeds** (VirusTotal, AbuseIPDB, Shodan)
- **Dark web monitoring** (Tor sites, data leak forums)

Instead of manually checking each source, dashboards aggregate and update data automatically, providing a unified intelligence feed.

2. Detect Threats Faster with Real-Time Alerts

Dashboards enable real-time threat tracking through:

✓ **Automated alerts for suspicious activity** (e.g., newly registered domains mimicking a company's brand)

✓ **Visual heatmaps of cyber threats** (e.g., phishing domains mapped to geographic locations)

✓ **Live sentiment analysis of social media posts** (e.g., tracking narratives around disinformation campaigns)

By automating these insights, analysts reduce response times and can mitigate threats before they escalate.

3. Improve Data Visualization & Reporting

Visualizing OSINT data makes it easier to interpret and communicate findings. Dashboards offer:

- **Interactive charts and graphs** (e.g., bar charts showing cyberattack trends)
- **Network graphs** (e.g., mapping relationships between threat actors and compromised domains)
- **Timeline analysis** (e.g., tracking an unfolding event across social media and news sources)

Such visual elements enhance situational awareness, making intelligence more accessible to decision-makers.

4. Automate Repetitive Intelligence Tasks

Manually collecting OSINT data is time-consuming. Dashboards automate tasks such as:

- **Scheduled API calls to intelligence feeds** (e.g., querying VirusTotal for new malicious URLs)
- **Automatic data collection from open sources** (e.g., scraping Telegram channels for cybercrime discussions)
- **Filtering and tagging high-risk entities** (e.g., flagging domains associated with known malware campaigns)

Automation saves valuable time, allowing analysts to focus on deeper analysis rather than data retrieval.

7.1.3 Use Cases of OSINT Dashboards in Intelligence Gathering

Cyber Threat Intelligence (CTI) Dashboards

- **Purpose**: Track cyber threats, botnets, and malicious domains
- **Data Sources**: VirusTotal, Shodan, AbuseIPDB, PassiveTotal

Key Features:

- Mapping hacker infrastructure (C2 servers, phishing domains)
- Tracking dark web discussions on cybercriminal forums
- Monitoring IP blacklists for new threats

Social Media OSINT Dashboards

- **Purpose**: Monitor public sentiment, disinformation campaigns, and digital threats
- **Data Sources**: Twitter API, Facebook Graph API, Reddit Scraper

Key Features:

- Hashtag tracking for emerging trends (e.g., protests, hacktivist campaigns)
- User behavior analysis (e.g., identifying fake/bot accounts spreading misinformation)
- Geolocating social media posts (e.g., detecting real-time crisis events)

Dark Web Monitoring Dashboards

- **Purpose**: Track illegal marketplaces, data leaks, and cybercrime discussions
- **Data Sources**: Tor hidden services, Onion sites, Pastebin dumps

Key Features:

- Detecting compromised credentials from dark web data leaks
- Monitoring cybercrime forums for discussions on hacking tools
- Tracking cryptocurrency transactions linked to ransomware

7.1.4 Designing an Effective OSINT Dashboard

To build a practical OSINT dashboard, analysts must consider:

Data Source Integration

A dashboard should seamlessly connect with OSINT tools and APIs, such as:

- Google Dorking queries for open-source intelligence
- VirusTotal & AbuseIPDB for domain reputation checks
- Telegram & Discord monitoring for real-time chatter

User-Friendly Visualization

Data should be presented intuitively, using:

- Graphs, heatmaps, and alerts for rapid analysis
- Custom filters for refining intelligence (e.g., searching by IP range, keywords)

- Interactive network diagrams for mapping cyber threat actors

Automated Workflows & Alerts

OSINT dashboards should support:

- Automated data ingestion from APIs and scraping tools
- Email/SMS alerts for critical intelligence (e.g., domain blacklisting)
- Scheduled report generation for stakeholders

7.1.5 Challenges & Ethical Considerations in OSINT Dashboards

While OSINT dashboards enhance intelligence gathering, they also come with risks:

Data Overload

- **Problem**: Too much data can overwhelm analysts
- **Solution**: Implement custom filters & machine learning models to prioritize threats

Legal & Ethical Boundaries

- **Problem**: Some OSINT tools may scrape private data (violating TOS of platforms)
- **Solution**: Follow ethical guidelines & use only publicly available intelligence sources

Securing Sensitive Intelligence

- **Problem**: Centralizing OSINT data can be a security risk
- **Solution**: Implement access controls, encryption, and audit logs

Conclusion: The Future of OSINT Dashboards

Why Do Dashboards Matter?

- They transform raw OSINT data into actionable intelligence
- They reduce manual work through automation
- They enable real-time threat monitoring & early detection

The Future of OSINT Dashboards

- AI-powered predictive intelligence for faster decision-making
- Cloud-based OSINT dashboards for global intelligence sharing
- Integration with machine learning models for automated anomaly detection

7.2 Tools for Building OSINT Dashboards (Streamlit, Flask, Django)

An OSINT dashboard is only as powerful as the tools used to build it. Choosing the right framework depends on functionality, scalability, and ease of deployment. In this chapter, we explore three popular Python frameworks for building OSINT dashboards—Streamlit, Flask, and Django—comparing their strengths, weaknesses, and ideal use cases.

By the end of this section, you'll understand:

- How to choose the right framework based on your OSINT needs
- How Streamlit simplifies rapid OSINT dashboard development
- When Flask is the best choice for lightweight OSINT applications
- How Django supports large-scale intelligence platforms

7.2.1 Choosing the Right Framework for OSINT Dashboards

Each OSINT project has unique requirements—some need quick data visualization, others require complex back-end logic. The choice between Streamlit, Flask, and Django depends on the following factors:

Feature	Streamlit 🔵	Flask ⚫	Django 🔵
Ease of Use	⭐⭐⭐⭐⭐ (Beginner-friendly)	⭐⭐⭐ (Moderate)	⭐⭐ (Steeper learning curve)
Best for	Fast, interactive dashboards	Lightweight web apps & APIs	Scalable, enterprise OSINT platforms
Data Visualization	⭐⭐⭐⭐⭐ (Built-in charts, maps)	⭐⭐⭐ (Requires JavaScript or plugins)	⭐⭐⭐ (Can integrate with JS libraries)
API & Backend	⭐⭐ (Limited API control)	⭐⭐⭐⭐ (Customizable API)	⭐⭐⭐⭐⭐ (Robust ORM & API capabilities)
Scalability	⭐⭐ (For small projects)	⭐⭐⭐ (Medium scale)	⭐⭐⭐⭐⭐ (Enterprise-level deployments)

7.2.2 Streamlit: Rapid OSINT Dashboard Development

Why Use Streamlit?

- Best for fast prototyping & visualization
- Requires minimal coding – great for analysts with Python knowledge
- Interactive & real-time updates

Installing Streamlit

pip install streamlit

Sample OSINT Dashboard in Streamlit

Let's build a simple dashboard that:

✓ Fetches threat intelligence from VirusTotal API

✓ Displays suspicious domain data

✓ Visualizes results with interactive charts

import streamlit as st
import requests

```
# Set up the Streamlit page
st.title("OSINT Dashboard - Threat Intelligence")
st.sidebar.header("Enter Domain to Investigate")

# Input field for domain lookup
domain = st.sidebar.text_input("Domain Name", "example.com")

# Function to fetch data from VirusTotal API
def check_domain_reputation(domain):
    API_KEY = "your_virustotal_api_key"
    url = f"https://www.virustotal.com/api/v3/domains/{domain}"
    headers = {"x-apikey": API_KEY}

    response = requests.get(url, headers=headers)
    return response.json()

# Display results
if st.sidebar.button("Check Domain"):
    data = check_domain_reputation(domain)
    st.write("### Threat Report for:", domain)
    st.json(data)
```

Why Choose Streamlit for OSINT?

- Fastest way to build an OSINT dashboard
- Auto-refresh & real-time updates
- Simple UI with minimal development time

Best for: Analysts who need quick, real-time data visualization with minimal coding.

7.2.3 Flask: Lightweight Framework for OSINT APIs & Dashboards

Why Use Flask?

- Lightweight, flexible, and easy to integrate with OSINT APIs
- Good for small to medium OSINT web apps
- More control over API requests & back-end processing

Installing Flask

pip install flask

Building a Flask-Based OSINT Dashboard

Let's create an OSINT web app that:

✓ Uses Flask to handle API requests

✓ Displays results in HTML format

✓ Fetches data from Shodan API

```python
from flask import Flask, request, render_template
import requests

app = Flask(__name__)

# Function to get IP reputation from Shodan API
def get_ip_reputation(ip):
    API_KEY = "your_shodan_api_key"
    url = f"https://api.shodan.io/shodan/host/{ip}?key={API_KEY}"
    response = requests.get(url)
    return response.json()

@app.route("/", methods=["GET", "POST"])
def index():
    data = None
    if request.method == "POST":
        ip = request.form["ip"]
        data = get_ip_reputation(ip)
    return render_template("dashboard.html", data=data)

if __name__ == "__main__":
    app.run(debug=True)
```

Flask Templates (dashboard.html)

```html
<!DOCTYPE html>
<html>
<head>
    <title>OSINT Dashboard</title>
```

```
</head>
<body>
    <h2>Enter an IP Address to Investigate</h2>
    <form method="post">
        <input type="text" name="ip" required>
        <button type="submit">Check</button>
    </form>

    {% if data %}
        <h3>Threat Report</h3>
        <pre>{{ data | tojson(indent=4) }}</pre>
    {% endif %}
</body>
</html>
```

Why Choose Flask for OSINT?

- More customization than Streamlit
- Supports complex API integrations
- Ideal for small OSINT web applications

Best for: OSINT professionals needing more flexibility in API handling and web development.

7.2.4 Django: Scalable OSINT Intelligence Platforms

Why Use Django?

- Best for large-scale OSINT platforms
- Built-in user authentication & database management
- Ideal for government agencies, cybersecurity firms, and enterprise OSINT

Installing Django

pip install django

Creating a Django-Based OSINT Dashboard

Initialize Django Project

```
django-admin startproject osint_dashboard
cd osint_dashboard
python manage.py startapp threatintel
```

Define Models for OSINT Data Storage (models.py)

```
from django.db import models

class ThreatIntel(models.Model):
    domain = models.CharField(max_length=255)
    risk_score = models.IntegerField()
    last_analysis_date = models.DateTimeField(auto_now=True)
```

Build Views & Templates for Dashboard (views.py)

```
from django.shortcuts import render
from .models import ThreatIntel

def dashboard(request):
    data = ThreatIntel.objects.all()
    return render(request, "dashboard.html", {"data": data})
```

Run Server & Access OSINT Dashboard

```
python manage.py runserver
```

Why Choose Django for OSINT?

✔ Handles large-scale OSINT data efficiently

✔ Best for multi-user authentication & role-based access control

✔ Ideal for cybersecurity teams and government intelligence analysts

Best for: Enterprise-level OSINT platforms with database-driven intelligence storage.

7.2.5 Comparing Streamlit, Flask & Django for OSINT

Framework	Best Use Case	Pros	Cons
Streamlit	Fast, simple OSINT dashboards	Easy setup, real-time visualization	Limited API/backend support
Flask	Custom OSINT APIs & web apps	Lightweight, flexible	Requires manual UI design
Django	Large-scale OSINT platforms	Scalable, robust security	Complex setup

Conclusion: Choosing the Best Framework for OSINT Dashboards

- Choose Streamlit if you need a fast, simple OSINT dashboard with real-time data.
- Choose Flask if you need a lightweight API-driven OSINT app with flexible customization.
- Choose Django if you're building a large-scale OSINT platform for enterprise use.

7.3 Automating Data Ingestion for Live Threat Monitoring

OSINT dashboards are only as useful as the data they process. Live threat monitoring requires continuous data ingestion from multiple sources, such as social media, cyber threat intelligence feeds, DNS records, and dark web monitoring tools. Automating this process ensures analysts receive real-time insights, helping them detect and respond to threats faster.

In this chapter, you will learn:

Why automated data ingestion is crucial for OSINT
Key data sources for live threat intelligence
How to set up automated data collection using Python
Best practices for handling large-scale OSINT data

7.3.1 Why Automate Data Ingestion for OSINT?

Manual data collection is inefficient, time-consuming, and prone to human error. In contrast, automated ingestion pipelines allow OSINT analysts to:

- Monitor multiple data sources in real-time
- Filter and prioritize high-risk intelligence
- Reduce manual intervention & improve response times

- Feed data into dashboards for visualization & analysis

For example, an automated pipeline can:

✓ Continuously pull malicious IP reports from AbuseIPDB

✓ Monitor Twitter for cyber attack discussions

✓ Scan newly registered phishing domains

∞ 7.3.2 Key Data Sources for Live OSINT Threat Monitoring

OSINT intelligence is scattered across different sources. Below are the most important ones for automated ingestion:

Source	Type of Threat Intelligence	Automation Method
VirusTotal	Malware, phishing domains, file hashes	API
Shodan	Open ports, exposed IoT devices	API
AbuseIPDB	Malicious IP addresses	API
Twitter API	Social media threat discussions	API
HaveIBeenPwned	Data breaches, leaked credentials	API
Censys	SSL certificates, network scans	API
Dark Web Forums	Leaked databases, cybercrime activity	Web Scraping
Passive DNS	Historical domain-IP mappings	API

By integrating these sources, analysts can track cyber threats in real time.

☐ 7.3.3 Setting Up Automated Data Ingestion with Python

1☐ Automating Threat Intelligence API Calls

Let's create a Python script that continuously fetches & updates OSINT threat data from APIs.

◆ Example: Automating VirusTotal Threat Intelligence Collection

```
import requests
import time
import json

API_KEY = "your_virustotal_api_key"
DOMAIN = "example.com"
VT_URL = f"https://www.virustotal.com/api/v3/domains/{DOMAIN}"

headers = {"x-apikey": API_KEY}

def fetch_virustotal_data():
    response = requests.get(VT_URL, headers=headers)
    if response.status_code == 200:
        return response.json()
    return None

while True:
    data = fetch_virustotal_data()
    if data:
        print(json.dumps(data, indent=4))  # Display results
    time.sleep(60)  # Fetch data every 60 seconds
```

✔ This script:

✔ Queries VirusTotal API for domain reputation

✔ Runs every 60 seconds to ensure live updates

✔ Prints structured JSON data for processing

2️⃣ Automating Social Media Threat Monitoring (Twitter API Example)

Cyber threats often emerge on social media platforms before traditional news sources report them. Automating Twitter monitoring allows analysts to detect:

✔ New malware campaigns (hashtags like #cyberattack)

✓ Hacker discussions (keywords like "zero-day exploit")

✓ Emerging phishing scams

◆ **Example: Twitter OSINT Automation with Tweepy**

import tweepy

 # Twitter API credentials
API_KEY = "your_api_key"
API_SECRET = "your_api_secret"
ACCESS_TOKEN = "your_access_token"
ACCESS_SECRET = "your_access_secret"

 # Authenticate
auth = tweepy.OAuthHandler(API_KEY, API_SECRET)
auth.set_access_token(ACCESS_TOKEN, ACCESS_SECRET)
api = tweepy.API(auth)

 # Define keywords to monitor
keywords = ["cyberattack", "phishing", "malware"]

 # Stream live tweets
class ThreatStreamListener(tweepy.StreamListener):
  def on_status(self, status):
    print(f"[ALERT] {status.user.screen_name}: {status.text}")

stream = tweepy.Stream(auth=api.auth, listener=ThreatStreamListener())
stream.filter(track=keywords, languages=["en"])

✅ **This script:**

✓ Monitors live Twitter feeds for cybersecurity discussions

✓ Prints alerts when relevant tweets are detected

✓ Can be extended to store data in a database

3️ Automating Dark Web Threat Monitoring

The dark web is a critical source of cyber threat intelligence, including:

✓ Data breaches (hacked credentials, leaked databases)

✓ Cybercrime markets (stolen credit cards, exploit kits)

✓ Hacker communications (planning of attacks, ransomware operators)

Since dark web sites require Tor access, we can automate monitoring using Scrapy + Tor.

◆ **Example: Scraping Dark Web Forums with Scrapy & Tor**

```
import scrapy

class DarkWebSpider(scrapy.Spider):
    name = "darkweb"
    allowed_domains = ["darkwebmarket.onion"]
    start_urls = ["http://darkwebmarket.onion/forums"]

    def parse(self, response):
        for post in response.css("div.post"):
            yield {
                "title": post.css("h2::text").get(),
                "content": post.css("p::text").get(),
            }
```

To run this on Tor, configure scrapy to use a Tor proxy (localhost:9050).

```
scrapy crawl darkweb --set HTTP_PROXY="socks5h://127.0.0.1:9050"
```

● ⚠ **Ethical Considerations:**

- Accessing dark web content may be illegal in some countries.
- Ensure compliance with all legal frameworks before scraping dark web sites.

🏛 7.3.4 Storing & Managing Live OSINT Data

Collected OSINT data should be stored securely for analysis and correlation.

◆ Using SQLite for Small OSINT Data Storage

```python
import sqlite3

conn = sqlite3.connect("osint_data.db")
cursor = conn.cursor()

cursor.execute("""
CREATE TABLE IF NOT EXISTS threats (
    id INTEGER PRIMARY KEY,
    source TEXT,
    data TEXT,
    timestamp DATETIME DEFAULT CURRENT_TIMESTAMP
)
""")
conn.commit()
```

◆ Using Elasticsearch for Large-Scale Threat Intelligence

```python
from elasticsearch import Elasticsearch

es = Elasticsearch(["http://localhost:9200"])
es.index(index="osint-threats", body={"source": "Twitter", "data": "Phishing alert",
"timestamp": "2025-02-23T10:00:00"})
```

✓ Best Practices for Automated OSINT Data Ingestion

✓ **Respect API Rate Limits** – Some OSINT APIs limit requests per hour. Implement rate limiting to avoid bans.

✓ **Use Background Jobs** – Automate ingestion using Celery or cron jobs for continuous updates.

✓ **Store Data Efficiently** – Use databases (SQLite, PostgreSQL) or big data storage (Elasticsearch).

✓ **Filter Noisy Data** – Apply keyword filtering to remove irrelevant intelligence.

✓ **Secure Sensitive Data** – Encrypt stored threat intelligence to prevent leaks.

✓ Conclusion: Automating Live OSINT Feeds for Better Threat Intelligence

📌 **Why Automate OSINT Ingestion?**

◆ Speeds up threat detection & response
◆ Reduces manual data collection efforts
◆ Ensures continuous monitoring of emerging cyber threats

7.4 Visualizing Intelligence Data in Real-Time

Collecting and analyzing OSINT data is crucial, but raw data can be overwhelming. Real-time visualization transforms complex intelligence into clear, actionable insights, enabling analysts to detect threats, track patterns, and respond faster. Whether monitoring cyber threats, mapping online discussions, or tracking domain abuse, a well-designed OSINT dashboard provides a dynamic and interactive view of intelligence data.

In this chapter, you will learn:

✅ Why real-time visualization is critical for OSINT

✅ Best tools for OSINT data visualization

✅ How to build interactive dashboards with Streamlit, Flask, and Plotly

✅ How to integrate live data sources into real-time charts and graphs

📌 **7.4.1 Why Real-Time Visualization Matters for OSINT**

OSINT investigations involve large amounts of data from multiple sources, such as:

◆ **Threat intelligence feeds** – Malicious IPs, phishing domains, leaked credentials
◆ **Social media monitoring** – Hashtags, mentions, and emerging cyber threats
◆ **Dark web monitoring** – Data breaches, hacker forum discussions
◆ **Geospatial intelligence** – Mapping suspicious activities or attacks

Analyzing raw text logs or spreadsheets is inefficient. Visualization simplifies data interpretation and helps analysts:

✔ **Detect trends and anomalies** – Identify sudden spikes in cyber attacks

✓ **Monitor live threat intelligence feeds** – Keep an eye on emerging threats

✓ **Geolocate incidents in real-time** – See where cyberattacks are occurring

✓ **Understand social network relationships** – Identify key influencers in disinformation campaigns

Example OSINT Visualization Use Cases

● **Tracking Phishing Campaigns** → A line graph showing the rise in phishing domains over time.

☐ **Monitoring Cyber Threats** → A heatmap displaying malware activity in different countries.

⬤ **Social Media Intelligence** → A network graph of hashtags and mentions related to cyberattacks.

☐ 7.4.2 Best Tools for Real-Time OSINT Data Visualization

Several Python-based visualization tools can transform OSINT data into interactive dashboards.

Tool	Best For	Key Features
Streamlit	Quick OSINT dashboard development	Auto-refresh, simple Python integration
Flask + Plotly/Dash	Custom web-based dashboards	Full control over UI, interactive charts
Grafana + Elasticsearch	Large-scale threat monitoring	Connects to multiple data sources
Matplotlib & Seaborn	Static OSINT reports	Customizable charts for PDF reports
Geopandas & Folium	Geospatial OSINT visualization	Interactive world maps for cyber incidents

For real-time monitoring, we will focus on Streamlit (for quick dashboards) and Flask with Plotly (for more customizable web applications).

🚀 7.4.3 Creating a Real-Time OSINT Dashboard with Streamlit

Streamlit is a lightweight, Python-based tool that allows you to create interactive dashboards with minimal coding.

Step 1: Install Streamlit

pip install streamlit requests pandas plotly

Step 2: Build a Live OSINT Threat Monitoring Dashboard

The following script creates a live threat intelligence dashboard that:

✓ Fetches malicious IP reports from AbuseIPDB

✓ Displays real-time updates in a data table

✓ Visualizes threat data with an interactive bar chart

◆ **OSINT Dashboard Example (Streamlit)**

```
import streamlit as st
import requests
import pandas as pd
import plotly.express as px

# API Key for AbuseIPDB (Replace with your own)
API_KEY = "your_abuseipdb_api_key"

# Function to fetch threat data
def fetch_threat_data():
    url = "https://api.abuseipdb.com/api/v2/reports"
    headers = {"Key": API_KEY, "Accept": "application/json"}
    response = requests.get(url, headers=headers)
    if response.status_code == 200:
        return response.json()["data"]
    return []

# Streamlit UI
st.title("□ Live OSINT Threat Intelligence Dashboard")
st.write("Monitoring real-time malicious IP reports")

# Fetch live data
```

```
data = fetch_threat_data()
df = pd.DataFrame(data)

# Display data table
st.dataframe(df)

# Create a bar chart of threat types
if not df.empty:
    fig = px.bar(df, x="ipAddress", y="reportCount", title="Top Reported Malicious IPs")
    st.plotly_chart(fig)

st.button("Refresh Data", on_click=fetch_threat_data)
```

What This Dashboard Does:

✓ Fetches live OSINT data from an API

✓ Displays a data table of reported IPs

✓ Plots a bar chart of top threats

✓ Auto-refreshes when clicking "Refresh Data"

● Want to run it?

Save the script as osint_dashboard.py, then run:

```
streamlit run osint_dashboard.py
```

☐ 7.4.4 Visualizing OSINT Data on Interactive Maps

For geospatial OSINT analysis, we can use Folium and Geopandas to map cyber threat activity.

Example: Mapping Cyber Threats Using Folium

```
import folium
import pandas as pd

# Sample OSINT data (malicious IPs and locations)
data = [
```

```
    {"ip": "192.168.1.1", "latitude": 37.7749, "longitude": -122.4194, "threat": "Phishing"},
    {"ip": "203.0.113.5", "latitude": 51.5074, "longitude": -0.1278, "threat": "Malware"},
]

# Create map
m = folium.Map(location=[20, 0], zoom_start=2)

# Add threat markers
for entry in data:
    folium.Marker(
        location=[entry["latitude"], entry["longitude"]],
        popup=f"IP: {entry['ip']}<br>Threat: {entry['threat']}",
        icon=folium.Icon(color="red"),
    ).add_to(m)

# Save map
m.save("osint_map.html")
```

● What This Does:

✔ Plots malicious IPs on an interactive world map

✔ Saves the map as osint_map.html

✔ Allows users to click on locations for threat details

⚙ 7.4.5 Integrating OSINT Visualization with Flask + Plotly

For a custom web-based OSINT dashboard, Flask + Plotly is a great combination.

Example: Flask + Plotly OSINT Dashboard

```
from flask import Flask, render_template
import plotly.express as px
import pandas as pd

app = Flask(__name__)

@app.route("/")
def index():
    data = {"Threat Type": ["Phishing", "Malware", "Ransomware"], "Count": [20, 15, 8]}
```

```
    df = pd.DataFrame(data)
    fig = px.pie(df, names="Threat Type", values="Count", title="OSINT Threat
Breakdown")
    graph_html = fig.to_html(full_html=False)
    return render_template("index.html", graph_html=graph_html)

if __name__ == "__main__":
    app.run(debug=True)
```

💡 This Flask app serves a real-time OSINT chart in a web browser.

✅ **Best Practices for Real-Time OSINT Visualization**

✔ **Use live data sources** – Ensure dashboards update dynamically.

✔ **Filter out noise** – Apply keyword filtering to remove irrelevant intelligence.

✔ **Ensure data security** – Do not expose sensitive OSINT data publicly.

✔ **Optimize performance** – Use caching or databases for large-scale data.

✔ **Customize for your needs** – Use Streamlit for fast prototypes, Flask for full web apps.

🚀 **Conclusion: Bringing OSINT Intelligence to Life**

📌 **Why Real-Time OSINT Visualization Matters**

✅ Transforms raw data into actionable insights

✅ Helps analysts track cyber threats dynamically

✅ Improves situational awareness with interactive dashboards

7.5 Integrating APIs for Live Data Feeds

Real-time OSINT (Open-Source Intelligence) dashboards rely on live data feeds to provide up-to-date intelligence on threats, social media activity, domain monitoring, and more. APIs (Application Programming Interfaces) are the key to pulling this live data into an OSINT dashboard, allowing analysts to automate intelligence gathering and respond to emerging threats quickly.

📌 In this chapter, you will learn:

✅ What live data feeds are and why they matter for OSINT

✅ How to integrate APIs into an OSINT dashboard

✅ Best OSINT APIs for threat intelligence, social media monitoring, and domain analysis

✅ Example Python scripts for live data ingestion

🔍 7.5.1 Why Live Data Feeds Matter for OSINT

OSINT is dynamic—cyber threats, disinformation campaigns, and security incidents evolve rapidly. A static dataset quickly becomes outdated, but real-time data feeds allow analysts to:

✓ **Monitor cyber threats as they happen** – Track phishing attacks, leaked credentials, and malware campaigns.

✓ **Detecting emerging social media trends** – Identify viral misinformation or coordinated campaigns.

✓ **Analyze domain and IP activity** – Keep an eye on newly registered domains or malicious infrastructure.

✓ **Improve response time** – Get live alerts on security risks instead of analyzing old data.

📌 Example Live OSINT Use Cases

● **Threat Intelligence Dashboards** – Pulling data from AbuseIPDB, VirusTotal, and AlienVault OTX to track malicious IPs and domains.

☐ **Social Media Monitoring** – Using Twitter and Reddit APIs to watch for hashtags, disinformation, or threats.

⬤ **Dark Web Monitoring** – Checking onion sites for leaked credentials or hacker forum discussions.

☐ 7.5.2 Best OSINT APIs for Live Data Feeds

To integrate real-time intelligence into an OSINT dashboard, we can use APIs from various sources.

API Name	Use Case	Data Provided
AbuseIPDB	Cyber threat intelligence	Malicious IP reports
VirusTotal	Malware & domain reputation	File, URL, and IP scans
Shodan	Internet-connected devices	Open ports, vulnerabilities
AlienVault OTX	Threat intelligence sharing	Latest cyber threat reports
Twitter API	Social media OSINT	Tweets, mentions, trends
Reddit API	Disinformation tracking	Posts, comments, user activity
Have I Been Pwned (HIBP)	Breach monitoring	Exposed emails & passwords
WhoisXML API	Domain intelligence	WHOIS, DNS, IP history

These APIs enable real-time intelligence gathering, helping OSINT analysts automate monitoring for cybersecurity, threat detection, and forensic investigations.

⚙ 7.5.3 How to Integrate Live APIs into an OSINT Dashboard

The key steps to integrating APIs into an OSINT dashboard:

Step 1: Install Required Python Libraries

Before fetching data, install the necessary Python libraries:

pip install requests pandas streamlit plotly

Step 2: Fetch Live Data from an OSINT API

◆ Example 1: Fetching Malicious IP Reports from AbuseIPDB

```
import requests
import pandas as pd

# API Key (replace with your own)
API_KEY = "your_abuseipdb_api_key"
```

```
# Fetch threat data
def get_malicious_ips():
    url = "https://api.abuseipdb.com/api/v2/reports"
    headers = {"Key": API_KEY, "Accept": "application/json"}
    response = requests.get(url, headers=headers)
    if response.status_code == 200:
        return response.json()["data"]
    return []

# Convert API response to a DataFrame
data = get_malicious_ips()
df = pd.DataFrame(data)
print(df.head())  # Display first few rows
```

✓ This script pulls live malicious IP reports from AbuseIPDB, useful for tracking cyber threats.

◆ **Example 2: Monitoring Cyber Threats with AlienVault OTX API**

```
import requests

OTX_API_KEY = "your_alienvault_api_key"
url = "https://otx.alienvault.com/api/v1/pulses/subscribed"

headers = {"X-OTX-API-KEY": OTX_API_KEY}
response = requests.get(url, headers=headers)

if response.status_code == 200:
    data = response.json()
    print("Latest Threat Reports:", data["results"])
else:
    print("Error:", response.status_code)
```

✓ This script fetches real-time threat intelligence reports from AlienVault OTX, a great source for emerging cyber threats.

◆ **Example 3: Fetching Live Social Media Data (Twitter API)**

```python
import tweepy

# Twitter API Keys (Replace with yours)
consumer_key = "your_consumer_key"
consumer_secret = "your_consumer_secret"
access_token = "your_access_token"
access_token_secret = "your_access_token_secret"

# Authenticate with Twitter API
auth = tweepy.OAuthHandler(consumer_key, consumer_secret)
auth.set_access_token(access_token, access_token_secret)
api = tweepy.API(auth)

# Fetch latest tweets with a keyword (e.g., "cyber attack")
tweets = api.search_tweets(q="cyber attack", count=10)

for tweet in tweets:
    print(f"{tweet.user.screen_name}: {tweet.text}\n")
```

✔ This script fetches live tweets on cybersecurity threats, useful for social media intelligence (SOCMINT).

🚀 7.5.4 Building a Live Threat Monitoring Dashboard (Streamlit + API Data)

Let's create a real-time OSINT dashboard that pulls live threat intelligence and visualizes it dynamically.

◆ Full Python Script (Streamlit + Live API Data)

```python
import streamlit as st
import requests
import pandas as pd
import plotly.express as px

# API Key for AbuseIPDB (Replace with your own)
API_KEY = "your_abuseipdb_api_key"

# Function to fetch real-time malicious IPs
def get_malicious_ips():
```

```
url = "https://api.abuseipdb.com/api/v2/reports"
headers = {"Key": API_KEY, "Accept": "application/json"}
response = requests.get(url, headers=headers)
if response.status_code == 200:
    return response.json()["data"]
return []

# Streamlit UI
st.title(" Real-Time OSINT Threat Intelligence Dashboard")
st.write("Live Monitoring of Malicious IP Reports")

# Fetch and display data
data = get_malicious_ips()
df = pd.DataFrame(data)

if not df.empty:
    st.dataframe(df)
    fig = px.bar(df, x="ipAddress", y="reportCount", title="Top Reported Malicious IPs")
    st.plotly_chart(fig)

st.button("Refresh Data", on_click=get_malicious_ips)
```

● How It Works:

✓ Fetches real-time OSINT threat data from AbuseIPDB

✓ Displays malicious IPs and their reports in a table

✓ Plots a bar chart of the most reported threats

✓ Allows on-demand data refresh with a button

To run the dashboard, save the script as osint_dashboard.py and run:

```
streamlit run osint_dashboard.py
```

⊘ Best Practices for OSINT API Integration

✓ **Use API rate limits wisely** – Avoid excessive API calls to prevent getting blocked.

✓ **Secure your API keys** – Store API keys in environment variables or config files.

✓ **Cache API responses** – Reduce the number of requests and speed up dashboard performance.

✓ **Filter data before visualization** – Avoid cluttering dashboards with unnecessary information.

🚀 **Conclusion: Powering OSINT with Live Data Feeds**

📌 **Why Live APIs Matter for OSINT**

✅ Enables real-time intelligence monitoring

✅ Automates cyber threat tracking

✅ Enhances decision-making for analysts

7.6 Case Study: Developing a Cyber Threat Intelligence Dashboard

A cybersecurity team needs a real-time cyber threat intelligence (CTI) dashboard that automates the collection, analysis, and visualization of OSINT data. The goal is to track cyber threats, monitor malicious IPs and domains, and analyze social media discussions related to cybersecurity.

This case study walks through how an OSINT analyst can develop a Cyber Threat Intelligence (CTI) dashboard using Python, live API integrations, and data visualization tools.

📷 7.6.1 The Problem Statement

The cybersecurity team faces multiple challenges in monitoring threats:

✓ **Too much raw data** – Manually analyzing IPs, domains, and social media threats is time-consuming.

✓ **No centralized monitoring** – Analysts check multiple sources separately (AbuseIPDB, VirusTotal, Twitter, etc.).

✓ Slow response time – Without automation, they fail to detect emerging cyber threats in real-time.

☉ The Solution:

Build an OSINT-powered Cyber Threat Intelligence Dashboard that:

✅ Monitors cyber threats dynamically

✅ Analyzes domain and IP reputation automatically

✅ Tracks social media threats (Twitter, Reddit) in real-time

✅ Provides an interactive UI for visualization & insights

☐ 7.6.2 Step 1: Setting Up the Development Environment

Before building the dashboard, we need to install key Python libraries:

pip install streamlit requests pandas plotly folium tweepy

◆ Required Technologies

- **Streamlit** → To build an interactive OSINT dashboard
- **Requests** → To fetch live data from OSINT APIs
- **Pandas** → For data processing & structuring
- **Plotly** → For interactive charts & data visualization
- **Folium** → To plot geolocation data of malicious IPs
- **Tweepy** → To fetch Twitter data for cyber threat monitoring

⚲ 7.6.3 Step 2: Integrating OSINT APIs for Live Data

The dashboard will collect data from:

API	Purpose	Use Case
AbuseIPDB	IP threat intelligence	Track malicious IPs
VirusTotal	Malware & domain reputation	Identify harmful URLs and files
AlienVault OTX	Cyber threat sharing	Detect emerging cyber threats
Twitter API	Social media intelligence	Monitor cybersecurity discussions

☐ 7.6.4 Step 3: Building the Cyber Threat Dashboard

1☐ Fetching Live Malicious IP Reports (AbuseIPDB API)

```
import requests
import pandas as pd

API_KEY = "your_abuseipdb_api_key"

def get_malicious_ips():
    url = "https://api.abuseipdb.com/api/v2/reports"
    headers = {"Key": API_KEY, "Accept": "application/json"}
    response = requests.get(url, headers=headers)
    if response.status_code == 200:
        return response.json()["data"]
    return []

# Convert data to Pandas DataFrame
data = get_malicious_ips()
df = pd.DataFrame(data)
print(df.head())
```

✔ This fetches real-time malicious IPs, useful for threat monitoring.

2☐ Checking Domain Reputation (VirusTotal API)

```
import requests
```

```
VT_API_KEY = "your_virustotal_api_key"
domain = "example.com"

def check_domain_reputation(domain):
    url = f"https://www.virustotal.com/api/v3/domains/{domain}"
    headers = {"x-apikey": VT_API_KEY}
    response = requests.get(url, headers=headers)
    return response.json() if response.status_code == 200 else None

# Fetch data
domain_data = check_domain_reputation(domain)
print(domain_data)
```

✔ This script checks whether a domain is blacklisted for malware.

3️⃣ Monitoring Twitter for Cyber Threat Intelligence

```
import tweepy

# Twitter API credentials
consumer_key = "your_consumer_key"
consumer_secret = "your_consumer_secret"
access_token = "your_access_token"
access_token_secret = "your_access_token_secret"

# Authenticate with Twitter API
auth = tweepy.OAuthHandler(consumer_key, consumer_secret)
auth.set_access_token(access_token, access_token_secret)
api = tweepy.API(auth)

# Fetch latest tweets on cybersecurity threats
tweets = api.search_tweets(q="cyber attack", count=10)

for tweet in tweets:
    print(f"{tweet.user.screen_name}: {tweet.text}\n")
```

✔ This script monitors cybersecurity discussions on Twitter in real-time.

🚀 7.6.5 Step 4: Building the Dashboard UI with Streamlit

Now, let's combine the OSINT data feeds into an interactive Streamlit dashboard.

◆ Full Python Script for the OSINT Dashboard

```python
import streamlit as st
import requests
import pandas as pd
import plotly.express as px
import folium
from streamlit_folium import folium_static

# API Keys
ABUSEIPDB_KEY = "your_abuseipdb_api_key"

# Function to get malicious IP reports
def get_malicious_ips():
    url = "https://api.abuseipdb.com/api/v2/reports"
    headers = {"Key": ABUSEIPDB_KEY, "Accept": "application/json"}
    response = requests.get(url, headers=headers)
    return response.json()["data"] if response.status_code == 200 else []

# Streamlit UI
st.title("□ Cyber Threat Intelligence Dashboard")
st.write("Live OSINT Monitoring of Cyber Threats")

# Fetch and display malicious IPs
data = get_malicious_ips()
df = pd.DataFrame(data)

if not df.empty:
    st.dataframe(df)

    # Visualize top reported malicious IPs
    fig = px.bar(df, x="ipAddress", y="reportCount", title="Top Malicious IPs")
    st.plotly_chart(fig)

    # Add malicious IPs to a map
    map = folium.Map(location=[20, 0], zoom_start=2)
    for _, row in df.iterrows():
```

```
folium.Marker(
    location=[row["latitude"], row["longitude"]],
    popup=f"IP: {row['ipAddress']}, Reports: {row['reportCount']}",
    icon=folium.Icon(color="red")
).add_to(map)

folium_static(map)

st.button("Refresh Data", on_click=get_malicious_ips)
```

◆ Running the Dashboard

Save the script as osint_dashboard.py and run:

```
streamlit run osint_dashboard.py
```

☞ 7.6.6 Key Features of the Final Dashboard

✅ Real-time OSINT monitoring of malicious IPs and domains

✅ Live threat visualization using bar charts and maps

✅ Automated intelligence gathering from AbuseIPDB, VirusTotal, Twitter API

✅ One-click refresh button for the latest cyber threat updates

📌 Lessons Learned & Best Practices

✔ **Automate OSINT workflows** → Reduces manual effort in cyber threat monitoring

✔ **Use multiple data sources** → Combining OSINT APIs gives better intelligence

✔ **Visualize data effectively** → Interactive dashboards help decision-making

✔ **Ensure ethical compliance** → Follow legal guidelines for OSINT data collection

🚀 Conclusion: Automating Cyber Threat Intelligence with OSINT

This case study demonstrates how OSINT automation and data visualization can enhance cyber threat intelligence operations.

8. Image & Metadata Analysis with Automated Tools

In this chapter, we explore the critical role of image and metadata analysis in OSINT, using automated tools to extract valuable intelligence from digital images and their associated metadata. You'll learn how to harness Python libraries like Pillow, OpenCV, and ExifTool to analyze image files, extract metadata (such as GPS coordinates, timestamps, and device information), and uncover hidden details that can lead to valuable insights. We'll also cover techniques for detecting image manipulation and verifying authenticity. By the end of this chapter, you will have the skills to automate the extraction and analysis of image metadata, enhancing your ability to track locations, identify sources, and verify content in an efficient, automated manner.

8.1 Understanding EXIF Metadata & Image Analysis

In OSINT investigations, images contain hidden metadata that can reveal crucial intelligence about their origin, the device used to capture them, and even their geographic location. This metadata, known as EXIF (Exchangeable Image File Format) data, is embedded in digital images and can provide valuable clues for threat intelligence, geolocation tracking, and forensic analysis.

In this chapter, we will explore:

✔ What EXIF metadata is and why it matters in OSINT

✔ How to extract EXIF data from images using Python

✔ How to analyze image manipulation and detect tampering

✔ Real-world applications of image forensics in OSINT

🔍 8.1.1 What is EXIF Metadata?

EXIF metadata is additional information stored in image files, primarily by cameras and smartphones. It contains details such as:

Metadata Type	Description
Camera Model	The device used to capture the image
Date & Time	When the image was taken
GPS Coordinates	Geolocation data (latitude & longitude)
Shutter Speed	Camera settings during capture
Software Used	Editing software (e.g., Photoshop)
Compression Type	Image format and encoding

This data can be critical for OSINT investigations, as it helps verify the authenticity of an image and track its origin.

☐☐ 8.1.2 How EXIF Metadata Helps in OSINT Investigations

📌 1. Geolocation Tracking

If an image contains GPS coordinates, investigators can pinpoint where it was taken. This is useful for:

✔ Locating individuals or objects in images

✔ Verifying the authenticity of news reports or claims

✔ Mapping intelligence on criminal activities or war zones

📌 2. Image Manipulation & Tampering Detection

Analyzing EXIF metadata can reveal:

✔ Whether an image was edited with software like Photoshop

✔ If the date/time was altered to mislead investigators

✓ Inconsistencies in camera settings that indicate fake or AI-generated images

📌 3. Identifying the Source Device

By extracting camera model and serial numbers, analysts can trace images back to specific devices. This can help in:

✓ Tracking down cybercriminals and fraudsters

✓ Investigating leaked documents with embedded images

✓ Unmasking fake social media accounts using stolen images

☐ 8.1.3 Extracting EXIF Metadata with Python

To automate EXIF metadata extraction, we use the Pillow and exifread libraries in Python.

◆ Install Required Libraries

```
pip install pillow exifread
```

◆ Extract EXIF Data from an Image

```python
from PIL import Image
import exifread

def extract_exif(image_path):
    with open(image_path, 'rb') as img_file:
        tags = exifread.process_file(img_file)

    for tag, value in tags.items():
        print(f"{tag}: {value}")

# Example usage
extract_exif("example.jpg")
```

✓ This script extracts all EXIF metadata from a given JPEG image.

🔎 8.1.4 Extracting GPS Coordinates from an Image

If an image contains GPS metadata, we can extract latitude and longitude for geolocation analysis.

```python
from PIL import Image
from PIL.ExifTags import TAGS, GPSTAGS

def get_exif_data(image_path):
    image = Image.open(image_path)
    exif_data = {}

    if image._getexif():
        for tag, value in image._getexif().items():
            tag_name = TAGS.get(tag, tag)
            exif_data[tag_name] = value
    return exif_data

def get_gps_coords(image_path):
    exif_data = get_exif_data(image_path)
    gps_info = exif_data.get("GPSInfo", {})

    if gps_info:
        lat = gps_info.get(2)  # Latitude
        lon = gps_info.get(4)  # Longitude
        lat_ref = gps_info.get(1)  # N or S
        lon_ref = gps_info.get(3)  # E or W

        lat = lat[0] + lat[1]/60 + lat[2]/3600
        lon = lon[0] + lon[1]/60 + lon[2]/3600

        if lat_ref != "N":
            lat = -lat
        if lon_ref != "E":
            lon = -lon

        return lat, lon
    return None

# Example usage
print(get_gps_coords("image_with_gps.jpg"))
```

✓ This extracts GPS coordinates and converts them into a usable latitude/longitude format.

☐ 8.1.5 Mapping Image Locations with Folium

Once we extract GPS coordinates, we can plot them on an interactive map using Folium.

◆ Install Folium

pip install folium

◆ Visualize GPS Coordinates on a Map

```
import folium

def plot_location(lat, lon):
    map = folium.Map(location=[lat, lon], zoom_start=15)
    folium.Marker([lat, lon], popup="Image Location").add_to(map)
    return map

# Example usage
lat, lon = get_gps_coords("image_with_gps.jpg")
if lat and lon:
    folium_map = plot_location(lat, lon)
    folium_map.save("image_location_map.html")
```

✓ This script creates an interactive map showing where the image was taken.

☐ 8.1.6 Detecting Image Manipulation

◆ Check for Photoshop Edits

If an image has been altered using Photoshop or other software, its EXIF metadata may contain editing traces.

```
def check_software_used(image_path):
    exif_data = get_exif_data(image_path)
```

```
software = exif_data.get("Software", "Unknown")
print(f"Software Used: {software}")

# Example usage
check_software_used("edited_image.jpg")
```

✓ This identifies whether an image was edited or manipulated.

□□♂□ 8.1.7 Real-World OSINT Applications

Use Case	How EXIF Data Helps
Tracking Cybercriminals	Identify where an image was taken, track devices used
Fake News Verification	Confirm if images are real or altered
Geolocation Analysis	Find locations based on GPS data
Threat Intelligence	Investigate images in cybercrime, terrorism, or fraud cases

Threat Intelligence   Investigate images in cybercrime, terrorism, or fraud cases

⟨✓⟩ Summary & Key Takeaways

✓ EXIF metadata contains hidden details about an image, including camera data, timestamps, and GPS coordinates.

✓ Python can automate EXIF data extraction for OSINT investigations.

✓ Geolocation tracking helps locate where an image was taken.

✓ EXIF analysis can detect image manipulation and editing history.

8.2 Extracting Image Metadata with Python

In OSINT investigations, extracting metadata from images can reveal valuable intelligence such as:

✓ **Device Information** – Camera model, manufacturer, and software used

✓ **Timestamps** – The exact date and time the image was captured or modified

✓ **Geolocation Data** – GPS coordinates that indicate where the image was taken

✓ **Editing History** – Whether the image has been altered using Photoshop or other software

Metadata analysis helps investigators verify images, track sources, and uncover hidden details. In this chapter, we will explore how to:

✓ Extract image metadata using Python

✓ Analyze EXIF data for OSINT investigations

✓ Automate metadata extraction for bulk image analysis

🔍 8.2.1 Understanding Image Metadata Formats

Image metadata is stored in different formats:

Metadata Type	Description	Common Formats
EXIF (Exchangeable Image File Format)	Stores camera details, timestamps, and GPS data	JPEG, TIFF, PNG
IPTC (International Press Telecommunications Council)	Stores captions, keywords, and author info	JPEG, PNG
XMP (Extensible Metadata Platform)	Metadata used in Adobe products	JPEG, PNG, PDF

☐ 8.2.2 Setting Up Python for Metadata Extraction

To extract metadata, we use the following Python libraries:

◆ **Pillow** – Extracts EXIF data from images

- **ExifRead** – Reads detailed EXIF metadata
- **Piexif** – Modifies and removes EXIF metadata

◆ Install Required Libraries

pip install pillow exifread piexif

☐ 8.2.3 Extracting Basic EXIF Metadata from an Image

◆ Using Pillow to Read EXIF Data

```
from PIL import Image
from PIL.ExifTags import TAGS

def extract_exif(image_path):
    image = Image.open(image_path)
    exif_data = image._getexif()

    if not exif_data:
        print("No EXIF metadata found.")
        return

    for tag, value in exif_data.items():
        tag_name = TAGS.get(tag, tag)
        print(f"{tag_name}: {value}")

# Example usage
extract_exif("image.jpg")
```

✓ This script extracts camera details, timestamps, and editing software from an image.

☐ 8.2.4 Extracting GPS Coordinates for Geolocation Analysis

Some images contain GPS metadata, which can help track the location where they were taken.

◆ Extract GPS Coordinates from an Image

```
from PIL import Image
```

```
from PIL.ExifTags import TAGS, GPSTAGS

def get_gps_data(image_path):
    image = Image.open(image_path)
    exif_data = image._getexif()

    if not exif_data:
        return None

    gps_info = {}
    for tag, value in exif_data.items():
        tag_name = TAGS.get(tag, tag)
        if tag_name == "GPSInfo":
            for key, val in value.items():
                gps_tag = GPSTAGS.get(key, key)
                gps_info[gps_tag] = val

    return gps_info

# Example usage
gps_data = get_gps_data("image.jpg")
print(gps_data)
```

✓ This script extracts latitude, longitude, and altitude from an image.

🔎 8.2.5 Converting GPS Data into Usable Coordinates

Raw GPS data is often stored in degrees, minutes, and seconds (DMS) format. We need to convert it into decimal format for mapping.

◆ Convert GPS Coordinates to Decimal Format

```
def convert_to_degrees(value):
    d, m, s = value
    return d + (m / 60.0) + (s / 3600.0)

def get_lat_lon(image_path):
    gps_data = get_gps_data(image_path)

    if not gps_data:
```

```
    print("No GPS data found.")
    return None

lat = convert_to_degrees(gps_data["GPSLatitude"])
lon = convert_to_degrees(gps_data["GPSLongitude"])

if gps_data["GPSLatitudeRef"] != "N":
    lat = -lat
if gps_data["GPSLongitudeRef"] != "E":
    lon = -lon

return lat, lon

# Example usage
latitude, longitude = get_lat_lon("image.jpg")
print(f"Latitude: {latitude}, Longitude: {longitude}")
```

✓ This script converts raw GPS data into decimal coordinates for mapping.

☐ 8.2.6 Mapping Image Locations Using Folium

Now that we have the GPS coordinates, we can plot them on a map.

◆ Install Folium for Mapping

```
pip install folium
```

◆ Visualize the Image Location on a Map

```
import folium

def plot_image_location(image_path):
    coords = get_lat_lon(image_path)
    if not coords:
        print("No location data found.")
        return

    lat, lon = coords
    map = folium.Map(location=[lat, lon], zoom_start=15)
    folium.Marker([lat, lon], popup="Image Location").add_to(map)
```

```
map.save("image_location.html")
```

```
# Example usage
plot_image_location("image.jpg")
```

✓ This script creates an interactive map showing where the image was taken.

□□♂□ 8.2.7 Detecting Image Editing & Tampering

◆ Identify Software Used for Editing

```
def check_editing_software(image_path):
    exif_data = get_exif_data(image_path)
    software = exif_data.get("Software", "Unknown")
    print(f"Editing Software: {software}")
```

```
# Example usage
check_editing_software("edited_image.jpg")
```

✓ This detects Photoshop edits or image modifications.

⚡ 8.2.8 Automating Metadata Extraction for Multiple Images

What if we need to analyze hundreds of images for OSINT? We can automate metadata extraction in bulk.

◆ Extract EXIF Data from Multiple Images in a Folder

```
import os
```

```
def batch_extract_exif(folder_path):
    for filename in os.listdir(folder_path):
        if filename.lower().endswith((".jpg", ".jpeg", ".png")):
            print(f"\nExtracting metadata for: {filename}")
            extract_exif(os.path.join(folder_path, filename))
```

```
# Example usage
batch_extract_exif("images_folder/")
```

✓ This script automatically scans all images in a folder and extracts metadata.

🔒 8.2.9 How to Remove EXIF Metadata for Privacy

Bad actors can use EXIF data for tracking people. We can remove EXIF metadata before sharing images online.

◆ Remove EXIF Metadata Using Piexif

```
import piexif

def remove_exif(image_path):
    piexif.remove(image_path)
    print(f"EXIF metadata removed from {image_path}")

# Example usage
remove_exif("image.jpg")
```

✓ This script strips all EXIF metadata from an image.

☐ 8.2.10 Real-World OSINT Applications

Use Case	How Metadata Helps
Tracking Criminals	Find where a suspect took an image
Fake News Verification	Check if images are real or altered
Threat Intelligence	Identify leaked images with metadata
Privacy Protection	Remove metadata before sharing images

✅ Summary & Key Takeaways

✓ Image metadata contains valuable intelligence (EXIF, GPS, timestamps).

✓ Python can automate metadata extraction for OSINT investigations.

✓ GPS data can reveal the location where an image was taken.

✓ Automating metadata analysis speeds up large-scale investigations.

✓ Removing metadata protects privacy and prevents tracking.

8.3 Automating Reverse Image Searches (Google, Yandex, Tineye)

Reverse image search is a powerful OSINT technique that allows analysts to:

✓ Identify the origin of an image

✓ Find visually similar images across the internet

✓ Detect fake profiles and stolen images

✓ Verify the authenticity of images in news and social media

Manually performing reverse image searches on platforms like Google Images, Yandex, and TinEye can be time-consuming. This chapter explores how to automate reverse image searches using Python.

🔍 8.3.1 What is Reverse Image Search?

Reverse image search engines analyze an image and return:

✓ Websites where the image appears

✓ Similar images from across the web

✓ Higher-resolution versions of the image

✓ Associated metadata (e.g., timestamps, EXIF data)

Popular Reverse Image Search Engines

Platform	Best Use Cases	Automation Methods
Google Images	General search, social media verification	Selenium, Google Lens API
Yandex Images	Best for finding similar images & faces	Direct URL submission
TinEye	Finds image modifications & source tracking	TinEye API

☐ 8.3.2 Automating Google Reverse Image Search

Google Images doesn't provide a public API for reverse image search, but we can automate the process using Selenium.

◆ Install Required Libraries

pip install selenium webdriver-manager

◆ Set Up Selenium for Google Image Search

```
from selenium import webdriver
from selenium.webdriver.common.by import By
from selenium.webdriver.common.keys import Keys
import time

def google_reverse_image_search(image_path):
    driver = webdriver.Chrome()
    driver.get("https://images.google.com")

    # Click on the camera icon
    search_by_image_button = driver.find_element(By.CLASS_NAME, "Gdd5U")
    search_by_image_button.click()

    # Upload image
    upload_tab = driver.find_element(By.LINK_TEXT, "Upload an image")
    upload_tab.click()

    file_input = driver.find_element(By.NAME, "encoded_image")
    file_input.send_keys(image_path)
```

```
time.sleep(5)  # Wait for results
print(driver.current_url)  # Print search results URL

driver.quit()
```

```
# Example usage
google_reverse_image_search("image.jpg")
```

✓ This script automates the process of uploading an image to Google Images.

◆ **Limitations**: Google may block bots, so using proxies and headless browsing may be necessary.

☐ 8.3.3 Automating Yandex Reverse Image Search

Yandex provides one of the best reverse image search engines, especially for facial recognition.

◆ Automate Yandex Reverse Image Search Using Selenium

```
def yandex_reverse_image_search(image_path):
    driver = webdriver.Chrome()
    driver.get("https://yandex.com/images/")

    # Click on the camera icon
    camera_button = driver.find_element(By.CLASS_NAME, "cbir-button")
    camera_button.click()

    # Upload image
    upload_input = driver.find_element(By.XPATH, "//input[@type='file']")
    upload_input.send_keys(image_path)

    time.sleep(5)  # Wait for results
    print(driver.current_url)  # Print search results URL

    driver.quit()
```

```
# Example usage
yandex_reverse_image_search("image.jpg")
```

✓ This script automates uploading an image to Yandex for reverse searching.

◆ **Why Use Yandex?**

✓ Best for finding similar faces

✓ Great for tracking stolen images

🔍 **8.3.4 Automating TinEye Reverse Image Search**

TinEye offers an API for automated searches, making it the best option for large-scale OSINT investigations.

◆ **Install the TinEye API**

pip install requests

◆ **Use the TinEye API for Reverse Image Search**

```
import requests

TINEYE_API_URL = "https://api.tineye.com/rest/search/"
TINEYE_API_KEY = "your_api_key_here"

def tineye_reverse_image_search(image_url):
    params = {
        "url": image_url,
        "api_key": TINEYE_API_KEY
    }
    response = requests.get(TINEYE_API_URL, params=params)
    results = response.json()
    print(results)

# Example usage
tineye_reverse_image_search("https://example.com/image.jpg")
```

✓ TinEye API allows large-scale image searches and provides detailed match results.

◆ **Advantages of TinEye API:**

✓ No need for Selenium (faster & more reliable)

✓ Can track image modifications

📠 8.3.5 Comparing the Reverse Image Search Methods

Method	Pros	Cons
Google Images (Selenium)	Best for general searches	May block bots, no API
Yandex (Selenium)	Excellent for face recognition	Russian-based, requires manual upload
TinEye API	Automated API access, tracks modifications	Requires API key, limited free searches

⚡ 8.3.6 Automating Reverse Image Search for Multiple Images

For OSINT investigations, we often need to check multiple images at once. We can automate bulk searches using a loop.

◆ Automate Google Reverse Image Search for Multiple Images

```
import os

def batch_google_search(folder_path):
    for filename in os.listdir(folder_path):
        if filename.lower().endswith((".jpg", ".jpeg", ".png")):
            print(f"Searching for: {filename}")
            google_reverse_image_search(os.path.join(folder_path, filename))

# Example usage
batch_google_search("images_folder/")
```

✓ This script automates reverse image search for an entire folder of images.

🕵️ 8.3.7 Real-World OSINT Applications

Use Case	How Reverse Image Search Helps
Fake Social Media Accounts	Detect stolen profile pictures
Tracking Stolen Images	Identify unauthorized use of images
Verifying News Reports	Find original sources of viral images
Locating Persons of Interest	Track online presence through images

✅ Summary & Key Takeaways

✔ Reverse image search is a critical OSINT tool for tracking images.

✔ Google, Yandex, and TinEye each have strengths:

- **Google** = Best for general searches
- **Yandex** = Best for face recognition
- **TinEye** = Best for tracking image edits

✔ Selenium can automate Google and Yandex searches, while TinEye has an API for bulk searches.

✔ Python can automate searches for multiple images to speed up investigations

8.4 Identifying Objects & Faces Using AI-Based Image Recognition

Artificial Intelligence (AI) and Machine Learning (ML) have revolutionized OSINT investigations by enabling automated image recognition, face detection, and object identification. These technologies allow analysts to:

✔ Detect and classify objects in images (e.g., weapons, vehicles, landmarks)

✔ Identify individuals using facial recognition

✔ Analyze large datasets of images efficiently

✓ Track people and objects across multiple images and videos

This chapter explores how to use Python-based AI tools for object and face recognition in OSINT investigations.

☐ 8.4.1 Understanding AI-Powered Image Recognition

AI image recognition uses deep learning models, such as Convolutional Neural Networks (CNNs), to analyze and classify images.

Method	Use Case in OSINT	Popular AI Models
Object Detection	Identifying vehicles, weapons, logos	YOLO, OpenCV, TensorFlow
Facial Recognition	Identifying individuals in images	FaceNet, DeepFace, dlib
Landmark Recognition	Geolocating images using landmarks	Google Vision, OpenCV
Text Detection (OCR)	Extracting text from images	Tesseract OCR, EasyOCR

☐ 8.4.2 Setting Up AI-Based Image Recognition in Python

To perform object and face recognition, we use the following Python libraries:

- **OpenCV** – For object and face detection
- **TensorFlow/Keras** – For deep learning-based image recognition
- **Face_recognition** – For facial recognition
- **YOLO (You Only Look Once)** – For real-time object detection

◆ Install Required Libraries

pip install opencv-python tensorflow keras face-recognition numpy

☐ 8.4.3 Detecting Objects in Images Using OpenCV

◆ Detect Objects Using a Pre-Trained Model

OpenCV provides pre-trained models that can recognize common objects.

```python
import cv2

# Load pre-trained model
net = cv2.dnn.readNetFromCaffe("MobileNetSSD_deploy.prototxt",
"MobileNetSSD_deploy.caffemodel")

# Load image
image = cv2.imread("image.jpg")
(h, w) = image.shape[:2]

# Convert image into a blob
blob = cv2.dnn.blobFromImage(image, 0.007843, (300, 300), 127.5)
net.setInput(blob)

# Perform object detection
detections = net.forward()

# Loop through detections
for i in range(detections.shape[2]):
    confidence = detections[0, 0, i, 2]
    if confidence > 0.5:
        idx = int(detections[0, 0, i, 1])
        box = detections[0, 0, i, 3:7] * [w, h, w, h]
        (startX, startY, endX, endY) = box.astype("int")

        # Draw bounding box
        label = f"Object {idx}: {confidence:.2f}"
        cv2.rectangle(image, (startX, startY), (endX, endY), (0, 255, 0), 2)
        cv2.putText(image, label, (startX, startY - 10), cv2.FONT_HERSHEY_SIMPLEX,
0.5, (0, 255, 0), 2)

cv2.imshow("Image", image)
cv2.waitKey(0)
cv2.destroyAllWindows()
```

✔ This script detects objects in an image using OpenCV's deep learning model.

🧍 8.4.4 Performing Facial Recognition Using Python

◆ Use the Face Recognition Library

```
import face_recognition
import cv2

# Load image
image = face_recognition.load_image_file("face.jpg")

# Detect faces
face_locations = face_recognition.face_locations(image)

# Draw boxes around faces
for (top, right, bottom, left) in face_locations:
    cv2.rectangle(image, (left, top), (right, bottom), (0, 255, 0), 2)

cv2.imshow("Face Recognition", image)
cv2.waitKey(0)
cv2.destroyAllWindows()
```

✓ This script detects faces in an image and draws bounding boxes.

⊙ 8.4.5 Identifying Specific Individuals Using AI

Facial recognition is useful for matching faces against known databases.

◆ Compare Faces to a Known Database

```
import face_recognition

# Load known image
known_image = face_recognition.load_image_file("known_person.jpg")
known_encoding = face_recognition.face_encodings(known_image)[0]

# Load unknown image
unknown_image = face_recognition.load_image_file("unknown_person.jpg")
unknown_encoding = face_recognition.face_encodings(unknown_image)[0]

# Compare faces
results = face_recognition.compare_faces([known_encoding], unknown_encoding)
```

```
if results[0]:
    print("Match found!")
else:
    print("No match.")
```

✓ This script compares an unknown face to a known database to find a match.

🚗 8.4.6 Detecting Vehicles, Weapons, and Objects in OSINT

◆ Use YOLO for Object Detection

YOLO (You Only Look Once) is a real-time object detection model.

```
import cv2
import numpy as np

# Load YOLO model
net = cv2.dnn.readNet("yolov3.weights", "yolov3.cfg")
layer_names = net.getLayerNames()
output_layers = [layer_names[i[0] - 1] for i in net.getUnconnectedOutLayers()]

# Load image
image = cv2.imread("street.jpg")
height, width, channels = image.shape

# Convert image to blob
blob = cv2.dnn.blobFromImage(image, 0.00392, (416, 416), swapRB=True, crop=False)
net.setInput(blob)
outs = net.forward(output_layers)

# Process detections
for out in outs:
    for detection in out:
        scores = detection[5:]
        class_id = np.argmax(scores)
        confidence = scores[class_id]

        if confidence > 0.5:
            # Draw bounding box
            center_x, center_y, w, h = detection[:4] * [width, height, width, height]
```

```
x = int(center_x - w / 2)
y = int(center_y - h / 2)

cv2.rectangle(image, (x, y), (x + w, y + h), (0, 255, 0), 2)
```

```
cv2.imshow("YOLO Object Detection", image)
cv2.waitKey(0)
cv2.destroyAllWindows()
```

✓ This script detects cars, people, weapons, and other objects in an image using YOLO.

□□♂□ 8.4.7 Real-World OSINT Applications

Use Case	How AI Helps
Identifying Criminals	Recognize suspects from surveillance footage
Tracking Military Movements	Detect military vehicles & equipment
Verifying News Footage	Identify fake or manipulated images
Human Trafficking Investigations	Detect missing persons in online images

✅ Summary & Key Takeaways

✓ AI image recognition helps in face identification, object detection, and location tracking.

✓ OpenCV and TensorFlow enable automated image analysis.

✓ Face_recognition allows comparing faces against databases.

✓ YOLO provides real-time object detection for OSINT.

✓ AI-powered OSINT improves efficiency in large-scale investigations.

8.5 Geolocation Tracking from Image Data

Geolocation tracking from images is a crucial OSINT technique that helps analysts determine where an image was taken based on:

✓ Embedded metadata (EXIF data)

✓ Visible landmarks, signs, and environmental clues

✓ Satellite imagery and mapping tools

✓ Reverse image search and AI-based scene recognition

This chapter explores Python-based methods to extract geolocation data from images, analyze landmarks, and use mapping tools for OSINT investigations.

🔍 8.5.1 Understanding Geolocation in OSINT

◆ How Can Images Reveal Their Location?

Method	How It Works	Example Tools
EXIF Metadata	Extracts GPS coordinates from image metadata	ExifTool, Pillow, exifread
Landmark Recognition	Identifies buildings, signs, landscapes	Google Vision API, OpenCV
Street Signs & License Plates	Reads signs and plates to determine location	Tesseract OCR, Google Lens
Satellite & Street View Matching	Compares images with Google Maps & OpenStreetMap	Google Earth, Mapillary
Weather & Shadows Analysis	Analyzes sun position and weather to estimate location	SunCalc, PyEphem

Some images contain embedded GPS coordinates, while others require contextual analysis.

☐ 8.5.2 Extracting GPS Coordinates from Image Metadata

Many modern cameras and smartphones store EXIF metadata, which includes:

✓ GPS latitude & longitude

✔ Device model

✔ Timestamp

✔ Camera settings

◆ Install Required Libraries

pip install pillow exifread

◆ Extract GPS Data from an Image

```
from PIL import Image
from PIL.ExifTags import TAGS, GPSTAGS

def get_exif_data(image_path):
    image = Image.open(image_path)
    exif_data = image._getexif()

    if not exif_data:
        return None

    exif = {TAGS[k]: v for k, v in exif_data.items() if k in TAGS}

    gps_info = {}
    if "GPSInfo" in exif:
        for key in exif["GPSInfo"].keys():
            label = GPSTAGS.get(key, key)
            gps_info[label] = exif["GPSInfo"][key]

    return gps_info

# Example usage
image_path = "image.jpg"
gps_data = get_exif_data(image_path)
print(gps_data)
```

✔ This script extracts GPS metadata from an image.

◆ How to Convert GPS Data to Latitude/Longitude?

GPS data is often stored in DMS (degrees, minutes, seconds) format. We can convert it to decimal coordinates:

```python
def convert_to_degrees(value):
    d, m, s = value
    return d + (m / 60.0) + (s / 3600.0)

def extract_lat_lon(gps_data):
    if not gps_data:
        return None

    lat = convert_to_degrees(gps_data["GPSLatitude"])
    lon = convert_to_degrees(gps_data["GPSLongitude"])

    if gps_data["GPSLatitudeRef"] == "S":
        lat = -lat
    if gps_data["GPSLongitudeRef"] == "W":
        lon = -lon

    return lat, lon

# Example usage
coords = extract_lat_lon(gps_data)
if coords:
    print(f"Latitude: {coords[0]}, Longitude: {coords[1]}")
```

✓ This script converts raw GPS data into latitude and longitude coordinates.

☐ 8.5.3 Mapping Image Locations with Google Maps API

Once we extract coordinates, we can plot them on a map using Google Maps.

◆ Install Google Maps API

```
pip install gmplot
```

◆ Plot GPS Coordinates on a Map

```python
import gmplot
```

```
# Example coordinates
latitude, longitude = 37.7749, -122.4194  # San Francisco

# Create a map centered on the location
gmap = gmplot.GoogleMapPlotter(latitude, longitude, 13)

# Add marker
gmap.marker(latitude, longitude, title="Image Location")

# Save the map
gmap.draw("map.html")
print("Map generated!")
```

✓ This script creates an interactive Google Map with the image's location.

☐ 8.5.4 Identifying Locations Using AI-Based Landmark Recognition

If an image does not contain EXIF GPS data, we can analyze landmarks, signs, and backgrounds.

◆ Use Google Vision API for Landmark Recognition

Google's Vision API can detect famous landmarks in an image.

```
from google.cloud import vision
import io

def detect_landmark(image_path):
    client = vision.ImageAnnotatorClient()

    with io.open(image_path, "rb") as image_file:
        content = image_file.read()

    image = vision.Image(content=content)
    response = client.landmark_detection(image=image)

    for landmark in response.landmark_annotations:
        print(f"Landmark: {landmark.description}")
        print(f"Location: {landmark.locations[0].lat_lng}")
```

```
# Example usage
detect_landmark("landmark.jpg")
```

✓ This script identifies landmarks and their coordinates from an image.

◆ **Use Cases:**

✓ Identifying famous buildings, statues, or natural landmarks

✓ Confirming geolocation of viral images

✓ Verifying photos used in misinformation campaigns

🔎 8.5.5 Extracting Geolocation Clues from Signs & License Plates

Street signs, billboards, and vehicle license plates provide valuable geolocation clues.

◆ **Use OCR to Extract Text from Images**

```
pip install pytesseract opencv-python

import cv2
import pytesseract

# Load image
image = cv2.imread("sign.jpg")
gray = cv2.cvtColor(image, cv2.COLOR_BGR2GRAY)

# Extract text using OCR
text = pytesseract.image_to_string(gray, lang="eng")
print(f"Extracted Text: {text}")
```

✓ This script extracts text from street signs and license plates for location analysis.

◆ **Use Cases:**

✓ Identifying city names, phone numbers, or addresses in the image

✔ Recognizing license plate numbers to trace vehicles

☐ 8.5.6 Using Satellite & Street View for Image Matching

Even without direct geolocation data, analysts can match images to satellite and street view.

◆ Use Google Street View API to Find Image Locations

import requests

API_KEY = "your_google_api_key"
latitude, longitude = 37.7749, -122.4194 # Example coords

url =
*f"https://maps.googleapis.com/maps/api/streetview?size=600x300&location={latitude},{l
ongitude}&key={API_KEY}"*

response = requests.get(url)

with open("streetview.jpg", "wb") as file:
   file.write(response.content)

print("Street View image saved!")

✔ This script downloads a Google Street View image of the location.

☐☐♂☐ 8.5.7 Real-World OSINT Applications

Use Case	How Geolocation Tracking Helps
Verifying Social Media Posts	Confirm if an image matches its claimed location
Tracking Criminal Activities	Identify locations from surveillance or leaked images
Disaster Response	Locate victims from social media images
Human Trafficking & Missing Persons	Identify surroundings from victim photos

✅ Summary & Key Takeaways

✓ Geolocation tracking is essential for verifying images in OSINT investigations.

✓ EXIF metadata can provide GPS coordinates directly.

✓ AI-based landmark detection helps when EXIF data is missing.

✓ Street signs, weather, and environment clues assist in geolocation.

✓ Satellite imagery and Google Maps APIs can be used for further analysis.

8.6 Case Study: Automating Image Analysis for Geospatial Intelligence

Geospatial intelligence (GEOINT) is a critical component of OSINT that involves extracting location-based insights from images. Analysts can use automated image analysis techniques to identify locations, detect objects, and derive intelligence from visual data.

In this case study, we will explore how automation improves geospatial analysis by:

✓ Extracting EXIF metadata to get GPS coordinates

✓ Identifying landmarks and geographic features using AI

✓ Using satellite and street view imagery to verify locations

✓ Automating reverse image searches for additional intelligence

We will develop a Python-based automation workflow to process images and extract geospatial intelligence efficiently.

🔎 8.6.1 Case Study Scenario

Scenario:

A cybersecurity firm is investigating a series of social media posts claiming to be from a conflict zone. They need to verify whether the images are genuine and locate where they were taken.

Key Objectives:

- Extract metadata to determine if the images contain embedded location data.
- Use AI-based object detection to identify landmarks or geographic features.
- Perform reverse image searches to check if the images were used before in misleading contexts.
- Cross-check satellite and street view imagery for location verification.

☐ 8.6.2 Automating Image Metadata Extraction

First, we automate EXIF metadata extraction to check for GPS coordinates, camera details, and timestamps.

◆ Install Required Libraries

pip install pillow exifread

◆ Extract GPS Coordinates from Image Metadata

```
from PIL import Image
from PIL.ExifTags import TAGS, GPSTAGS

def extract_exif_data(image_path):
    image = Image.open(image_path)
    exif_data = image._getexif()

    if not exif_data:
        return None

    metadata = {TAGS.get(k, k): v for k, v in exif_data.items()}

    gps_data = {}
    if "GPSInfo" in metadata:
        for key, value in metadata["GPSInfo"].items():
            label = GPSTAGS.get(key, key)
            gps_data[label] = value
```

```
    return gps_data
```

```
# Example usage
image_path = "suspect_image.jpg"
gps_info = extract_exif_data(image_path)
print(gps_info)
```

✓ This script extracts GPS coordinates and other metadata from the image.

◆ **Convert GPS Data to Latitude/Longitude**

```
def convert_to_degrees(value):
    d, m, s = value
    return d + (m / 60.0) + (s / 3600.0)
```

```
def get_lat_lon(gps_data):
    if not gps_data:
        return None

    lat = convert_to_degrees(gps_data["GPSLatitude"])
    lon = convert_to_degrees(gps_data["GPSLongitude"])

    if gps_data["GPSLatitudeRef"] == "S":
        lat = -lat
    if gps_data["GPSLongitudeRef"] == "W":
        lon = -lon

    return lat, lon
```

```
# Example usage
coordinates = get_lat_lon(gps_info)
if coordinates:
    print(f"Latitude: {coordinates[0]}, Longitude: {coordinates[1]}")
```

✓ This converts raw GPS data into usable latitude and longitude coordinates.

🔎 **8.6.3 Automating Landmark Recognition**

If an image lacks GPS data, we can analyze its contents using AI-powered landmark detection.

◆ Use Google Vision API for Landmark Recognition

Google Vision API can identify famous buildings, natural landmarks, and geographic features.

```
from google.cloud import vision
import io

def detect_landmarks(image_path):
    client = vision.ImageAnnotatorClient()

    with io.open(image_path, "rb") as image_file:
        content = image_file.read()

    image = vision.Image(content=content)
    response = client.landmark_detection(image=image)

    for landmark in response.landmark_annotations:
        print(f"Landmark: {landmark.description}")
        print(f"Location: {landmark.locations[0].lat_lng}")

# Example usage
detect_landmarks("suspect_image.jpg")
```

✔ This script identifies landmarks and their coordinates, helping verify the image's location.

☐ 8.6.4 Automating Reverse Image Search for Verification

To check if the image has been used before, we automate reverse image search using Google or Yandex.

◆ Google Reverse Image Search Automation

```
import webbrowser
```

```
def google_reverse_image_search(image_path):
    search_url = f"https://www.google.com/searchbyimage?image_url={image_path}"
    webbrowser.open(search_url)

# Example usage
google_reverse_image_search("suspect_image.jpg")
```

✓ This opens Google Reverse Image Search, checking if the image was previously published.

☐ 8.6.5 Cross-Checking with Satellite & Street View

We use Google Maps API to match extracted coordinates with satellite imagery and street view.

◆ Plot Image Location on Google Maps

```
import gmplot

latitude, longitude = 34.0522, -118.2437  # Example coordinates

gmap = gmplot.GoogleMapPlotter(latitude, longitude, 13)
gmap.marker(latitude, longitude, title="Suspect Image Location")
gmap.draw("map.html")
print("Google Map generated!")
```

✓ This creates an interactive map to verify if the image matches real-world locations.

▥ 8.6.6 Automating the Entire Workflow

To streamline the analysis, we create a full automation pipeline that:

✓ Extracts EXIF metadata

✓ Identifies landmarks using AI

✓ Performs reverse image search

✓ Cross-checks satellite and street view

◆ Full Python Workflow for Automated GEOINT

```python
import os
from PIL import Image
from google.cloud import vision
import webbrowser

# Step 1: Extract Metadata
def extract_metadata(image_path):
    image = Image.open(image_path)
    exif_data = image._getexif()

    if not exif_data:
        return None

    metadata = {TAGS.get(k, k): v for k, v in exif_data.items()}
    return metadata

# Step 2: Identify Landmarks
def detect_landmarks(image_path):
    client = vision.ImageAnnotatorClient()
    with open(image_path, "rb") as image_file:
        content = image_file.read()
    image = vision.Image(content=content)
    response = client.landmark_detection(image=image)
    return response.landmark_annotations

# Step 3: Reverse Image Search
def reverse_image_search(image_path):
    search_url = f"https://www.google.com/searchbyimage?image_url={image_path}"
    webbrowser.open(search_url)

# Run the Automated Workflow
def automated_geoint_analysis(image_path):
    print("Extracting metadata...")
    metadata = extract_metadata(image_path)
    print(metadata)

    print("Detecting landmarks...")
    landmarks = detect_landmarks(image_path)
```

```
for landmark in landmarks:
    print(f"Landmark Detected: {landmark.description}")

print("Performing reverse image search...")
reverse_image_search(image_path)

# Example Usage
image_path = "suspect_image.jpg"
automated_geoint_analysis(image_path)
```

✓ This automates the entire OSINT geospatial analysis process!

✅ Case Study Results & Key Takeaways

✓ Automating GEOINT reduces manual workload and improves accuracy.

✓ EXIF metadata extraction provides direct GPS data when available.

✓ AI-based image recognition helps analyze images without metadata.

✓ Reverse image search helps verify whether images are reused or misleading.

✓ Google Maps API integration cross-checks real-world locations.

9. Dark Web Monitoring with Python Scripts

In this chapter, we dive into the complex and often elusive world of dark web monitoring using Python scripts. The dark web contains a wealth of unindexed, anonymous information that is valuable for intelligence gathering, but accessing it requires specialized tools and techniques. You'll learn how to automate the process of scanning dark web forums, marketplaces, and other hidden services using Python-based tools such as requests, BeautifulSoup, and Tor for anonymous browsing. We'll also discuss how to monitor specific keywords, track suspicious activity, and extract relevant data while maintaining ethical standards and privacy. By the end of this chapter, you'll be equipped with the tools to automate dark web monitoring, allowing you to uncover threats, track illicit activities, and enhance your overall OSINT capabilities.

9.1 Challenges of Dark Web Monitoring & Data Extraction

The dark web is a hidden part of the internet that requires specialized tools like Tor to access. It hosts a variety of forums, marketplaces, and communication channels used for both legitimate and illicit activities. For OSINT analysts, monitoring the dark web can provide critical intelligence on cyber threats, financial fraud, and criminal activities.

However, dark web monitoring presents significant challenges, including:

✔ **Technical Barriers** – Accessing and crawling dark web sites is difficult due to network restrictions.

✔ **Legal & Ethical Risks** – OSINT analysts must ensure compliance with laws while gathering intelligence.

✔ **Data Extraction Issues** – Many dark web sites use CAPTCHAs, hidden links, and login barriers.

✔ **Anonymity of Users** – Tracing users is difficult due to encryption and anonymous networks.

✔ **Volatile Content** – Dark web sites often disappear, requiring real-time monitoring.

In this chapter, we will explore these challenges and discuss strategies to safely and effectively collect intelligence from the dark web.

⚠ 9.1.1 Legal & Ethical Considerations

Before diving into dark web monitoring, OSINT professionals must be aware of legal and ethical boundaries.

📜 Key Legal Concerns:

✓ **Accessing the Dark Web** – Simply browsing is legal in most countries, but downloading illegal content can lead to prosecution.

✓ **Data Collection** – Some jurisdictions restrict the collection and storage of dark web data.

✓ **Undercover Investigations** – Engaging with illicit groups may require law enforcement approval.

✓ **Privacy Laws** – Scraping user data or monitoring individuals may violate GDPR or other privacy laws.

🔍 Ethical Guidelines for OSINT Analysts:

✓ **Stay Within Legal Boundaries** – Consult with legal experts if unsure about data collection methods.

✓ **Do Not Participate in Illicit Activities** – Avoid engaging with illegal marketplaces or forums.

✓ **Protect Your Identity** – Use secure and anonymous methods to avoid exposure.

☐ 9.1.2 Accessing the Dark Web for OSINT

To monitor the dark web, analysts must use Tor (The Onion Router) to access .onion websites.

◆ Setting Up Tor in Python

Install the required tools:

```
sudo apt update && sudo apt install tor
pip install requests[socks]
```

Configure Tor to route Python requests through an anonymous connection:

```
import requests

proxies = {
    "http": "socks5h://127.0.0.1:9050",
    "https": "socks5h://127.0.0.1:9050",
}

url = "http://exampledarkwebsite.onion"

response = requests.get(url, proxies=proxies)
print(response.text)
```

✓ This script allows anonymous browsing of dark web sites using Tor proxies.

🚧 9.1.3 Technical Barriers in Dark Web Scraping

Unlike traditional web scraping, dark web monitoring faces several challenges:

1️⃣ Websites Disappear Frequently

✓ Many dark web markets and forums shut down unexpectedly, requiring continuous monitoring.

✓ Solution: Automate data collection at regular intervals.

2️⃣ CAPTCHA & Login Restrictions

✓ Dark web sites often block automated bots with CAPTCHAs.

✓ Solution: Use headless browsers like Selenium or human-in-the-loop CAPTCHA solvers.

3️⃣ Hidden Links & Dynamic Content

✓ Many pages require JavaScript execution to load content.

✓ Solution: Use Selenium or tools like Scrapy-Splash to handle JavaScript-heavy pages.

🔎 9.1.4 Extracting & Analyzing Dark Web Data

Once we access a dark web page, we need to extract relevant intelligence.

◆ Scraping Dark Web Marketplaces

Example script to scrape a dark web forum:

```
from bs4 import BeautifulSoup
import requests

url = "http://exampledarkwebforum.onion"

proxies = {"http": "socks5h://127.0.0.1:9050", "https": "socks5h://127.0.0.1:9050"}

response = requests.get(url, proxies=proxies)
soup = BeautifulSoup(response.text, "html.parser")

# Extract post titles
for post in soup.find_all("h2"):
    print(post.text)
```

✓ This script extracts forum discussions, which could include cybercrime topics, data leaks, and hacking tutorials.

⚡ 9.1.5 Analyzing Dark Web Threat Intelligence

After extracting data, we need to analyze it for actionable insights.

◆ Identifying Keywords in Dark Web Posts

```
from collections import Counter
import re

text = """Selling stolen credit cards. Hacking services available. Buy ransomware kits here."""
```

```
words = re.findall(r"\w+", text.lower())
common_terms = Counter(words).most_common(5)

print("Top Keywords in Forum Post:", common_terms)
```

✓ This helps detect cybercrime-related keywords and trending threats.

◆ Detecting Dark Web Mentions of a Target

We can monitor mentions of company names, leaked credentials, or financial data.

```
target_keywords = ["companyX", "leaked database", "stolen credentials"]

for word in words:
    if word in target_keywords:
        print(f"ALERT: Found {word} in dark web post!")
```

✓ This alerts analysts if a company's data appears on dark web forums.

☐ 9.1.6 Security Best Practices for Dark Web Monitoring

Monitoring the dark web comes with risks. Here's how to protect yourself:

◆ Use a Secure Setup

✓ Always access the dark web through Tor or a secure VPS.

✓ Avoid using personal devices for OSINT investigations.

◆ Protect Your Identity

✓ Use a dedicated OSINT email and pseudonymous accounts.

✓ Do not use your real name or IP address.

◆ Encrypt & Secure Data Storage

✓ Any data collected should be stored in an encrypted database to prevent leaks.

✓ Avoid downloading illegal files, as possession could be a crime.

🏛 Conclusion & Next Steps

Dark web monitoring is an essential OSINT technique but comes with technical, legal, and security challenges.

Key Takeaways:

✓ Accessing the dark web requires Tor and special configurations.

✓ Many sites block scraping using CAPTCHAs and login barriers.

✓ Keyword analysis can help identify cyber threats and data breaches.

✓ Security precautions are necessary to protect your identity and system.

9.2 Automating Dark Web Site Crawling with Python

The dark web contains vast amounts of intelligence related to cybercrime, financial fraud, and illicit activities. However, manually monitoring dark web sites is inefficient and time-consuming. Automation helps OSINT analysts crawl and extract data from dark web forums, marketplaces, and hidden services.

In this chapter, we will cover:

✓ How to access and navigate dark web sites using Python

✓ Automating Tor connections for anonymous crawling

✓ Extracting forum posts, product listings, and leaked data

✓ Handling CAPTCHAs, login pages, and dynamic content

✓ Storing and analyzing dark web data

By the end, you'll have a Python-based dark web crawler that can automate intelligence gathering while maintaining security and anonymity.

☐ 9.2.1 Setting Up a Secure Environment for Crawling

◆ Installing Required Tools

To interact with the dark web, we need:

1☐ **Tor** – Routes traffic anonymously.
2☐ **Stem** – A Python library for controlling Tor.
3☐ **Requests** – Sends web requests via Tor.
4☐ **BeautifulSoup** – Extracts content from HTML pages.

☐ **Install the required libraries:**

```
sudo apt update && sudo apt install tor
pip install requests[socks] stem beautifulsoup4
```

◆ Configuring Tor for Python

Start Tor in the background:

```
tor &
```

Check if Tor is working by sending a request through its proxy:

```
import requests

proxies = {
    "http": "socks5h://127.0.0.1:9050",
    "https": "socks5h://127.0.0.1:9050",
}

response = requests.get("http://check.torproject.org", proxies=proxies)
print(response.text)
```

✔ If Tor is working, the response should confirm "You are using Tor".

☐ 9.2.2 Automating Dark Web Crawling

Now, let's automate the crawling of .onion sites.

◆ Basic Dark Web Crawler

This script accesses dark web marketplaces and extracts listings or forum posts.

```
from bs4 import BeautifulSoup
import requests

# Set up Tor proxy
proxies = {
    "http": "socks5h://127.0.0.1:9050",
    "https": "socks5h://127.0.0.1:9050",
}

# Dark web site (replace with a real .onion site)
url = "http://exampledarkmarket.onion"

# Send request through Tor
response = requests.get(url, proxies=proxies)
soup = BeautifulSoup(response.text, "html.parser")

# Extract titles from the page
for title in soup.find_all("h2"):
    print("Listing Found:", title.text)
```

✓ This extracts product listings or forum post titles from a dark web page.

🔐 9.2.3 Handling Login Pages & Session-Based Crawling

Some dark web sites require login credentials before allowing access.

◆ Automating Login to a Dark Web Forum

We can submit login forms using session-based authentication:

```
session = requests.Session()
session.proxies = proxies

login_url = "http://exampleforum.onion/login"
```

```
login_data = {"username": "your_username", "password": "your_password"}

# Perform login request
response = session.post(login_url, data=login_data)
print("Login Response:", response.status_code)

# Access a protected page after login
protected_url = "http://exampleforum.onion/private"
protected_page = session.get(protected_url)
print("Protected Page Content:", protected_page.text)
```

✓ This maintains an active session after logging in, allowing us to crawl private forums.

☐ 9.2.4 Handling CAPTCHAs & Anti-Scraping Measures

◆ 1☐☐ Using a CAPTCHA Solving Service

Some sites block automated bots by displaying CAPTCHAs.

To solve CAPTCHAs, we can use services like 2Captcha or Anti-Captcha:

```
import requests

API_KEY = "your_2captcha_api_key"
captcha_image_url = "http://exampleforum.onion/captcha.jpg"

# Request CAPTCHA solution
captcha_id = requests.post("http://2captcha.com/in.php", data={
    "key": API_KEY,
    "method": "post",
    "body": captcha_image_url
}).text

# Get the solved CAPTCHA
solution =
requests.get(f"http://2captcha.com/res.php?key={API_KEY}&id={captcha_id}").text
print("CAPTCHA Solved:", solution)
```

✓ This submits CAPTCHA images for human solving and returns the correct text.

◆ 2□□ Using a Headless Browser to Solve CAPTCHAs

We can use Selenium to manually solve CAPTCHAs in a browser:

```
from selenium import webdriver

options = webdriver.FirefoxOptions()
options.add_argument("--headless")  # Run browser in background
options.set_preference("network.proxy.type", 1)
options.set_preference("network.proxy.socks", "127.0.0.1")
options.set_preference("network.proxy.socks_port", 9050)

driver = webdriver.Firefox(options=options)
driver.get("http://exampleforum.onion")

input("Solve the CAPTCHA manually, then press Enter...")

# Extract forum content
print(driver.page_source)
```

✓ This allows manual CAPTCHA solving, after which automation continues.

📁 9.2.5 Storing & Analyzing Dark Web Data

Extracted data can be saved and analyzed for intelligence reports.

◆ Storing Data in CSV Format

```
import csv

data = [("Username", "Post Content"),
      ("User1", "Selling stolen credentials"),
      ("User2", "Hacking services available")]

with open("darkweb_data.csv", "w", newline="") as file:
   writer = csv.writer(file)
   writer.writerow(["Username", "Post Content"])
   writer.writerows(data)
```

print("Data saved successfully!")

✓ This saves forum discussions, marketplace listings, and leaked credentials.

🏛 9.2.6 Automating the Entire Dark Web Crawling Workflow

To make crawling fully automated, we combine all steps into a single script.

◆ Full Dark Web Crawler in Python

```
from bs4 import BeautifulSoup
import requests
import csv

# Set up Tor proxy
proxies = {
    "http": "socks5h://127.0.0.1:9050",
    "https": "socks5h://127.0.0.1:9050",
}

# Dark web target site
url = "http://exampleforum.onion"

# Send request through Tor
response = requests.get(url, proxies=proxies)
soup = BeautifulSoup(response.text, "html.parser")

# Extract forum posts
data = []
for post in soup.find_all("div", class_="post"):
    username = post.find("span", class_="user").text
    content = post.find("p", class_="message").text
    data.append((username, content))

# Save extracted data
with open("darkweb_forum_posts.csv", "w", newline="") as file:
    writer = csv.writer(file)
    writer.writerow(["Username", "Post Content"])
    writer.writerows(data)
```

print("Dark web data saved!")

✓ This crawls a dark web forum, extracts usernames & posts, and saves them to CSV.

✅ Conclusion & Next Steps

Key Takeaways:

✓ Tor proxies allow anonymous crawling.

✓ Session-based authentication helps access restricted pages.

✓ CAPTCHA bypassing ensures continuous crawling.

✓ Extracted data can be stored & analyzed for cyber threat intelligence.

9.3 Extracting Intelligence from Onion Sites via Tor API

The dark web hosts a wealth of intelligence, from cybercrime marketplaces to leaked data repositories. Extracting actionable intelligence from .onion sites requires secure access, automation, and data processing techniques. While traditional web scraping methods can work, using the Tor API enhances anonymity, efficiency, and reliability when interacting with dark web sites.

In this chapter, we will cover:

✓ How to interact with the Tor network programmatically using the Tor API

✓ Automating connections to onion sites securely

✓ Extracting forum posts, product listings, and leaked credentials

✓ Handling anti-crawling measures, captchas, and login barriers

✓ Storing and structuring extracted dark web intelligence

By the end of this chapter, you will have a Python-based Tor API framework for securely gathering OSINT from the dark web.

9.3.1 Understanding the Tor API & Its Benefits

The Tor API (via the Stem library) allows Python scripts to communicate directly with the Tor network, offering key benefits:

✅ **Control Over Tor Circuits** – Programmatically change IP addresses & exit nodes
✅ **Automated Connection Handling** – Restart Tor connections when blocked
✅ **Better Anonymity** – Prevents direct interactions with dark web sites
✅ **Efficient Crawling** – Avoids manual browser-based operations

To utilize this API, we use Stem, a Python library that interfaces with the Tor daemon.

9.3.2 Setting Up the Tor API for Python

◆ Install Required Libraries

```
sudo apt update && sudo apt install tor
pip install stem requests[socks] beautifulsoup4
```

◆ Configuring Tor to Allow API Control

Modify the Tor configuration file (torrc):

```
sudo nano /etc/tor/torrc
```

Add the following lines at the end of the file:

```
ControlPort 9051
CookieAuthentication 1
```

Save the file and restart Tor:

```
sudo systemctl restart tor
```

✓ Now, Python can interact with the Tor network via port 9051.

9.3.3 Connecting to Onion Sites via the Tor API

We can now access .onion sites programmatically through Tor's SOCKS5 proxy.

◆ Establishing a Tor Connection

```
import requests

# Define Tor proxy settings
proxies = {
    "http": "socks5h://127.0.0.1:9050",
    "https": "socks5h://127.0.0.1:9050",
}

# Test access to an onion site
url = "http://exampledarkmarket.onion"
response = requests.get(url, proxies=proxies)

print("Dark Web Response:", response.text)
```

✔ If successful, this returns the HTML content of the dark web site.

□ 9.3.4 Automating IP Address Rotation for Anonymity

Dark web sites often block repeated requests from the same IP. We can rotate IP addresses using the Tor API.

◆ Changing Tor Exit Nodes

```
from stem.control import Controller

def change_tor_ip():
    with Controller.from_port(port=9051) as controller:
        controller.authenticate()  # Authenticate with Tor
        controller.signal("NEWNYM")  # Request new identity
        print("Tor IP Address Changed!")

change_tor_ip()
```

✔ This forces Tor to assign a new exit node and refresh anonymity.

□□♂□ 9.3.5 Extracting Intelligence from Onion Sites

Now, let's extract data from dark web marketplaces and forums.

◆ Scraping Dark Web Forums

```
from bs4 import BeautifulSoup
import requests

# Onion site URL
url = "http://exampleforum.onion"

# Send request through Tor
response = requests.get(url, proxies=proxies)
soup = BeautifulSoup(response.text, "html.parser")

# Extract forum post titles
for post in soup.find_all("h2"):
    print("Forum Post:", post.text)
```

✓ This script retrieves forum posts from a dark web discussion board.

◆ Extracting Leaked Data from Dark Web Marketplaces

```
# Extract leaked email addresses from an onion marketplace
for listing in soup.find_all("div", class_="leak"):
    title = listing.find("h2").text
    details = listing.find("p").text
    print(f"Leaked Data: {title} - {details}")
```

✓ This identifies leaked credentials, stolen databases, or compromised accounts.

🎁 9.3.6 Handling Login Forms & Authentication

Many dark web sites require user authentication before accessing sensitive content.

◆ Automating Login Requests

```
session = requests.Session()
session.proxies = proxies
```

```
login_url = "http://exampleforum.onion/login"
login_data = {"username": "user123", "password": "securepassword"}

# Perform login request
response = session.post(login_url, data=login_data)
print("Login Response:", response.status_code)

# Access a protected page
protected_url = "http://exampleforum.onion/private"
protected_page = session.get(protected_url)
print("Protected Page Content:", protected_page.text)
```

✓ This script logs into a dark web forum and extracts protected content.

🏛 9.3.7 Storing & Structuring Extracted Intelligence

Collected data must be organized for analysis.

◆ Storing Data in JSON Format

```
import json

data = [{"username": "User1", "post": "Selling stolen credentials"},
    {"username": "User2", "post": "Hacking services available"}]

with open("darkweb_data.json", "w") as file:
    json.dump(data, file, indent=4)

print("Data saved successfully!")
```

✓ This creates a structured intelligence database from extracted content.

☐ 9.3.8 Overcoming Dark Web Anti-Scraping Measures

Dark web sites actively block automated scrapers. Here's how to bypass common restrictions:

◆ CAPTCHA Handling

- Use 2Captcha API to solve CAPTCHAs automatically.
- Use Selenium for manual CAPTCHA entry.

◆ JavaScript-Based Content Handling

Use Selenium with a headless browser to render JavaScript content.

◆ Randomized User-Agent Strings

headers = {"User-Agent": "Mozilla/5.0 (Windows NT 10.0; Win64; x64)"}
requests.get(url, proxies=proxies, headers=headers)

✓ This mimics human browsing behavior to avoid detection.

✅ Conclusion & Next Steps

Key Takeaways:

✓ The Tor API allows secure, anonymous crawling of onion sites.

✓ Automating IP address rotation prevents blocking.

✓ Data extraction from forums & marketplaces reveals valuable OSINT.

✓ Handling authentication & captchas improves access to restricted areas.

✓ Storing data in JSON or CSV ensures structured analysis.

9.4 Tracking Cryptocurrency Transactions in the Dark Web

Cryptocurrency plays a vital role in dark web transactions, enabling anonymous payments for illicit goods and services. Tracking these transactions is a crucial aspect of OSINT investigations, allowing analysts to follow the money and uncover criminal activities such as:

- Money laundering through tumblers/mixers
- Ransomware payments to threat actors
- Illicit purchases on dark web marketplaces

- Fraudulent financial activities using crypto

This chapter explores how to track Bitcoin and other cryptocurrencies using Python and blockchain analysis tools.

9.4.1 Understanding How Cryptocurrency Works on the Dark Web

Unlike traditional banking, cryptocurrency transactions are pseudo-anonymous—they don't reveal personal identities but are publicly recorded on the blockchain. Bitcoin (BTC) remains the most commonly used cryptocurrency on the dark web, though others like Monero (XMR), Ethereum (ETH), and Litecoin (LTC) are also popular.

◆ How Criminals Obfuscate Transactions

To avoid tracking, criminals use various techniques, including:

✅ **Bitcoin Tumblers & Mixers** – Services that mix BTC from multiple users to obscure the original source.
✅ **Privacy Coins (e.g., Monero)** – Coins designed for complete anonymity, unlike Bitcoin's transparent ledger.
✅ **Multiple Wallet Hops** – Moving funds through multiple addresses to make tracing difficult.
✅ **Exchanges & OTC Trades** – Converting crypto into fiat through underground exchanges.

Despite these obfuscation tactics, blockchain analysis tools can still provide key intelligence.

9.4.2 Setting Up Blockchain Analysis Tools in Python

We will use Python APIs to track cryptocurrency transactions. Here's how to set up:

◆ Install Required Libraries

pip install blockchain requests pandas

✅ This installs the Blockchain API and data processing tools.

👓 9.4.3 Tracking Bitcoin Transactions Using Blockchain APIs

We can track Bitcoin transactions using the Blockchain.com API.

◆ Fetching Transaction Details

```python
import requests

# Target Bitcoin address (example)
btc_address = "1A1zP1eP5QGefi2DMPTfTL5SLmv7DivfNa"

# Blockchain.com API endpoint
url = f"https://blockchain.info/rawaddr/{btc_address}"

# Fetch transaction data
response = requests.get(url)
data = response.json()

# Extract and display transaction details
for tx in data["txs"][:5]:  # Show first 5 transactions
    print(f"Transaction Hash: {tx['hash']}")
    print(f"Amount Received: {tx['result'] / 100000000} BTC")
    print(f"Date: {tx['time']}")
    print("-" * 50)
```

✓ This script extracts Bitcoin transaction details from public blockchains.

🔍 9.4.4 Identifying Suspicious Transactions

Investigators look for patterns in Bitcoin transactions that indicate illicit activity.

◆ Key Indicators of Criminal Transactions

🏛 **Large deposits into new wallets** → Potential laundering

🏛 **Frequent small transactions** → Mixing service usage

🏛 **Funds moving through known illicit addresses** → Possible darknet market activity

We can flag suspicious transactions by analyzing transaction flows.

◆ Checking if an Address is Blacklisted

```
# Example blacklist of known dark web wallets
blacklisted_addresses = ["3QJmV3qfvL9SuYo34YihAf3sRCW3qSinyC",
"1KAt6STtisWMMVo5XGdos9P7DBNNsFfjx7"]

def check_blacklist(btc_address):
    if btc_address in blacklisted_addresses:
        print(f"⚠ ALERT: {btc_address} is linked to dark web activities!")
    else:
        print(f"{btc_address} is not in the blacklist.")

# Check a specific address
check_blacklist("3QJmV3qfvL9SuYo34YihAf3sRCW3qSinyC")
```

✓ This alerts analysts if a Bitcoin address is associated with illicit transactions.

💰 9.4.5 Tracing Bitcoin Transactions on the Dark Web

To map money movements, we can visualize Bitcoin transactions using Graphviz.

◆ Install Graphviz for Visualization

```
pip install graphviz
```

◆ Generating a Bitcoin Transaction Flow Graph

```
from graphviz import Digraph

# Create a directed graph
dot = Digraph()

# Example transactions (Bitcoin addresses)
dot.edge("DarkWebVendor1", "Buyer1", label="0.5 BTC")
dot.edge("DarkWebVendor1", "Buyer2", label="1.2 BTC")
dot.edge("Buyer2", "Mixer", label="1.2 BTC")
dot.edge("Mixer", "NewWallet1", label="1.0 BTC")
dot.edge("Mixer", "NewWallet2", label="0.2 BTC")
```

```
# Render graph
dot.render("bitcoin_flow", format="png", view=True)
```

✓ This generates a flowchart of Bitcoin transactions, revealing money laundering paths.

☐ 9.4.6 Tracking Monero (XMR) Transactions

Monero (XMR) is designed for untraceable transactions, making it a favorite for dark web criminals. However, forensic techniques like statistical analysis and timing correlations can sometimes reveal hidden connections.

While Bitcoin transactions are fully transparent, Monero uses:

✅ **Ring signatures** – Mixing multiple transactions together
✅ **Stealth addresses** – Generating one-time use addresses
✅ **Confidential transactions** – Hiding transaction amounts

Tracking Monero requires specialized tools like Chainalysis and CipherTrace, though open-source alternatives are limited.

📠 9.4.7 Case Study: Investigating a Dark Web Ransomware Payment

Let's examine a real-world OSINT case study involving Bitcoin ransom payments.

◆ The Scenario:

- A ransomware gang demands 5 BTC from a victim.
- The victim makes a payment to a Bitcoin address provided by the attackers.
- The OSINT analyst must track where the funds go.

◆ Investigating the Ransomware Payment

```
ransom_address = "34xp4vRoCGJym3xR7yCVPFHoCNxv4Twseo"

# Fetch transaction details
url = f"https://blockchain.info/rawaddr/{ransom_address}"
response = requests.get(url)
data = response.json()
```

```
# Print transaction flow
for tx in data["txs"][:5]:
    print(f"Transaction Hash: {tx['hash']}")
    print(f"Amount Sent: {tx['result'] / 100000000} BTC")
    print(f"Timestamp: {tx['time']}")
    print("-" * 50)
```

✓ This maps ransom payments, helping analysts track attacker-controlled wallets.

✅ Conclusion & Next Steps

🚀 Key Takeaways:

✓ Cryptocurrencies power dark web transactions, making them a crucial OSINT target.

✓ Bitcoin transactions are publicly traceable, while Monero is more private.

✓ Using Python, we can fetch blockchain transaction data and identify suspicious financial activity.

✓ Mapping cryptocurrency flows helps track money laundering and illicit payments.

9.5 Monitoring Marketplaces & Leaked Database Dumps

Dark web marketplaces serve as hubs for buying and selling stolen credentials, financial data, hacking tools, counterfeit documents, and illicit goods. Additionally, data breaches often result in leaked database dumps containing sensitive user information, which are sold or freely distributed on forums and marketplaces.

For OSINT analysts, monitoring these marketplaces and leaked databases is crucial for:

✅ Identifying compromised personal or corporate data

✅ Tracking cybercriminal activity and emerging threats

✅ Preventing fraud, identity theft, and financial crime

✅ Supporting law enforcement and cybersecurity operations

In this chapter, we will explore how to automate dark web marketplace monitoring and extract intelligence from leaked database dumps using Python and OSINT tools.

☐ 9.5.1 Understanding Dark Web Marketplaces & Data Leaks

◆ How Dark Web Marketplaces Work

Dark web marketplaces operate like black-market versions of eBay or Amazon, often featuring:

- User profiles & feedback ratings for sellers
- Bitcoin, Monero, or privacy coin payments
- Hidden URLs (.onion sites) requiring Tor access
- Escrow services to facilitate anonymous transactions

Examples of illicit goods & services sold:

🏧 Stolen credentials (email, social media, banking accounts)
🏧 Credit card dumps & skimming data
🏧 Malware, exploits, & hacking tools
🏧 Fake IDs & counterfeit documents

◆ The Risk of Leaked Database Dumps

Leaked database dumps often include:

- **Emails & passwords** (plaintext or hashed)
- Financial data, social security numbers
- Internal company databases
- **PII** (Personally Identifiable Information)

These leaks pose serious security risks and require constant monitoring.

☐ 9.5.2 Setting Up a Dark Web Monitoring Environment

To monitor dark web marketplaces and leaked database dumps, we will:

- Use the Tor network to access .onion sites
- Scrape marketplace listings for relevant data
- Search for leaked credentials in public breach dumps

- Automate alerts for new data leaks

◆ Install Required Libraries

pip install requests[socks] beautifulsoup4 pandas
sudo apt install tor

◆ Configure Tor for Python Access

Edit the torrc file:

sudo nano /etc/tor/torrc

Add:

ControlPort 9051
CookieAuthentication 1

Then restart Tor:

sudo systemctl restart tor

✅ Now, Python can connect to the Tor network.

9.5.3 Extracting Intelligence from Dark Web Marketplaces

◆ Connecting to a Dark Web Marketplace

```
import requests

# Define Tor proxy settings
proxies = {
    "http": "socks5h://127.0.0.1:9050",
    "https": "socks5h://127.0.0.1:9050",
}

# Example onion marketplace URL
url = "http://examplemarket.onion"
```

```
# Fetch the page
response = requests.get(url, proxies=proxies)
print(response.text)
```

✓ This retrieves marketplace HTML content.

◆ Scraping Marketplace Listings for Stolen Data

```
from bs4 import BeautifulSoup

# Parse HTML
soup = BeautifulSoup(response.text, "html.parser")

# Extract product listings
for listing in soup.find_all("div", class_="product-listing"):
    title = listing.find("h2").text
    price = listing.find("span", class_="price").text
    seller = listing.find("span", class_="seller").text

    print(f"Product: {title}, Price: {price}, Seller: {seller}")
```

✓ This extracts listings for stolen credentials, credit card data, and hacking tools.

◆ Monitoring Specific Keywords on Marketplaces

We can track specific keywords (e.g., "stolen PayPal accounts").

```
keywords = ["PayPal", "credit card dump", "SSN database"]

# Search marketplace listings
for listing in soup.find_all("div", class_="product-listing"):
    title = listing.find("h2").text.lower()
    for keyword in keywords:
        if keyword.lower() in title:
            print(f"⚠ ALERT: Found {keyword} - {title}")
```

✓ This flags high-risk stolen data in marketplace listings.

🔍 9.5.4 Extracting Leaked Credentials from Database Dumps

◆ Searching Public Data Leak Repositories

Many breached databases appear on dark web forums, Telegram channels, and GitHub. OSINT analysts often search sites like:

- Have I Been Pwned API (https://haveibeenpwned.com)
- Dehashed API (https://www.dehashed.com)
- Leaked source sites & Telegram dump channels

◆ Checking if an Email is in a Data Breach

```python
import requests

# Target email
email = "target@example.com"

# Have I Been Pwned API
api_url = f"https://haveibeenpwned.com/api/v3/breachedaccount/{email}"

headers = {"hibp-api-key": "YOUR_API_KEY"}  # Requires API key
response = requests.get(api_url, headers=headers)

if response.status_code == 200:
    print(f"⚠ ALERT: {email} is in a data breach!")
    print(response.json())  # Display breach details
else:
    print("✅ Email not found in any breaches.")
```

✔ This checks if an email is in known data breaches.

🖥 9.5.5 Automating Alerts for New Leaked Databases

Instead of manually checking for leaked databases, we can automate alerts.

◆ Email Alert System for New Leaks

```
import smtplib
from email.mime.text import MIMEText

def send_alert(leak_info):
    sender_email = "your_alerts@gmail.com"
    receiver_email = "your_email@example.com"
    msg = MIMEText(f"New Data Leak Found: {leak_info}")
    msg["Subject"] = "⚠ Dark Web Data Leak Alert!"
    msg["From"] = sender_email
    msg["To"] = receiver_email

    with smtplib.SMTP("smtp.gmail.com", 587) as server:
        server.starttls()
        server.login("your_alerts@gmail.com", "yourpassword")
        server.sendmail(sender_email, receiver_email, msg.as_string())

# Example use case
send_alert("Leaked 10,000 credit card numbers on ExampleMarket.onion")
```

✓ This sends alerts when new leaks are detected.

🏧 9.5.6 Storing & Analyzing Dark Web Data

Collected data should be structured for analysis.

◆ Save Marketplace Listings to a CSV File

```
import pandas as pd

data = [{"Title": "Stolen PayPal Account", "Price": "$200", "Seller": "DarkSeller123"},
    {"Title": "SSN Database Dump", "Price": "$500", "Seller": "DataLeaker"}]

df = pd.DataFrame(data)
df.to_csv("darkweb_listings.csv", index=False)

print("Marketplace data saved!")
```

✓ This creates a structured database of dark web listings.

✅ Conclusion & Next Steps

🚀 Key Takeaways:

✓ Dark web marketplaces are hubs for stolen credentials, financial data, and illicit services.

✓ Leaked database dumps pose serious cybersecurity threats.

✓ Python can scrape dark web marketplaces, extract stolen data, and monitor new leaks.

✓ Automating alerts ensures rapid threat detection.

9.6 Case Study: Automating Dark Web Intelligence Collection

The dark web is a hidden part of the internet where cybercriminals trade stolen data, illicit goods, hacking tools, and leaked databases. Manually monitoring dark web sites is time-consuming, risky, and inefficient, making automation a crucial element of OSINT operations.

This case study demonstrates how a cybersecurity team used Python automation to:

✅ Monitor dark web marketplaces for stolen credentials

✅ Track leaked database dumps for sensitive information

✅ Extract and analyze intelligence from .onion sites

✅ Generate automated alerts when new threats emerge

By leveraging Python, Tor, web scraping, and API integrations, this approach significantly improved intelligence collection efficiency and enhanced threat response capabilities.

🗂️ 9.6.1 Background: The Challenge of Dark Web Monitoring

A financial organization detected multiple fraud cases related to compromised customer accounts. Investigations suggested that customer credentials were being sold on dark web marketplaces and forums.

The company's Threat Intelligence Team faced several challenges:

● **Manual monitoring was slow & inefficient** – Analysts had to manually visit dark web forums and marketplaces to check for stolen data.

● **Data was constantly changing** – New leaks appeared daily, making real-time monitoring essential.

● **Accessing dark web sites required anonymity** – Traditional web crawling tools could not access .onion sites securely.

● **Large data volumes made analysis difficult** – Extracting useful intelligence from vast amounts of dark web content was complex.

To solve these issues, the team built an automated intelligence collection system using Python.

9.6.2 Designing the OSINT Automation System

The automation framework consisted of four key components:

1 **Dark Web Access & Scraping** → Python + Tor to extract marketplace listings

2 **Leaked Database Analysis** → API integrations for breach detection

3 **Threat Intelligence Storage** → SQL database to structure stolen data findings

4 **Automated Alert System** → Email & Slack notifications for security teams

9.6.3 Step 1: Setting Up Secure Dark Web Access

Since dark web sites require Tor for access, the first step was configuring Python to route traffic through Tor.

◆ Install Required Tools

pip install requests[socks] beautifulsoup4 pandas
sudo apt install tor

◆ Configure Tor for Python Access

Edit the Tor configuration file:

sudo nano /etc/tor/torrc

Add:

ControlPort 9051
CookieAuthentication 1

Then restart Tor:

sudo systemctl restart tor

Now, Python scripts can anonymously browse .onion sites.

□□ 9.6.4 Step 2: Scraping Dark Web Marketplaces for Stolen Data

To monitor stolen credit cards, passwords, and personal data, the team scraped dark web marketplace listings.

◆ Connecting to a Dark Web Site

```
import requests

# Define Tor proxy settings
proxies = {
    "http": "socks5h://127.0.0.1:9050",
    "https": "socks5h://127.0.0.1:9050",
}

# Example dark web marketplace URL
url = "http://examplemarket.onion"

# Fetch the page
response = requests.get(url, proxies=proxies)
print(response.text)  # Display HTML content
```

◆ Extracting Marketplace Listings

Once connected, the team extracted stolen data listings.

```
from bs4 import BeautifulSoup
```

```
# Parse HTML
soup = BeautifulSoup(response.text, "html.parser")

# Extract product listings
for listing in soup.find_all("div", class_="product-listing"):
    title = listing.find("h2").text
    price = listing.find("span", class_="price").text
    seller = listing.find("span", class_="seller").text

    print(f"Product: {title}, Price: {price}, Seller: {seller}")
```

✓ This script automatically collects new listings for stolen credentials.

◆ Monitoring Specific Keywords (e.g., "bank accounts", "SSN")

The team configured the bot to track high-risk keywords in stolen data listings.

```
keywords = ["bank account", "credit card", "social security number"]

for listing in soup.find_all("div", class_="product-listing"):
    title = listing.find("h2").text.lower()
    for keyword in keywords:
        if keyword.lower() in title:
            print(f"⚠ ALERT: Found {keyword} - {title}")
```

✓ If a stolen customer record was found, the security team was alerted.

📁 9.6.5 Step 3: Tracking Leaked Database Dumps

To detect if customer credentials were compromised, the system checked leaked database dumps via OSINT APIs.

◆ Searching Public Data Breach Repositories

The team used Have I Been Pwned API to verify compromised emails.

```
import requests
```

```
email = "customer@example.com"
api_url = f"https://haveibeenpwned.com/api/v3/breachedaccount/{email}"

headers = {"hibp-api-key": "YOUR_API_KEY"}  # Requires API key
response = requests.get(api_url, headers=headers)

if response.status_code == 200:
    print(f"⚠ ALERT: {email} is in a data breach!")
    print(response.json())  # Display breach details
else:
    print("✅ No breach found.")
```

✓ This allowed real-time detection of leaked credentials.

🏧 9.6.6 Step 4: Storing Intelligence Data for Analysis

All scraped listings and leaked credentials were stored in a SQL database for further analysis.

◆ Save Marketplace Data to a CSV File

```
import pandas as pd

data = [{"Title": "Stolen PayPal Account", "Price": "$200", "Seller": "DarkSeller123"},
    {"Title": "SSN Database Dump", "Price": "$500", "Seller": "DataLeaker"}]

df = pd.DataFrame(data)
df.to_csv("darkweb_listings.csv", index=False)

print("Marketplace data saved!")
```

✓ This allowed the security team to analyze dark web trends over time.

🔒 9.6.7 Step 5: Automating Alerts for New Threats

To immediately respond to new dark web threats, an email alert system was integrated.

◆ Send an Alert When Stolen Data is Detected

```python
import smtplib
from email.mime.text import MIMEText

def send_alert(leak_info):
    sender_email = "your_alerts@gmail.com"
    receiver_email = "security_team@example.com"
    msg = MIMEText(f"New Dark Web Leak Found: {leak_info}")
    msg["Subject"] = "⚠ Dark Web Intelligence Alert!"
    msg["From"] = sender_email
    msg["To"] = receiver_email

    with smtplib.SMTP("smtp.gmail.com", 587) as server:
        server.starttls()
        server.login("your_alerts@gmail.com", "yourpassword")
        server.sendmail(sender_email, receiver_email, msg.as_string())

# Example use case
send_alert("Leaked 10,000 credit card numbers on ExampleMarket.onion")
```

✓ This automated alerts whenever new stolen data appeared.

✅ Conclusion: How Automation Improved OSINT Workflows

By implementing this automated OSINT system, the team:

✓ Reduced manual dark web monitoring time by 80%

✓ Identified leaked customer credentials before fraud occurred

✓ Tracked new stolen data in real-time

✓ Automated alerts for immediate threat response

10. Using Machine Learning for OSINT Insights

In this chapter, we explore the integration of machine learning (ML) techniques into OSINT workflows to unlock deeper insights from large datasets. You'll learn how to apply ML algorithms to categorize, analyze, and identify patterns in data collected from open sources, including social media, websites, and the dark web. We'll cover key concepts such as natural language processing (NLP) for text analysis, clustering for identifying trends, and sentiment analysis for gauging public opinion. Using Python and libraries like Scikit-learn and TensorFlow, you'll learn how to build models that can automate the identification of threats, track emerging topics, and generate actionable intelligence. By the end of this chapter, you will be equipped to leverage machine learning in your OSINT processes, enhancing your ability to detect complex patterns and provide more sophisticated intelligence insights.

10.1 How Machine Learning Enhances OSINT Investigations

The sheer volume of open-source intelligence (OSINT) data collected from websites, social media, dark web forums, leaked databases, and threat reports is overwhelming. Manual analysis is time-consuming and often fails to detect hidden patterns in large datasets. Machine Learning (ML) revolutionizes OSINT investigations by automating data processing, anomaly detection, predictive analysis, and pattern recognition.

This chapter explores how ML enhances OSINT by:

✅ Automating data classification (fake news detection, sentiment analysis, entity recognition)

✅ Identifying hidden connections between entities (people, organizations, domains, and financial transactions)

✅ Detecting cyber threats and fraud patterns

✅ Predicting future trends in intelligence data

By integrating Python-based ML libraries such as Scikit-Learn, TensorFlow, and NLP models, OSINT analysts can improve intelligence accuracy and response time.

📌 10.1.1 Why Use Machine Learning for OSINT?

1️⃣ Processing Large-Scale Data Efficiently

OSINT involves big data from multiple sources (social media, news, forums, databases). ML automates data processing, allowing analysts to focus on high-priority threats.

2️⃣ Detecting Anomalies & Threats

ML models can detect suspicious activities, such as fake accounts, phishing domains, and cyberattack patterns, by recognizing behavioral deviations.

3️⃣ Uncovering Hidden Connections

Graph-based ML models analyze relationships between entities (e.g., cybercriminal networks, money laundering activities) using data from social media, blockchain transactions, and domain registries.

4️⃣ Predictive Intelligence & Risk Assessment

ML enables predictive analysis, helping security teams anticipate future cyber threats, misinformation campaigns, and geopolitical risks.

10.1.2 Key Machine Learning Techniques in OSINT

1️⃣ Natural Language Processing (NLP) for Text Analysis

◆ **Use case**: Detecting fake news, propaganda, sentiment trends, and extremist content from social media and news sources.

✓ Example ML models used:

- BERT/GPT → Contextual text understanding
- TF-IDF + Logistic Regression → Fake news classification
- Sentiment Analysis with Vader/Transformers

◆ **Example**: Identifying Fake News using Python

```
from sklearn.feature_extraction.text import TfidfVectorizer
from sklearn.linear_model import LogisticRegression

# Sample dataset
documents = ["Breaking: Government collapse! Click here", "Official news: Economic
growth reported"]
labels = [1, 0]  # 1 = Fake, 0 = Real

# Convert text to numerical features
vectorizer = TfidfVectorizer()
X = vectorizer.fit_transform(documents)

# Train a simple model
model = LogisticRegression()
model.fit(X, labels)

# Test on new data
new_text = ["Urgent: Click to win money now!"]
new_X = vectorizer.transform(new_text)
prediction = model.predict(new_X)

print("Fake News Detected" if prediction[0] == 1 else "Legitimate News")
```

✓ **Impact**: Automated content verification to filter out disinformation.

2️⃣ Image Recognition & Metadata Analysis

◆ **Use case**: Identifying deepfake images, tracking geolocation from images, and reverse image search.

✓ Example ML models used:

- **YOLO, OpenCV, TensorFlow** → Object recognition in images
- **EXIF & Geolocation Analysis** → Extracting metadata

Deepfake Detection Models

◆ **Example**: Identifying Objects in OSINT Images

```
import cv2

# Load pre-trained YOLO model
net = cv2.dnn.readNet("yolov3.weights", "yolov3.cfg")

# Process an image
image = cv2.imread("suspicious_vehicle.jpg")
height, width, _ = image.shape

# Detect objects
blob = cv2.dnn.blobFromImage(image, 0.00392, (416, 416), swapRB=True, crop=False)
net.setInput(blob)
output_layers = net.getUnconnectedOutLayersNames()
detections = net.forward(output_layers)

# Print detected objects
for detection in detections:
    print("Detected object:", detection)
```

✓ **Impact**: Detects objects in images for law enforcement and cyber threat intelligence.

3️⃣ Network & Social Graph Analysis

◆ **Use case**: Identifying fake accounts, bot networks, and influence operations.

✓ **Example ML models used:**

- **Graph Neural Networks (GNNs)** → Analyzing relationships

- **PageRank Algorithm** → Identifying influential nodes

- **Community Detection (Louvain Algorithm)** → Clustering similar entities

◆ **Example**: Detecting Fake Social Media Accounts

```
import networkx as nx
```

```
# Create a graph of social media accounts
G = nx.Graph()
G.add_edges_from([
    ("UserA", "UserB"), ("UserA", "UserC"), ("UserD", "UserE"),
    ("Bot1", "Bot2"), ("Bot2", "Bot3"), ("Bot3", "Bot1")])

# Detect suspicious clusters (botnets)
communities = nx.community.louvain_communities(G)

print("Detected Social Media Communities:", communities)
```

✓ **Impact**: Detects bot networks & fake accounts used for misinformation.

4️ Cyber Threat Intelligence (CTI) & Anomaly Detection

◆ **Use case**: Identifying phishing domains, ransomware activity, and cyber attack patterns.

✓ **Example ML models used:**

- **Random Forest / XGBoost** → Predicting phishing domains
- **Time-Series Anomaly Detection** → Detecting suspicious web traffic
- **Unsupervised Learning (Isolation Forests, DBSCAN)** → Detecting outliers in cybersecurity logs

◆ **Example**: Detecting Phishing Domains with Machine Learning

```
from sklearn.ensemble import RandomForestClassifier
import pandas as pd

# Sample phishing dataset (Domain, Features, Label)
data = pd.DataFrame({
    "Domain": ["paypal-secure-login.com", "microsoft-support.xyz", "google.com"],
    "Length": [24, 20, 10],  # Domain length
    "Contains_Dash": [1, 1, 0],  # Presence of hyphen
    "Is_Phishing": [1, 1, 0]  # 1 = Phishing, 0 = Safe
```

```
})

# Train a phishing detection model
X = data[["Length", "Contains_Dash"]]
y = data["Is_Phishing"]
model = RandomForestClassifier()
model.fit(X, y)

# Test on new domains
new_data = pd.DataFrame({"Length": [15], "Contains_Dash": [0]})
prediction = model.predict(new_data)

print("⚠ Phishing Detected!" if prediction[0] == 1 else "✅ Safe Domain")
```

✓ **Impact**: Automates phishing domain detection to prevent cyberattacks.

🚀 Conclusion: The Future of OSINT with AI & Machine Learning

◆ Machine Learning transforms OSINT investigations by automating:

✓ Fake news detection & misinformation tracking

✓ Social media monitoring & bot detection

✓ Threat intelligence from cyberattack patterns

✓ Image recognition & geolocation tracking

◆ Challenges & Ethical Considerations

✓ **Bias in AI models** → False positives in misinformation tracking

✓ **Privacy concerns** → OSINT investigations should respect ethical boundaries

✓ **Legal restrictions** → Some ML-based OSINT techniques may violate terms of service

◆ The Future of OSINT with AI

✓ **Deepfake detection** → AI tools to analyze synthetic media

✓ **AI-powered cyber defense** → Real-time anomaly detection in threat intelligence

✓ **Automation at scale** → Cloud-based OSINT AI tools for law enforcement & cybersecurity

By combining Python, Machine Learning, and OSINT methodologies, analysts can automate intelligence gathering, improve threat detection, and stay ahead of adversaries in the digital battlefield. 🚀

10.2 Data Classification & Clustering for OSINT Analysis

Open-source intelligence (OSINT) investigations often deal with vast amounts of unstructured data from social media, news articles, dark web forums, domain registrations, and leaked databases. Manually sorting through this data is inefficient. This is where Machine Learning (ML) techniques like classification and clustering become powerful tools for OSINT analysts.

- Classification helps label and categorize data into predefined groups (e.g., identifying phishing emails, fake news, or extremist content).
- Clustering uncovers hidden patterns, relationships, and anomalies in large datasets (e.g., detecting coordinated misinformation campaigns or cybercriminal networks).

By leveraging Python and ML libraries like Scikit-Learn, TensorFlow, and NLP models, analysts can automate threat detection, group similar intelligence, and generate actionable insights efficiently.

📌 **10.2.1 Classification vs. Clustering in OSINT**

Feature	Classification	Clustering
Definition	Assigns labels to data	Groups similar data points
Use Cases	Fake news detection, spam filtering, sentiment analysis	Identifying bot networks, threat actor grouping, anomaly detection
Examples	"Is this domain malicious?" (Yes/No)	"Which domains are related to the same attacker?"
Algorithms	Logistic Regression, Random Forest, Neural Networks	K-Means, DBSCAN, Hierarchical Clustering

☐ 10.2.2 Classification Techniques in OSINT

1☐ Fake News Detection with NLP

Fake news spreads rapidly across social media, impacting OSINT investigations related to disinformation campaigns, cyber warfare, and political influence operations.

✓ **Solution**: Use Natural Language Processing (NLP) to classify news articles as real or fake based on text patterns.

◆ Python Implementation: Detecting Fake News

```
from sklearn.feature_extraction.text import TfidfVectorizer
from sklearn.naive_bayes import MultinomialNB

# Sample dataset (text, label: 1 = Fake, 0 = Real)
news_articles = ["Government collapse imminent!", "Stock market sees steady growth."]
labels = [1, 0]

# Convert text into numerical vectors
vectorizer = TfidfVectorizer()
X = vectorizer.fit_transform(news_articles)

# Train a Naive Bayes classifier
model = MultinomialNB()
model.fit(X, labels)
```

```python
# Test new article
new_text = ["Breaking: Economic crisis deepens!"]
new_X = vectorizer.transform(new_text)
prediction = model.predict(new_X)

print("📰 Fake News Detected!" if prediction[0] == 1 else "✅ Legitimate News")
```

✓ **Impact**: Helps intelligence analysts automatically filter misinformation.

2️⃣ Identifying Phishing Domains & Malicious URLs

Cybercriminals use phishing domains to steal credentials, spread malware, and conduct cyberattacks.

✓ **Solution**: Train a classifier to detect phishing domains based on domain length, presence of special characters, and WHOIS data.

◆ Python Implementation: Detecting Phishing Domains

```python
from sklearn.ensemble import RandomForestClassifier
import pandas as pd

# Sample phishing dataset (Domain, Features, Label)
data = pd.DataFrame({
    "Domain": ["paypal-secure-login.com", "microsoft-support.xyz", "google.com"],
    "Length": [24, 20, 10],  # Domain length
    "Contains_Dash": [1, 1, 0],  # Presence of hyphen
    "Is_Phishing": [1, 1, 0]  # 1 = Phishing, 0 = Safe
})

# Train a phishing detection model
X = data[["Length", "Contains_Dash"]]
y = data["Is_Phishing"]
model = RandomForestClassifier()
model.fit(X, y)

# Test on new domains
new_data = pd.DataFrame({"Length": [15], "Contains_Dash": [0]})
prediction = model.predict(new_data)
```

print("⚠ Phishing Domain Detected!" if prediction[0] == 1 else "✓ Safe Domain")

✓ **Impact**: Automates phishing detection for cybersecurity threat intelligence.

🔍 10.2.3 Clustering Techniques in OSINT

1️⃣ Identifying Bot Networks on Social Media

OSINT analysts track coordinated bot campaigns spreading misinformation or manipulating public opinion.

✓ **Solution**: Clustering techniques (DBSCAN, K-Means, Graph Analysis) group similar bot-like behaviors based on tweet frequency, network structure, and content patterns.

◆ **Python Implementation: Detecting Social Media Bots with Clustering**

```
import networkx as nx
from networkx.algorithms import community

# Create a social network graph
G = nx.Graph()
G.add_edges_from([
    ("UserA", "UserB"), ("UserA", "UserC"), ("UserD", "UserE"),
    ("Bot1", "Bot2"), ("Bot2", "Bot3"), ("Bot3", "Bot1")])

# Detect suspicious clusters (botnets)
bot_communities = community.louvain_communities(G)

print("🖥 Detected Social Media Bot Communities:", bot_communities)
```

✓ **Impact**: Helps track bot-driven influence operations.

2️⃣ Clustering Dark Web Marketplaces & Cybercrime Forums

Threat actors operate dark web marketplaces to sell stolen credentials, hacking tools, and illicit services.

✓ Solution: Cluster threat actors based on forum activity, cryptocurrency transactions, and selling patterns.

◆ Python Implementation: Clustering Dark Web Data

```
from sklearn.cluster import KMeans
import numpy as np

# Sample dark web vendor activity data (Transactions, Avg Sale Value)
data = np.array([[50, 300], [200, 1500], [10, 50], [400, 5000]])

# Apply K-Means clustering
kmeans = KMeans(n_clusters=2)
clusters = kmeans.fit_predict(data)

print("🔎 Clustered Threat Actors:", clusters)
```

✓ Impact: Helps track cybercriminal networks and fraud patterns.

3⃣ Detecting Anomalous Financial Transactions

Financial intelligence analysts monitor money laundering, fraud, and terrorist financing using OSINT.

✓ Solution: Unsupervised anomaly detection models (Isolation Forests, DBSCAN) detect suspicious financial transactions.

◆ Python Implementation: Identifying Suspicious Transactions

```
from sklearn.ensemble import IsolationForest
import pandas as pd

# Sample transaction dataset (Amount, Frequency)
data = pd.DataFrame({"Amount": [500, 1500, 50, 10000], "Frequency": [10, 2, 50, 1]})

# Train Isolation Forest model
model = IsolationForest(contamination=0.2)
```

model.fit(data)

 # Detect anomalies
anomalies = model.predict(data)

print("🖥 Anomalous Transactions Detected:", anomalies)

✔ **Impact**: Helps identify suspicious financial patterns in OSINT.

🚀 **Conclusion: The Power of ML-Based Classification & Clustering in OSINT**

◆ **Classification Techniques Enable:**

✔ **Fake news detection** → Prevents misinformation spread

✔ **Phishing detection** → Automates cybersecurity intelligence

✔ **Threat classification** → Identifies cyber threats faster

◆ **Clustering Techniques Reveal:**

✔ **Bot networks & influence campaigns** → Detects disinformation operations

✔ **Dark web & fraud networks** → Tracks cybercriminal activity

✔ **Financial anomalies** → Exposes suspicious money transfers

◆ **The Future of OSINT ML Analysis:**

✔ Real-time classification & clustering using AI-powered threat monitoring systems

✔ Deep learning for advanced pattern recognition in cyber intelligence

✔ Automated OSINT dashboards integrating ML-driven insights

By integrating Machine Learning with OSINT, analysts accelerate intelligence gathering, detect emerging threats, and stay ahead of adversaries in the digital battlefield. 🚀

10.3 Sentiment Analysis for Social Media Intelligence

Social media platforms generate vast amounts of real-time data, making them valuable sources for open-source intelligence (OSINT). However, manually analyzing thousands of tweets, posts, and comments is impractical. This is where sentiment analysis—a natural language processing (NLP) technique—becomes a crucial tool for OSINT analysts.

Sentiment analysis helps intelligence teams determine public sentiment, track geopolitical risks, detect disinformation campaigns, and analyze online extremism. By using Python and NLP libraries (NLTK, VADER, TextBlob, and transformers), analysts can automate the classification of social media posts into positive, negative, or neutral sentiments.

📌 10.3.1 Understanding Sentiment Analysis in OSINT

Sentiment analysis, also known as opinion mining, evaluates the tone, mood, and attitude expressed in textual data. It helps analysts:

✅ Monitor public perception of political events, brands, or cyber threats

✅ Detect rising tensions or hate speech in social movements

✅ Identify potential misinformation or propaganda

✅ Gauge sentiment towards cyber incidents, vulnerabilities, and data leaks

Types of Sentiment Analysis in OSINT:

Sentiment Analysis Type	Use Case in OSINT
Polarity Analysis (Positive, Negative, Neutral)	Identifying public reaction to an event or incident
Emotion Detection (Anger, Fear, Joy, Sadness)	Tracking emotional reactions to crises or cyberattacks
Aspect-Based Sentiment Analysis (ABSA)	Analyzing opinions on specific topics like cybersecurity threats or political policies
Sarcasm Detection	Filtering out misleading or sarcastic comments in intelligence gathering

10.3.2 Implementing Sentiment Analysis with Python

1⃞ Basic Sentiment Analysis Using TextBlob

TextBlob is a simple NLP library that can analyze the sentiment of a given text.

◆ **Python Implementation: Classifying Social Media Sentiment**

```python
from textblob import TextBlob

# Sample tweets
tweets = [
    "The government is failing us! Total disaster! #corruption",
    "Amazing step towards a safer future! #progress",
    "Not sure how I feel about this new policy."
]

# Analyze sentiment
for tweet in tweets:
    sentiment = TextBlob(tweet).sentiment.polarity
    if sentiment > 0:
        print(f"✓ Positive: {tweet}")
    elif sentiment < 0:
        print(f"▨ Negative: {tweet}")
    else:
        print(f"☐ Neutral: {tweet}")
```

✓ **Impact**: Helps categorize large amounts of text into positive, negative, or neutral categories automatically.

2⃞ Real-Time Twitter Sentiment Analysis with VADER

VADER (Valence Aware Dictionary and sEntiment Reasoner) is optimized for analyzing short social media texts.

◆ **Python Implementation: Analyzing Sentiment of Tweets in Real-Time**

```
from vaderSentiment.vaderSentiment import SentimentIntensityAnalyzer

# Initialize VADER
analyzer = SentimentIntensityAnalyzer()

# Sample tweet analysis
tweet = "Breaking: Major cyberattack hits financial institutions. Panic everywhere!
#CyberThreat"
sentiment = analyzer.polarity_scores(tweet)

# Categorize sentiment
if sentiment['compound'] >= 0.05:
    print("✅ Positive Sentiment")
elif sentiment['compound'] <= -0.05:
    print("🚨 Negative Sentiment")
else:
    print("⬜ Neutral Sentiment")
```

✓ **Impact**: Helps OSINT teams track reactions to global events, cyberattacks, or political unrest in real time.

📊 10.3.3 Advanced Sentiment Analysis with Machine Learning

For more accurate sentiment analysis, OSINT analysts can use supervised machine learning models trained on large datasets.

1️⃣ Training a Sentiment Classifier with Scikit-Learn

◆ Python Implementation: Machine Learning-Based Sentiment Analysis

```
from sklearn.feature_extraction.text import TfidfVectorizer
from sklearn.naive_bayes import MultinomialNB
from sklearn.pipeline import make_pipeline

# Training data (sample)
X_train = ["The new policy is fantastic!", "This is the worst decision ever.", "I have no
opinion on this matter."]
y_train = [1, 0, 2]  # 1 = Positive, 0 = Negative, 2 = Neutral
```

```
# Create a model pipeline
model = make_pipeline(TfidfVectorizer(), MultinomialNB())
model.fit(X_train, y_train)

# Test new tweet
tweet = ["I strongly oppose this new legislation!"]
prediction = model.predict(tweet)

sentiments = {0: "🔹 Negative", 1: "✅ Positive", 2: "🔸 Neutral"}
print("Sentiment:", sentiments[prediction[0]])
```

✓ **Impact**: Provides a more scalable and accurate approach for sentiment classification.

☐ 10.3.4 OSINT Use Cases for Sentiment Analysis

1☐ Tracking Disinformation & Propaganda Campaigns

- Governments and cybersecurity agencies use sentiment analysis to detect coordinated misinformation campaigns.
- **Example**: Analyzing bot-driven narratives during elections.

2☐ Monitoring Cybersecurity Threat Sentiment

- OSINT analysts track hacker forums, security blogs, and social media to assess sentiment towards new vulnerabilities or breaches.
- **Example**: Spike in negative sentiment towards a company may indicate an ongoing cyberattack.

3☐ Detecting Political Unrest & Extremist Activity

- Intelligence agencies analyze sentiment trends to predict protests, civil unrest, or radicalization efforts.
- **Example**: Negative and fear-driven sentiment spikes in a region may indicate potential violent activity.

🚀 10.3.5 Future of Sentiment Analysis in OSINT

✓ Real-time AI-powered social media monitoring

✓ Deep learning for emotion recognition in OSINT

✓ Combining sentiment analysis with geospatial intelligence

Sentiment analysis is a game-changer for OSINT analysts, automating intelligence gathering, detecting threats early, and enhancing situational awareness. 🚀

10.4 Image Recognition & Deep Learning in OSINT

Images and videos are powerful sources of open-source intelligence (OSINT), often containing crucial details about individuals, locations, objects, and events. However, manually analyzing large volumes of visual data is impractical. This is where image recognition and deep learning come into play.

Using deep learning techniques like Convolutional Neural Networks (CNNs), Optical Character Recognition (OCR), and Object Detection models (YOLO, Faster R-CNN, OpenCV), OSINT analysts can:

✓ Detect objects (weapons, vehicles, flags) in images

✓ Recognize faces in surveillance footage

✓ Extract text (license plates, street signs) from images

✓ Track visual propaganda and deepfake content

By integrating Python with TensorFlow, OpenCV, and pre-trained AI models, OSINT investigations can automate image intelligence, enhancing situational awareness and threat detection.

📌 10.4.1 Understanding Image Recognition in OSINT

Image recognition uses deep learning algorithms to analyze visual data and identify objects, patterns, or text.

Image Recognition Type	Use Case in OSINT
Face Recognition	Identifying individuals in protests, criminal investigations
Object Detection	Detecting weapons, vehicles, or tactical gear in surveillance footage
OCR (Optical Character Recognition)	Extracting text from leaked documents, license plates, street signs
Reverse Image Search	Tracking misinformation, deepfakes, and source verification
Geospatial Analysis from Images	Identifying locations based on landmarks, terrain, or metadata

☐ 10.4.2 Implementing Image Recognition for OSINT

1☐ Object Detection Using YOLOv8

YOLO (You Only Look Once) is a powerful deep learning model for real-time object detection.

◆ Python Implementation: Detecting Objects in Images

```python
from ultralytics import YOLO
import cv2

# Load YOLOv8 model
model = YOLO("yolov8n.pt")

# Load image
image_path = "suspicious_vehicle.jpg"
image = cv2.imread(image_path)

# Perform object detection
results = model(image)

# Display results
results.show()
```

✔ **Impact**: Helps OSINT analysts identify weapons, license plates, or suspicious objects in surveillance images.

2️⃣ Face Recognition for Intelligence Gathering

Facial recognition is used in criminal investigations, protest tracking, and security analysis.

◆ Python Implementation: Recognizing Faces in Images

```
import face_recognition

# Load known image (database of suspects)
known_image = face_recognition.load_image_file("suspect.jpg")
known_encoding = face_recognition.face_encodings(known_image)[0]

# Load unknown image
unknown_image = face_recognition.load_image_file("event_photo.jpg")
unknown_encoding = face_recognition.face_encodings(unknown_image)[0]

# Compare faces
results = face_recognition.compare_faces([known_encoding], unknown_encoding)

print("🖼 Match Found!" if results[0] else "✖ No Match")
```

✔ **Impact**: Automates tracking of known individuals in public events, social media, and surveillance footage.

3️⃣ Extracting Text from Images Using OCR

OCR (Optical Character Recognition) is used to extract text from documents, signs, or screenshots for OSINT investigations.

◆ Python Implementation: Extracting Text from an Image

```
import pytesseract
from PIL import Image
```

```
# Load image
image = Image.open("leaked_document.png")

# Extract text
text = pytesseract.image_to_string(image)

print("Extracted Text:", text)
```

✓ **Impact**: Helps intelligence analysts extract useful information from leaked documents, IDs, or handwritten notes.

☐ 10.4.3 OSINT Use Cases for Deep Learning in Image Recognition

1☐ Geolocation Intelligence from Images

- OSINT analysts use image metadata (EXIF data) and satellite imagery to determine the location of an event.
- **Example**: Analyzing social media images to verify claims about a military strike.

2☐ Tracking Misinformation & Deepfake Images

- Deep learning models detect AI-generated deepfake content used for propaganda or fraud.
- **Example**: Identifying altered images spreading misinformation on social media.

3☐ Analyzing Weapons & Vehicles in Conflict Zones

- Object detection models identify military equipment, license plates, and convoy movements in war zones.
- **Example**: Tracking insurgent activity in Syria through satellite images.

🚀 10.4.4 Future of Image Recognition in OSINT

✓ AI-powered image verification to combat fake news

✓ Real-time surveillance integration for threat monitoring

✓ Automated recognition of cyber threat actors from dark web images

By leveraging deep learning and image recognition, OSINT analysts can enhance intelligence collection, improve threat detection, and automate large-scale image analysis. 🚀

10.5 Automating Threat Detection with AI Models

Threat detection is a critical component of open-source intelligence (OSINT), requiring analysts to sift through vast amounts of data across social media, forums, the dark web, and network traffic. Traditional manual methods are time-consuming and inefficient. This is where Artificial Intelligence (AI) models come into play.

By leveraging machine learning (ML), deep learning (DL), and natural language processing (NLP), OSINT analysts can automate threat detection, risk assessment, and anomaly identification. AI models can process text, images, videos, and network traffic, helping security teams identify cyber threats, terrorism indicators, and misinformation campaigns with greater speed and accuracy.

📌 10.5.1 How AI Enhances Threat Detection in OSINT

AI-powered threat detection helps OSINT analysts in various ways:

AI Model Type	Use Case in OSINT Threat Detection
Natural Language Processing (NLP)	Detecting hate speech, radicalization, and disinformation
Sentiment Analysis	Monitoring public reaction to cyber threats and geopolitical events
Anomaly Detection (ML Algorithms)	Identifying suspicious activity in social media or network traffic
Image Recognition (CNNs, YOLO)	Detecting weapons, military assets, and geolocation data in images
Dark Web Crawlers (AI + Scraping)	Automating searches for leaked credentials and cybercrime discussions

☐ 10.5.2 Implementing AI-Powered Threat Detection with Python

1☐ NLP-Based Threat Detection Using Transformers

AI models like BERT, GPT, and RoBERTa can analyze text data to detect cyber threats, terrorism-related discussions, and disinformation.

◆ Python Implementation: Identifying Suspicious Conversations

```
from transformers import pipeline

# Load AI-powered text classification model
nlp_model = pipeline("text-classification", model="bhadresh-savani/distilbert-threat-text-classifier")

# Sample social media post
post = "We are planning a cyberattack against financial institutions. Spread the word."

# Analyze text for threats
result = nlp_model(post)
print(result)
```

✓ **Impact**: Automates the detection of cyber threats, violent extremism, and illicit activities in OSINT investigations.

2️ Detecting Anomalies in Cyber Threat Data

Anomaly detection helps identify unusual patterns in network traffic, financial transactions, or dark web forums.

◆ Python Implementation: Detecting Anomalous Activity

```
import numpy as np
from sklearn.ensemble import IsolationForest

# Sample dataset of normal vs suspicious activity
X_train = np.array([[1.1], [1.3], [1.2], [1.4], [8.9]])  # The last value is an anomaly

# Train anomaly detection model
model = IsolationForest(contamination=0.2)
model.fit(X_train)

# Predict anomalies
```

```
X_test = np.array([[1.2], [9.0]])
predictions = model.predict(X_test)
```

```
print("🖥 Anomalous activity detected!" if -1 in predictions else "✓ No threats detected")
```

✓ **Impact**: Helps OSINT analysts detect unusual behaviors in cyber threat intelligence data.

3⃣ Using AI for Dark Web Threat Monitoring

AI-driven dark web crawlers help track criminal activities, leaked credentials, and threat actor discussions.

◆ **Python Implementation: Automating Dark Web Monitoring**

```python
from bs4 import BeautifulSoup
import requests

# Tor proxy setup for dark web access
proxies = {
    "http": "socks5h://127.0.0.1:9050",
    "https": "socks5h://127.0.0.1:9050"
}

# Example onion site
url = "http://exampleonionsite.onion"

# Scrape dark web content
response = requests.get(url, proxies=proxies)
soup = BeautifulSoup(response.text, "html.parser")

# Extract intelligence
print(soup.text)
```

✓ **Impact**: Automates tracking of stolen data, cybercrime marketplaces, and ransomware groups on the dark web.

☐ 10.5.3 Real-World OSINT Use Cases for AI in Threat Detection

1️ Cyber Threat Intelligence & Dark Web Monitoring

- AI models analyze hacker forums, paste sites, and ransomware groups to detect emerging threats.
- **Example**: Tracking mentions of zero-day vulnerabilities in underground markets.

2️ Counterterrorism & Extremist Content Monitoring

- NLP and image recognition detect terrorist propaganda, radicalization indicators, and encrypted communications.
- **Example**: AI scans social media for recruitment messages from extremist groups.

3️ Misinformation & Disinformation Campaign Detection

- AI models identify fake news, deepfake videos, and bot-driven propaganda.
- Example: Detecting coordinated fake accounts pushing a political narrative.

🚀 10.5.4 The Future of AI in OSINT Threat Detection

✔ Advanced AI-driven cyber threat intelligence platforms

✔ Deepfake detection to counter misinformation

✔ Automated AI-powered risk assessment dashboards

AI-powered threat detection revolutionizes OSINT, allowing intelligence teams to analyze massive data streams, detect threats faster, and enhance security operations. 🚀

10.6 Case Study: Applying AI to Detect Disinformation Campaigns

Disinformation campaigns have become a significant threat to national security, elections, corporate reputations, and public trust. State-sponsored actors, cybercriminals, and propaganda networks use social media, news websites, and forums to spread false narratives, manipulate public opinion, and destabilize societies.

AI-powered OSINT techniques can help identify, track, and counteract disinformation by detecting bot-driven propaganda, fake news articles, coordinated campaigns, and deepfake media. In this case study, we will explore how AI is used to detect and analyze a large-scale disinformation operation.

📌 **10.6.1 The Disinformation Campaign Scenario**

🖥️ **Situation Overview**

A suspected disinformation network has been pushing false narratives about a geopolitical crisis on Twitter, Facebook, and Telegram. The campaign:

✅ Uses fake social media accounts to amplify misinformation

✅ Spreads deepfake images to manipulate public perception

✅ Employs bots and automated accounts to boost engagement

✅ Targets specific political groups and communities

🎯 **Objective:**

The OSINT investigation aims to detect, analyze, and attribute the disinformation campaign using AI-driven tools for:

✔ Bot detection in social media networks

✔ Fake news identification using NLP models

✔ Deepfake image analysis

✔ Network mapping of accounts spreading false narratives

10.6.2 AI-Powered Disinformation Detection Techniques

1️⃣ Detecting Bot-Driven Disinformation on Social Media

Most disinformation campaigns rely on bots to artificially amplify content. These bots often:

- Post at unnatural time intervals
- Use automated scripts to engage with posts

- Share identical content across multiple accounts

◆ Python Implementation: Identifying Twitter Bots with AI

```
import tweepy
from sklearn.ensemble import RandomForestClassifier
import numpy as np

# Twitter API authentication (use your credentials)
api_key = "your_api_key"
api_secret = "your_api_secret"
access_token = "your_access_token"
access_secret = "your_access_secret"

auth = tweepy.OAuthHandler(api_key, api_secret)
auth.set_access_token(access_token, access_secret)
api = tweepy.API(auth)

# Fetch user activity data
user = api.get_user(screen_name="suspicious_account")
features = np.array([[user.followers_count, user.statuses_count, user.friends_count]])

# Load AI bot detection model
model = RandomForestClassifier()
model.fit(training_data, labels)

# Predict if the account is a bot
prediction = model.predict(features)
print("🤖 Bot detected!" if prediction == 1 else "✅ Human user")
```

✔ **Impact**: Helps identify coordinated bot networks amplifying disinformation.

2️⃣ Detecting Fake News with NLP-Based AI Models

AI-powered Natural Language Processing (NLP) models can analyze text to determine if it contains misinformation, conspiracy theories, or propaganda.

◆ Python Implementation: Classifying Fake News with AI

```
from transformers import pipeline

# Load pre-trained AI model for fake news detection
fake_news_detector = pipeline("text-classification", model="lvwerra/distilbert-fake-news")

# Analyze a suspicious article
article = "Government sources confirm that a secret invasion is happening tomorrow."
result = fake_news_detector(article)

print(result)
```

✓ **Impact**: Automates real-time detection of false information spreading online.

3⃣ Identifying Deepfake Images in Disinformation Campaigns

Disinformation campaigns often use AI-generated deepfake images to fabricate events or misrepresent individuals.

◆ **Python Implementation: Detecting Deepfake Images with AI**

```
import cv2
import tensorflow as tf

# Load AI deepfake detection model
deepfake_model = tf.keras.models.load_model("deepfake_detector.h5")

# Load suspect image
image = cv2.imread("suspicious_photo.jpg")
image = cv2.resize(image, (224, 224))
image = image / 255.0
image = image.reshape(1, 224, 224, 3)

# Predict deepfake probability
prediction = deepfake_model.predict(image)
print("🖼 Deepfake detected!" if prediction > 0.5 else "✅ Genuine image")
```

✓ **Impact**: Helps OSINT analysts detect fake visuals used in propaganda efforts.

☐ 10.6.3 Mapping the Disinformation Network

Once bots, fake news, and deepfake media sources are identified, analysts must trace connections between accounts, websites, and actors involved.

- Graph analytics and network mapping tools like Gephi, NetworkX, and Maltego help visualize relationships.
- AI can analyze interactions between accounts to identify central nodes in disinformation networks.

◆ Python Implementation: Network Mapping of a Disinformation Campaign

```
import networkx as nx

# Create graph
G = nx.Graph()

# Add nodes (accounts spreading disinformation)
G.add_nodes_from(["account_1", "account_2", "bot_3", "fake_news_site"])

# Add connections
G.add_edges_from([("account_1", "bot_3"), ("account_2", "fake_news_site")])

# Visualize network
nx.draw(G, with_labels=True)
```

✓ **Impact**: Helps map relationships between disinformation actors, aiding intelligence analysis.

▥ 10.6.4 Case Study Findings & Insights

After analyzing the disinformation campaign using AI-powered OSINT methods, the investigation revealed:

🚨 500+ bot accounts spreading false narratives
🖥 3 major fake news websites generating misleading content
☐☐ Deepfake images used to fabricate events
☐ Strong ties to a foreign influence campaign

By automating the detection, classification, and network analysis of disinformation, AI allows OSINT analysts to combat influence operations at scale.

🚀 10.6.5 Future of AI in Disinformation Detection

✔ AI-powered real-time misinformation tracking systems

✔ Automated deepfake detection to counter visual propaganda

✔ Intelligent bot detection and influence network mapping

As disinformation campaigns grow more sophisticated, AI-driven OSINT solutions will play a crucial role in safeguarding public discourse, democracy, and cybersecurity. 🚀

11. OSINT Data Visualization & Reporting

In this chapter, we focus on transforming raw OSINT data into clear, actionable insights through effective data visualization and reporting techniques. Using Python libraries such as Matplotlib, Seaborn, and Plotly, we'll guide you in creating compelling charts, graphs, and interactive visuals that make complex data easy to understand and communicate. You'll learn how to visualize trends, relationships, and anomalies within your data, enabling stakeholders to quickly grasp key findings. Additionally, we'll explore how to automate the generation of detailed reports, integrating visuals with narrative explanations, to create comprehensive intelligence briefings. By the end of this chapter, you will be equipped to produce professional, data-driven reports and visuals that enhance your OSINT analysis and support informed decision-making.

11.1 The Importance of Data Visualization in Intelligence

In OSINT (Open-Source Intelligence), analysts deal with massive amounts of structured and unstructured data from multiple sources, including social media, dark web forums, network logs, financial transactions, and geopolitical reports. However, raw data alone is not enough—extracting insights and patterns from this data requires effective visualization techniques.

Data visualization transforms complex intelligence into graphs, maps, dashboards, and charts, enabling analysts to:

✓ Identify trends and anomalies

✓ Detect threat patterns in real-time

✓ Communicate findings effectively to decision-makers

This chapter explores why data visualization is crucial for OSINT, key visualization techniques, and how to automate visual reporting to improve intelligence workflows.

📌 **11.1.1 Why Visualization Matters in OSINT?**

1️⃣ Identifying Hidden Patterns in Large Datasets

OSINT investigations involve analyzing thousands—or even millions—of data points. Without visualization, detecting trends, relationships, and outliers is nearly impossible.

Example:

- A raw dataset of cyber attack logs may not reveal much at first glance.
- A heatmap of attack origins can highlight hotspots of malicious activity.

◆ **Visualization Example: Cyber Attack Heatmap**

```
import pandas as pd
import matplotlib.pyplot as plt
import seaborn as sns

# Sample dataset
data = {'Country': ['USA', 'Russia', 'China', 'Iran', 'Germany'],
    'Attack_Count': [1500, 2300, 1800, 900, 700]}

df = pd.DataFrame(data)

# Create heatmap
plt.figure(figsize=(10,5))
sns.barplot(x=df['Country'], y=df['Attack_Count'], palette='Reds')
plt.title("Cyber Attacks by Country")
plt.show()
```

✓ **Impact**: Helps analysts visually spot high-risk regions quickly.

2️⃣ Making Complex Intelligence Easy to Understand

Data visualization helps convert technical intelligence into actionable insights that security teams, policymakers, and executives can understand.

Example:

- A timeline of coordinated disinformation campaigns can reveal patterns in propaganda distribution.
- A network graph of threat actors can expose connections between cybercriminals.

◆ Visualization Example: Threat Actor Network Graph

```
import networkx as nx
import matplotlib.pyplot as plt

# Create graph
G = nx.Graph()

# Add nodes (threat actors)
G.add_nodes_from(["Threat_Actor_A", "Threat_Actor_B", "Forum_1",
"Dark_Web_Site"])

# Add edges (relationships)
G.add_edges_from([("Threat_Actor_A", "Forum_1"), ("Threat_Actor_B",
"Dark_Web_Site")])

# Draw graph
plt.figure(figsize=(6,6))
nx.draw(G, with_labels=True, node_color='red', edge_color='black', font_size=10)
plt.show()
```

✓ **Impact**: Provides an intuitive way to track relationships between threat actors.

3️ Enabling Real-Time Threat Monitoring

Cyber threats, misinformation campaigns, and geopolitical risks evolve in real-time. Visualization dashboards help analysts monitor intelligence dynamically.

Example:

- A real-time dashboard tracking ransomware attacks globally.
- A social media sentiment analysis graph detecting disinformation campaigns.

◆ Visualization Example: Real-Time Sentiment Analysis

```
import matplotlib.pyplot as plt
import random

# Simulated sentiment scores over time
```

```
time = list(range(1, 11))
sentiment_scores = [random.uniform(-1, 1) for _ in range(10)]

# Create line plot
plt.plot(time, sentiment_scores, marker='o', linestyle='-', color='blue')
plt.axhline(y=0, color='black', linestyle='--', label="Neutral Sentiment")
plt.title("Social Media Sentiment Over Time")
plt.xlabel("Time (Hours)")
plt.ylabel("Sentiment Score (-1 to +1)")
plt.legend()
plt.show()
```

✓ **Impact**: Detects rising negative sentiment spikes, which may indicate misinformation or cyber threats.

☐ 11.1.2 Key Visualization Techniques in OSINT

📊 1. Charts & Graphs for Trend Analysis

- **Line Charts**: Track sentiment, hacking activity, or misinformation trends over time.
- **Bar Charts**: Compare cyber threats by region, platform, or attack type.

🔎 2. Geospatial Mapping for Threat Intelligence

- **Heatmaps**: Visualize cyber attacks, protests, or dark web leaks by location.
- **Geolocation Tracking**: Plot social media activity or leaked credentials on a map.

☐ 3. Network Graphs for Social Media & Threat Actor Analysis

- Visualizing relationships between hackers, fake news sources, and compromised accounts.
- Mapping dark web forums where stolen credentials are traded.

🚀 11.1.3 Automating OSINT Data Visualization

◆ Python Libraries for OSINT Visualization

Library	Best Used For
matplotlib	Simple plots, charts, and histograms
seaborn	Heatmaps, statistical visualizations
plotly	Interactive dashboards and real-time updates
networkx	Graph-based intelligence mapping
folium	Geospatial mapping and OSINT geolocation tracking

folium Geospatial mapping and OSINT geolocation tracking

◆ Python Example: Automating Intelligence Visualization

```
import pandas as pd
import seaborn as sns
import matplotlib.pyplot as plt

# Sample OSINT data (phishing domains)
data = {'Month': ['Jan', 'Feb', 'Mar', 'Apr', 'May'],
     'Phishing_Attacks': [300, 450, 520, 490, 600]}

df = pd.DataFrame(data)

# Create visualization
plt.figure(figsize=(8,5))
sns.lineplot(x=df['Month'], y=df['Phishing_Attacks'], marker="o", color="red")
plt.title("Phishing Attacks Over Time")
plt.show()
```

✓ **Impact**: Provides an automated way to track phishing trends and respond proactively.

⊙ Conclusion: Why OSINT Analysts Must Use Visualization

Data visualization is a game-changer in OSINT, allowing analysts to:

✔ Identify intelligence trends quickly

✔ Track cyber threats in real-time

✔ Communicate insights effectively to decision-makers

By automating OSINT data visualization, analysts can improve threat detection, intelligence reporting, and decision-making processes. 🚀

11.2 Using Matplotlib & Seaborn for Graphical OSINT Representation

OSINT investigations generate vast amounts of data from social media platforms, dark web forums, network traffic, financial transactions, and other intelligence sources. However, raw datasets are difficult to interpret without visualization.

Two powerful Python libraries, Matplotlib and Seaborn, allow OSINT analysts to create insightful graphs, charts, and heatmaps to:

✅ Identify trends in cyber threats, fraud, and disinformation campaigns

✅ Compare data points from multiple intelligence sources

✅ Detect anomalies in social media activity, domain registrations, or attack patterns

This chapter will explore how Matplotlib and Seaborn can be used to enhance OSINT analysis through bar charts, line graphs, scatter plots, heatmaps, and network visualizations.

📌 **11.2.1 Why Use Matplotlib & Seaborn in OSINT?**

1️ Matplotlib: The Foundation for OSINT Data Visualization

Matplotlib is a low-level visualization library that allows complete customization of charts and graphs.

✓ **Best for**: Basic plots, time series analysis, network graphs, and geospatial data

✓ **Strengths**: Highly customizable, works well with other OSINT libraries like Pandas & NumPy

2️⃣ Seaborn: High-Level Statistical Visualization for OSINT

Seaborn is built on top of Matplotlib and offers advanced statistical plots for OSINT analysis.

✓ **Best for**: Heatmaps, correlation matrices, and trend analysis

✓ **Strengths**: Built-in themes, easy-to-use functions, and better aesthetics

🏛 11.2.2 Creating OSINT Visualizations with Matplotlib

1️⃣ Line Chart: Tracking Cyber Threat Activity Over Time

A line chart is useful for monitoring hacking attempts, phishing attacks, or data breaches over a period.

◆ **Python Implementation: Cyber Attack Trends**

```
import matplotlib.pyplot as plt

# Sample OSINT data (cyber attack incidents per month)
months = ["Jan", "Feb", "Mar", "Apr", "May", "Jun"]
attacks = [120, 150, 180, 220, 280, 300]

plt.figure(figsize=(8,5))
plt.plot(months, attacks, marker='o', linestyle='-', color='red', label="Cyber Attacks")
plt.xlabel("Month")
plt.ylabel("Number of Attacks")
plt.title("Cyber Attack Trends Over Time")
plt.legend()
plt.grid(True)
plt.show()
```

✓ **Impact**: Shows rising attack trends, allowing analysts to predict future cyber threats.

2️⃣ Bar Chart: Comparing OSINT Threat Intelligence Sources

A bar chart can compare threat intelligence sources, social media platforms, or attack vectors.

◆ Python Implementation: Dark Web vs. Social Media Threat Sources

```
# Sample OSINT data (threat sources)
sources = ["Dark Web", "Social Media", "Forum Posts", "Leaked Databases"]
incidents = [500, 700, 400, 600]

plt.figure(figsize=(8,5))
plt.bar(sources, incidents, color=['black', 'blue', 'purple', 'red'])
plt.xlabel("Threat Source")
plt.ylabel("Reported Incidents")
plt.title("Comparison of OSINT Threat Intelligence Sources")
plt.show()
```

✓ **Impact**: Highlights which sources contribute most to intelligence operations.

3️⃣ Scatter Plot: Detecting Anomalies in Phishing Attacks

A scatter plot helps identify unusual spikes in phishing activity, domain registrations, or fraudulent transactions.

◆ Python Implementation: Phishing Attacks vs. Suspicious Domain Registrations

```
import numpy as np

# Generate random sample data for phishing incidents
phishing_attacks = np.random.randint(10, 200, 50)
suspicious_domains = np.random.randint(5, 180, 50)

plt.figure(figsize=(8,5))
plt.scatter(phishing_attacks, suspicious_domains, color='red', alpha=0.6)
plt.xlabel("Phishing Attacks")
plt.ylabel("Suspicious Domain Registrations")
plt.title("Phishing Attacks vs. Suspicious Domains")
```

```
plt.grid(True)
plt.show()
```

✓ **Impact**: Identifies correlations between cyber incidents and domain registration activity.

🏛 11.2.3 Advanced OSINT Visualizations with Seaborn

1️⃣ Heatmap: Identifying High-Risk Cybercrime Locations

A heatmap can highlight cybercrime hotspots based on attack frequency.

◆ Python Implementation: Heatmap of Cyber Attacks by Region

```
import seaborn as sns
import pandas as pd

# Sample dataset (cyber attack frequencies by country)
data = {"Country": ["USA", "Russia", "China", "Germany", "Brazil"],
        "Attacks": [1500, 2000, 1800, 800, 900]}

df = pd.DataFrame(data)

# Create heatmap
plt.figure(figsize=(8,5))
sns.heatmap(df.pivot_table(index="Country", values="Attacks"), cmap="Reds",
annot=True)
plt.title("Cyber Attack Frequency by Country")
plt.show()
```

✓ **Impact**: Pinpoints geographic regions with high cyber threat activity.

2️⃣ Pair Plot: Analyzing OSINT Data Relationships

Pair plots are useful for finding hidden correlations between intelligence factors.

◆ Python Implementation: Correlation Between Cybercrime Factors

```
# Sample dataset (simulating different OSINT factors)
data = pd.DataFrame({
    "Phishing_Attacks": np.random.randint(10, 200, 50),
    "Malware_Cases": np.random.randint(5, 180, 50),
    "Data_Breaches": np.random.randint(20, 220, 50)
})

sns.pairplot(data, diag_kind="kde")
plt.show()
```

✓ **Impact**: Helps detect connections between cyber incidents.

📊 11.2.4 Automating OSINT Dashboards with Matplotlib & Seaborn

By integrating Matplotlib and Seaborn into Flask, Streamlit, or Jupyter Notebooks, OSINT analysts can create interactive intelligence dashboards.

◆ Python Implementation: Automating OSINT Reports

```
import streamlit as st

st.title("OSINT Cyber Threat Dashboard")

# Generate random phishing data
data = pd.DataFrame({
    "Month": ["Jan", "Feb", "Mar", "Apr", "May"],
    "Phishing_Attacks": [300, 450, 520, 490, 600]
})

# Plot using Seaborn
st.line_chart(data.set_index("Month"))
```

✓ **Impact**: Allows intelligence teams to visualize cyber threat activity dynamically.

🚀 Conclusion: Enhancing OSINT with Data Visualization

Using Matplotlib and Seaborn, OSINT analysts can:

✓ Detect trends in cybercrime, fraud, and disinformation campaigns

✓ Monitor intelligence data in real-time

✓ Automate intelligence reporting for decision-makers

By integrating AI-powered analytics and OSINT dashboards, analysts can make data-driven intelligence decisions faster and more efficiently. 🚀

11.3 Creating Interactive Data Reports with Plotly & Tableau

Open-Source Intelligence (OSINT) investigations generate large datasets from various sources, including social media, dark web forums, cyber threat reports, and domain lookups. However, raw data is often complex, making it difficult for analysts to identify patterns, detect anomalies, and communicate findings effectively.

Interactive data visualization tools like Plotly and Tableau allow OSINT analysts to create dynamic reports, dashboards, and visualizations that improve decision-making and intelligence sharing.

This chapter explores:

✅ How Plotly enables interactive charts and graphs in Python

✅ How Tableau transforms OSINT data into actionable insights

✅ Practical examples of automated interactive OSINT reports

📌 11.3.1 Why Use Interactive Reports for OSINT?

While static charts (Matplotlib, Seaborn) are useful, interactive reports provide more flexibility by allowing analysts to:

✓ Drill down into data (e.g., filtering threat intelligence by time, location, or severity)

✓ Hover & zoom to explore cyber incidents in depth

✓ Automate real-time OSINT dashboards that update dynamically

🆚 Matplotlib vs. Plotly vs. Tableau

Feature	Matplotlib	Plotly	Tableau
Static Charts	✅ Yes	✅ Yes	❌ No
Interactive Reports	❌ No	✅ Yes	✅ Yes
Drill-down Filters	❌ No	✅ Yes	✅ Yes
Real-time Data	❌ No	✅ Yes	✅ Yes
User-Friendly UI	❌ No	❌ No (Code-based)	✅ Yes (Drag & Drop)

📊 11.3.2 Interactive OSINT Visualizations with Plotly

Plotly is a Python-based interactive visualization library that enables analysts to create dynamic dashboards for cyber intelligence.

1️⃣ Line Chart: Monitoring Cyber Attacks in Real-Time

A Plotly line chart can track cyber threats over time, helping analysts detect attack spikes.

◆ Python Implementation: Plotly Line Chart for Cyber Attacks

```
import plotly.express as px
import pandas as pd

# Sample OSINT data (cyber attacks per day)
data = pd.DataFrame({
    "Date": pd.date_range(start="2024-01-01", periods=10, freq='D'),
    "Cyber_Attacks": [100, 150, 180, 210, 250, 300, 270, 290, 350, 400]
})

# Create interactive line chart
fig = px.line(data, x="Date", y="Cyber_Attacks", title="Cyber Attacks Over Time")
fig.show()
```

✔ **Impact**: Analysts can zoom in/out, filter dates, and analyze attack trends dynamically.

2️⃣ Heatmap: Detecting OSINT Intelligence Hotspots

A heatmap can highlight regions with high cyber activity, making it easier to focus on threat zones.

◆ Python Implementation: Heatmap for Cyber Incidents by Country

```python
import plotly.graph_objects as go

# Sample OSINT data
countries = ["USA", "Russia", "China", "Germany", "Brazil"]
incidents = [1500, 2000, 1800, 800, 900]

fig = go.Figure(data=go.Heatmap(z=incidents, x=countries, colorscale='Reds'))
fig.update_layout(title="Cyber Incident Heatmap by Country")
fig.show()
```

✓ **Impact**: Detects high-risk locations for cybercrime, data breaches, and malware attacks.

3️⃣ Scatter Plot: Identifying Anomalies in Threat Intelligence

A scatter plot helps find unusual spikes in phishing activity, domain registrations, or fraud cases.

◆ Python Implementation: Suspicious Cybercrime Patterns

```python
import numpy as np

# Generate random data
data = pd.DataFrame({
    "Phishing_Attacks": np.random.randint(10, 200, 50),
    "Suspicious_Transactions": np.random.randint(5, 180, 50)
})

fig = px.scatter(data, x="Phishing_Attacks", y="Suspicious_Transactions",
title="Phishing Attacks vs. Suspicious Transactions")
fig.show()
```

✓ **Impact**: Detects correlations between phishing attempts and fraudulent financial transactions.

📊 11.3.3 Interactive OSINT Dashboards with Tableau

☐ What is Tableau?

Tableau is a powerful data visualization tool that enables drag-and-drop dashboard creation for OSINT intelligence sharing.

✓ **Best for**: Non-programmers, real-time dashboards, executive reports

✓ **Strengths**: Integrates with databases, APIs, and CSV/JSON files

🚀 Building an OSINT Dashboard in Tableau

1️⃣ Step 1: Import OSINT Data

✅ **Connect to sources**: CSV, JSON, APIs (Twitter, Shodan, VirusTotal)
✅ Load datasets like phishing reports, leaked databases, or dark web monitoring logs

2️⃣ Step 2: Create Interactive Charts

✅ **Bar charts**: Compare cyber threats across platforms (Dark Web vs. Social Media)
✅ **Geo Maps**: Track cybercrime by country
✅ **Time Series** Graphs: Monitor hacking activity trends

3️⃣ Step 3: Add Filters & Interactive Elements

✅ Add search bars, sliders, date filters to refine intelligence reports

✅ Enable live updates to monitor cyber threats in real-time

📊 11.3.4 Automating OSINT Reports with Plotly & Tableau

📌 Automating Interactive Reports in Python

Plotly can be integrated with Streamlit to build real-time OSINT dashboards.

◆ Python Implementation: OSINT Intelligence Dashboard

```
import streamlit as st
import plotly.express as px

st.title("OSINT Cyber Threat Dashboard")

# Sample dataset
data = pd.DataFrame({
    "Month": ["Jan", "Feb", "Mar", "Apr", "May"],
    "Phishing_Attacks": [300, 450, 520, 490, 600]
})

# Plot using Plotly
fig = px.line(data, x="Month", y="Phishing_Attacks", title="Phishing Attack Trends")

st.plotly_chart(fig)
```

✓ **Impact**: Analysts can share interactive reports with cyber intelligence teams.

🚀 Conclusion: Enhancing OSINT with Interactive Reports

Using Plotly and Tableau, OSINT analysts can:

✓ Create dynamic threat intelligence dashboards

✓ Monitor cybercrime trends in real-time

✓ Automate intelligence reports for decision-makers

By integrating interactive data visualizations, OSINT professionals can detect cyber threats faster and respond more effectively. 🚀

11.4 Automating Report Generation & PDF Exports

OSINT (Open-Source Intelligence) investigations generate large amounts of data, requiring structured reports for decision-making and intelligence sharing. Automating the report generation and PDF export process ensures that analysts can produce consistent, well-formatted, and real-time intelligence reports with minimal effort.

In this chapter, you will learn how to:

✓ Automate report generation using Python

✓ Convert OSINT data into well-structured PDF reports

✓ Integrate graphs, tables, and insights into reports

☐ 11.4.1 Why Automate OSINT Report Generation?

Manually compiling OSINT data into reports is:

✗ **Time-consuming** – Formatting text, tables, and visuals takes hours
✗ **Error-prone** – Copy-pasting data can introduce mistakes
✗ **Inefficient** – Reports quickly become outdated

By automating the report generation process, OSINT analysts can:

✓ Generate reports instantly from live data sources

✓ Ensure reports follow a consistent format

✓ Export findings on-demand in PDF format

📌 11.4.2 Tools for Automating OSINT Reports

Several Python libraries can be used to automate OSINT report generation:

Tool	Purpose
reportlab	Create and format PDFs
pdfkit	Convert HTML reports into PDFs
Pandas	Process OSINT data (tables, CSVs, JSON)
Matplotlib	Generate static charts for reports
Plotly	Embed interactive charts into HTML reports
Jinja2	Automate report templates with placeholders

📑 11.4.3 Automating PDF Report Generation with Python

📌 **Example**: Generating a PDF OSINT Report with ReportLab

Step 1: Install ReportLab

pip install reportlab

Step 2: Generate a Basic OSINT Report in PDF

```
from reportlab.lib.pagesizes import letter
from reportlab.pdfgen import canvas

def create_osint_report(filename):
    c = canvas.Canvas(filename, pagesize=letter)
    c.setFont("Helvetica", 14)

    # Title
    c.drawString(100, 750, "OSINT Intelligence Report")
    c.setFont("Helvetica", 12)
    c.drawString(100, 730, "Generated by: OSINT Automation Tool")
```

```
# Sample intelligence data
c.drawString(100, 700, "Cyber Threat Intelligence:")
c.drawString(120, 680, "- Phishing incidents detected: 324")
c.drawString(120, 660, "- Malware campaigns identified: 57")
c.drawString(120, 640, "- High-risk IPs tracked: 1,245")

c.save()

# Generate report
create_osint_report("osint_report.pdf")
print("OSINT report generated successfully!")
```

✓ **Impact**: This script automatically creates a structured OSINT report in PDF format.

📖 11.4.4 Adding Data Tables to PDF Reports

OSINT reports often contain structured data, such as lists of malicious IPs, phishing domains, or leaked credentials. We can automate table generation in PDFs.

Step 1: Install ReportLab's Table Module

```
pip install reportlab
```

Step 2: Generate a Report with a Table

```
from reportlab.lib.pagesizes import letter
from reportlab.pdfgen import canvas
from reportlab.platypus import Table, TableStyle
from reportlab.lib import colors

def create_osint_report_with_table(filename):
    c = canvas.Canvas(filename, pagesize=letter)
    c.setFont("Helvetica", 14)
    c.drawString(100, 750, "OSINT Intelligence Report")

    # Sample table data
    data = [["Threat Type", "Count"],
        ["Phishing Attacks", "324"],
        ["Malware Campaigns", "57"],
        ["High-risk IPs", "1,245"]]
```

```
    # Create table
    table = Table(data, colWidths=[200, 100])
    table.setStyle(TableStyle([
        ('BACKGROUND', (0, 0), (-1, 0), colors.grey),
        ('TEXTCOLOR', (0, 0), (-1, 0), colors.whitesmoke),
        ('ALIGN', (0, 0), (-1, -1), 'CENTER'),
        ('FONTNAME', (0, 0), (-1, 0), 'Helvetica-Bold'),
        ('BOTTOMPADDING', (0, 0), (-1, 0), 12),
        ('BACKGROUND', (0, 1), (-1, -1), colors.beige),
    ]))

    table.wrapOn(c, 50, 500)
    table.drawOn(c, 100, 600)

    c.save()

create_osint_report_with_table("osint_report_with_table.pdf")
print("OSINT report with table generated successfully!")
```

✔ **Impact**: Generates a well-structured report with tables summarizing key intelligence findings.

📊 11.4.5 Converting HTML OSINT Reports into PDF

Many OSINT dashboards use web-based reports (e.g., Flask/Streamlit dashboards). We can convert HTML reports into PDFs using pdfkit.

Step 1: Install pdfkit & wkhtmltopdf

```
pip install pdfkit
sudo apt-get install wkhtmltopdf  # (Linux/macOS users)
```

Step 2: Convert HTML Reports into PDF

```
import pdfkit

# Sample OSINT report in HTML
html_report = """
<html>
```

```
<head><title>OSINT Report</title></head>
<body>
   <h1>OSINT Intelligence Report</h1>
   <p><strong>Generated on:</strong> 2025-02-23</p>
   <h2>Threat Intelligence Summary</h2>
   <ul>
      <li>Phishing Attacks: 324</li>
      <li>Malware Campaigns: 57</li>
      <li>High-risk IPs: 1,245</li>
   </ul>
</body>
</html>
"""


# Save HTML to file
with open("report.html", "w") as file:
   file.write(html_report)


# Convert HTML to PDF
pdfkit.from_file("report.html", "osint_html_report.pdf")


print("HTML-based OSINT report exported to PDF!")
```

✓ **Impact**: Converts live OSINT data dashboards into PDF reports for intelligence sharing.

▥ 11.4.6 Automating Scheduled Report Exports

OSINT analysts often need daily/weekly/monthly reports. We can automate this process using Python's schedule library.

Step 1: Install schedule

```
pip install schedule
```

Step 2: Schedule Report Generation Every 24 Hours

```
import schedule
import time
```

```
def generate_report():
    create_osint_report_with_table("daily_osint_report.pdf")
    print("Daily OSINT report generated.")

# Schedule report every day at 8 AM
schedule.every().day.at("08:00").do(generate_report)

while True:
    schedule.run_pending()
    time.sleep(60)
```

✓ **Impact**: Automatically exports OSINT reports at scheduled intervals.

🚀 **Conclusion: Automating OSINT Reporting for Efficiency**

By automating report generation and PDF exports, OSINT analysts can:

✓ Save time by eliminating manual reporting

✓ Ensure accuracy with real-time intelligence updates

✓ Deliver professional, structured reports for decision-makers

With Python libraries like ReportLab, pdfkit, and Jinja2, OSINT professionals can automate intelligence reporting workflows for maximum efficiency. 🚀

11.5 Integrating Geospatial Data for Mapping Intelligence

In OSINT (Open-Source Intelligence), geospatial data plays a critical role in tracking threats, analyzing incidents, and visualizing intelligence on maps. By integrating geospatial data into OSINT workflows, analysts can:

✓ Identify the location of cyber threats, social media trends, or leaked information

✓ Track movements of persons of interest or analyze crime patterns

✓ Monitor geopolitical risks using live data feeds

This chapter covers:

✓ Sources of geospatial OSINT data

✓ Using Python to process and visualize geospatial intelligence

✓ Automating map generation with APIs and Python libraries

🔎 11.5.1 Understanding Geospatial Data in OSINT

Geospatial intelligence (GEOINT) is essential in modern OSINT operations. Analysts use it to:

◆ Track digital footprints (social media check-ins, IP geolocation, EXIF metadata)
◆ Map cyber threats (malware C2 servers, phishing domains, fraud hotspots)
◆ Analyze physical security risks (protests, conflicts, disaster zones)

📌 Sources of OSINT Geospatial Data

Source	Type of Data
Social Media APIs	Geotagged tweets, posts, live locations
IP Geolocation APIs	Physical locations of IP addresses
EXIF Metadata	GPS coordinates from images
Open Data Sources	Crime data, disaster reports, government datasets
Dark Web Markets	Locations of illicit transactions (e.g., crypto ATMs)
Threat Intelligence Feeds	Locations of phishing servers, botnets

☐ 11.5.2 Python Libraries for Geospatial OSINT

Several Python libraries help process and visualize geospatial data:

Library	Purpose
geopy	Geocoding IPs, addresses, and coordinates
folium	Interactive maps with markers and layers
geopandas	Handling geospatial data in Pandas format
shapely	Processing geometric data (polygons, boundaries)
gmplot	Plotting data on Google Maps
Basemap	Creating advanced geospatial visualizations

☐ 11.5.3 Automating Geolocation Analysis with Python

📌 Example 1: IP Geolocation Analysis Using geopy

Many OSINT investigations involve tracking IP addresses to their physical locations.

Step 1: Install Geopy

pip install geopy

Step 2: Convert an IP Address to a Physical Location

```
from geopy.geocoders import Nominatim

def get_location(ip_address):
    geolocator = Nominatim(user_agent="osint_geo")
    location = geolocator.geocode(ip_address)
    if location:
        return location.address, location.latitude, location.longitude
    else:
        return "Location not found"

# Example Usage
```

```
ip = "8.8.8.8"  # Google DNS IP
address, lat, lon = get_location(ip)
print(f"IP Address: {ip}")
print(f"Location: {address}")
print(f"Coordinates: {lat}, {lon}")
```

✔ **Impact**: Quickly converts IP addresses to physical locations for OSINT analysis.

☐ 11.5.4 Mapping Geospatial Intelligence with Python

Once geospatial data is extracted, analysts visualize it on maps for pattern recognition and tracking.

📌 Example 2: Creating an Interactive OSINT Map Using folium

Step 1: Install Folium

```
pip install folium
```

Step 2: Plot Geospatial OSINT Data on a Map

```
import folium

# Define coordinates (example: Phishing C2 Server Locations)
locations = [
    {"lat": 40.7128, "lon": -74.0060, "label": "C2 Server - New York"},
    {"lat": 51.5074, "lon": -0.1278, "label": "C2 Server - London"},
    {"lat": 35.6895, "lon": 139.6917, "label": "C2 Server - Tokyo"}
]

# Create a map centered at a global view
osint_map = folium.Map(location=[20, 0], zoom_start=2)

# Add location markers
for loc in locations:
    folium.Marker([loc["lat"], loc["lon"]], popup=loc["label"]).add_to(osint_map)

# Save map as HTML
osint_map.save("osint_map.html")
```

print("Geospatial OSINT Map generated successfully!")

✔ **Impact**: Plots geospatial OSINT data (e.g., phishing servers, threat actors, IP traces) on an interactive map.

☐ 11.5.5 Extracting Geolocation from Image EXIF Data

Many images contain hidden GPS metadata that can reveal where they were taken.

📌 Example 3: Extracting GPS Data from Images

Step 1: Install EXIF Extraction Library

pip install exifread

Step 2: Extract GPS Data from an Image

```
import exifread

def get_exif_gps(image_path):
    with open(image_path, 'rb') as img_file:
        tags = exifread.process_file(img_file)

        # Extract GPS data
        if "GPS GPSLatitude" in tags and "GPS GPSLongitude" in tags:
            lat = tags["GPS GPSLatitude"]
            lon = tags["GPS GPSLongitude"]
            return lat, lon
        else:
            return "No GPS data found"

# Example usage
image_path = "suspect_photo.jpg"
print(get_exif_gps(image_path))
```

✔ **Impact**: Detects hidden geolocation data in images for forensic OSINT investigations.

☐ 11.5.6 Automating Threat Mapping with APIs

Many OSINT investigations use live geospatial data from APIs, such as:

✅ **Google Maps API** – Reverse geocoding & location data
✅ **OpenStreetMap API** – Open-source maps for investigations
✅ **Shodan API** – Mapping cyber threats by IP
✅ **Twitter API** – Geotagged tweets for OSINT

📌 **Example 4: Mapping Live Twitter Data with Python**

Step 1: Install Twitter API Client

pip install tweepy

Step 2: Retrieve Geotagged Tweets

```
import tweepy

# Twitter API Keys
API_KEY = "your_api_key"
API_SECRET = "your_api_secret"
ACCESS_TOKEN = "your_access_token"
ACCESS_SECRET = "your_access_secret"

# Authenticate Twitter API
auth = tweepy.OAuthHandler(API_KEY, API_SECRET)
auth.set_access_token(ACCESS_TOKEN, ACCESS_SECRET)
api = tweepy.API(auth)

# Search for geotagged tweets
tweets = api.search_tweets(q="earthquake", geocode="37.7749,-122.4194,100km", count=10)
for tweet in tweets:
    print(f"User: {tweet.user.screen_name}, Location: {tweet.user.location}, Text: {tweet.text}")
```

✓ **Impact**: Extracts real-time geotagged tweets for OSINT monitoring (e.g., protests, emergencies, cyber threats).

🚀 **Conclusion: The Power of Geospatial Intelligence in OSINT**

By integrating geospatial data into OSINT workflows, analysts can:

✓ Track cyber threats, social media movements, and physical risks

✓ Visualize intelligence findings on interactive maps

✓ Extract location metadata from images and live data sources

With Python libraries and APIs, geospatial intelligence becomes a powerful tool for investigations, threat detection, and decision-making. 🚀

11.6 Case Study: Generating an Automated OSINT Intelligence Report

In modern OSINT (Open-Source Intelligence) investigations, gathering intelligence is only half the battle. The real challenge lies in structuring, analyzing, and presenting data in a way that provides actionable insights. Analysts often spend hours compiling intelligence reports manually, but automation can significantly streamline this process.

This case study demonstrates how an OSINT analyst can:

✓ Collect data from multiple sources (social media, geospatial data, threat intelligence feeds)

✓ Analyze and visualize findings (charts, maps, and sentiment analysis)

✓ Automatically generate a well-structured intelligence report (in PDF or HTML format)

By the end of this case study, you'll learn how to build a fully automated OSINT reporting system using Python.

🔎 11.6.1 The OSINT Investigation Scenario

🕵️ Case Study: Identifying a Potential Cyber Threat

An OSINT analyst working for a cyber threat intelligence (CTI) team has been tasked with monitoring a suspected phishing campaign targeting financial institutions. The analyst must:

● Track mentions of phishing domains on Twitter & Reddit
● Identify IP addresses and geolocations of malicious domains
● Generate a report summarizing the findings

Instead of manually collecting data and writing reports, the analyst decides to automate the entire process using Python.

📌 11.6.2 Step 1: Gathering OSINT Data from Multiple Sources

✓ 1. Collecting Social Media Mentions of Phishing Domains

Extracting tweets containing phishing-related keywords

```
import tweepy

# Twitter API Credentials (Replace with your keys)
API_KEY = "your_api_key"
API_SECRET = "your_api_secret"
ACCESS_TOKEN = "your_access_token"
ACCESS_SECRET = "your_access_secret"

# Authenticate with Twitter API
auth = tweepy.OAuthHandler(API_KEY, API_SECRET)
auth.set_access_token(ACCESS_TOKEN, ACCESS_SECRET)
api = tweepy.API(auth)

# Search for phishing-related tweets
query = "phishing OR fake login site OR financial scam"
tweets = api.search_tweets(q=query, count=10)

# Store extracted tweets
tweet_data = []
for tweet in tweets:
    tweet_data.append(f"{tweet.user.screen_name}: {tweet.text}\n")
```

print("Social media mentions collected successfully!")

✔ **Impact**: Retrieves real-time social media intelligence for phishing domain tracking.

✔ 2. Extracting IP Addresses & Geolocation of Malicious Domains

Using WHOIS & Shodan APIs, the analyst can retrieve IP addresses, hosting information, and geolocations of phishing domains.

import requests

```
# Shodan API Key (Replace with your key)
SHODAN_API_KEY = "your_shodan_api_key"

# Function to fetch domain details
def get_shodan_info(domain):
    url = f"https://api.shodan.io/dns/domain/{domain}?key={SHODAN_API_KEY}"
    response = requests.get(url)
    return response.json()

# Example usage
domain = "example-phishing-site.com"
shodan_data = get_shodan_info(domain)

print(f"Domain: {domain}")
print(f"IP Addresses: {shodan_data.get('data', [])}")
```

✔ **Impact**: Extracts threat intelligence data (IP, location, hosting provider) from phishing domains.

📌 11.6.3 Step 2: Visualizing Intelligence Findings

Once data is collected, it needs to be visualized before being included in the report.

✔ 1. Generating a Map of Phishing Server Locations

import folium

```
# Define phishing server locations
locations = [
    {"lat": 37.7749, "lon": -122.4194, "label": "Phishing Server - San Francisco"},
    {"lat": 51.5074, "lon": -0.1278, "label": "Phishing Server - London"},
]

# Create an interactive map
map_osint = folium.Map(location=[20, 0], zoom_start=2)

# Add markers
for loc in locations:
    folium.Marker([loc["lat"], loc["lon"]], popup=loc["label"]).add_to(map_osint)

# Save the map
map_osint.save("phishing_map.html")

print("Map of phishing servers generated successfully!")
```

✓ **Impact**: Plots phishing servers on an interactive map to identify global patterns.

✓ 2. Creating a Sentiment Analysis Chart

Sentiment analysis can evaluate the tone of social media discussions regarding phishing campaigns.

```
from textblob import TextBlob
import matplotlib.pyplot as plt

# Sample tweets
tweets = ["Beware of this phishing scam! It's spreading fast!",
        "I think I almost got phished today... scary stuff!",
        "Just received a suspicious email asking for my bank details."]

# Sentiment Analysis
sentiments = [TextBlob(tweet).sentiment.polarity for tweet in tweets]

# Visualizing Sentiments
plt.bar(range(len(tweets)), sentiments, color=['red' if s < 0 else 'green' for s in sentiments])
```

```
plt.xlabel("Tweet")
plt.ylabel("Sentiment Score")
plt.title("Sentiment Analysis of Phishing Discussions")
plt.show()
```

✓ **Impact**: Analyzes public sentiment about phishing campaigns.

📌 11.6.4 Step 3: Automating Intelligence Report Generation

✓ 1. Formatting Intelligence Findings into a PDF Report

The intelligence report must be structured, including text summaries, charts, and maps.

```
from fpdf import FPDF

# Create PDF report
pdf = FPDF()
pdf.set_auto_page_break(auto=True, margin=15)
pdf.add_page()
pdf.set_font("Arial", size=12)

# Title
pdf.cell(200, 10, "OSINT Intelligence Report: Phishing Campaign Analysis", ln=True,
align="C")
pdf.ln(10)

# Section 1: Social Media Mentions
pdf.cell(200, 10, "1. Social Media Mentions", ln=True, align="L")
pdf.multi_cell(0, 10, "\n".join(tweet_data))
pdf.ln(5)

# Section 2: Phishing Domain Analysis
pdf.cell(200, 10, "2. Phishing Domain Analysis", ln=True, align="L")
pdf.multi_cell(0, 10, f"Domain: {domain}\nIP Addresses: {shodan_data.get('data', [])}")
pdf.ln(5)

# Save report
pdf.output("OSINT_Intelligence_Report.pdf")
print("OSINT Intelligence Report generated successfully!")
```

✓ **Impact**: Generates a structured intelligence report in PDF format, summarizing findings.

🚀 **Conclusion: The Power of OSINT Automation in Reporting**

This case study demonstrated how an OSINT analyst can:

✅ Automate intelligence collection from social media & threat feeds

✅ Visualize intelligence findings using maps & sentiment analysis

✅ Generate an OSINT report automatically in PDF format

By automating intelligence reporting, analysts save time, reduce errors, and improve decision-making.

- ◆ Manual reporting time: 5-6 hours
- ◆ Automated reporting time: 5-10 minutes

💡 **Future Enhancements:**

- ◆ Integrate AI for deeper threat analysis
- ◆ Generate interactive HTML reports with live dashboards

OSINT automation isn't just a luxury—it's a necessity for modern intelligence analysts. 🚀

12. Case Study: Automating an Intelligence Operation

In this final chapter, we bring everything together with a practical case study that demonstrates the full power of OSINT automation. You'll walk through a real-world scenario where Python scripts, APIs, web scraping, machine learning, and data visualization tools are integrated to automate an intelligence operation from start to finish. We'll guide you through the entire process—beginning with data collection, followed by analysis, threat detection, and the creation of a final report. By examining each stage of the operation, you'll see how the techniques covered throughout the book come to life in a cohesive, automated workflow. By the end of this chapter, you will have a comprehensive understanding of how to apply OSINT automation in a real-world setting, empowering you to carry out your own intelligence operations with efficiency and precision.

12.1 Defining the Investigation Scope & Objectives

Before automating an OSINT (Open-Source Intelligence) investigation, it's crucial to establish a clear scope and well-defined objectives. A poorly scoped investigation can lead to information overload, irrelevant data, or even legal and ethical pitfalls.

This chapter will guide you through:

✓ How to define the key objectives of an OSINT operation

✓ Setting clear parameters for data collection & analysis

✓ Ensuring compliance with legal and ethical standards

✓ Choosing the right OSINT tools based on investigation goals

By structuring your investigation properly, you can optimize intelligence gathering, enhance efficiency, and ensure meaningful insights.

🔎 **12.1.1 Understanding the Need for a Defined Scope**

OSINT investigations often involve vast amounts of public data, ranging from social media posts and domain records to leaked databases and darknet marketplaces. Without a well-defined scope, analysts may:

✘ Waste time collecting irrelevant information

✘ Violate ethical or legal boundaries

✘ Miss critical intelligence due to unfocused searches

✘ Overload themselves with too much raw data

Defining an investigation scope helps:

✓ **Prioritize data sources** (social media, domain records, leaked credentials, etc.)
✓ **Establish time frames** (e.g., past 30 days of activity)
✓ **Set geographic boundaries** (local, national, global)
✓ **Determine key intelligence objectives** (e.g., identifying a threat actor)

🔎 12.1.2 Key Questions to Define an OSINT Investigation

Before launching an automated OSINT operation, analysts should ask:

✔ 1. What is the main goal of this OSINT investigation?

- Are you tracking a cyber threat actor?
- Are you monitoring disinformation campaigns?
- Are you identifying data leaks or breached credentials?

✔ 2. What are the primary data sources?

- Social media (Twitter, LinkedIn, Reddit)
- Domain records (WHOIS, Shodan)
- Dark web marketplaces & forums
- News articles & blog posts
- Leaked database dumps

✔ 3. What time frame should be considered?

- Last 24 hours (real-time intelligence)
- Last 30 days (trend analysis)
- Last 6 months or more (historical patterns)

✔ 4. What geographic boundaries apply?

- Global (international cybercrime trends)
- National (threats targeting a specific country)
- Local (criminal activity in a specific city)

✔ 5. What ethical and legal considerations must be addressed?

- Is consent required for certain types of data?
- Are there restrictions on scraping certain websites?
- Is the investigation compliant with GDPR, CCPA, or other regulations?

🔎 12.1.3 Case Example: Defining Scope for a Cyber Threat Investigation

□□♂□ Scenario: Investigating a Ransomware Group

An OSINT analyst is tasked with gathering intelligence on a ransomware group targeting financial institutions.

Step 1: Define the Objective

✔ Identify ransomware group members & affiliations

✔ Track communication channels & dark web activities

✔ Monitor leaked data and extortion attempts

Step 2: Identify Data Sources

✔ Dark web forums (ransomware gang announcements)

✔ Twitter, Telegram & hacking communities

✔ Breach databases (to find leaked credentials)

✔ Cryptocurrency transactions (following ransom payments)

Step 3: Set Time Frame & Geographic Scope

✔ Past 6 months of ransomware activity

✔ Global focus, but prioritize North America & Europe

Step 4: Address Legal & Ethical Considerations

✔ Avoid hacking or unauthorized access to private systems

✔ Use publicly available or legally accessible data

✔ Follow corporate & legal policies on OSINT investigations

✔ **Final Scope**: The investigation will focus on monitoring ransomware-related social media activity, dark web forum discussions, leaked data, and cryptocurrency transactions over the past 6 months.

🔎 12.1.4 Selecting the Right OSINT Tools Based on Scope

Once the investigation scope is set, the next step is selecting the appropriate automation tools.

✔ OSINT Tools Based on Investigation Type

Investigation Type	Recommended Tools
Social Media Monitoring	Tweepy (Twitter), Facebook Graph API, Reddit API
Domain & IP Tracking	WHOIS Lookup, Shodan, VirusTotal API
Dark Web Intelligence	OnionScan, Tor API, Hunchly
Data Leak Monitoring	Have I Been Pwned API, DeHashed
Threat Intelligence	MISP, AlienVault OTX, IBM X-Force
Cryptocurrency Analysis	Blockchain Explorers, Chainalysis API

🔎 12.1.5 Automating Scope Definition with Python

To ensure consistency in defining an OSINT investigation scope, analysts can create a Python script that automates scope documentation.

✔ Example: Automating Scope Documentation in JSON

```
import json

# Define investigation parameters
osint_scope = {
    "Objective": "Identify ransomware group activities and track cryptocurrency transactions.",
    "Data Sources": ["Dark web forums", "Twitter", "Telegram", "Cryptocurrency blockchains"],
    "Time Frame": "Last 6 months",
    "Geographic Focus": "Global, with priority on North America & Europe",
    "Legal Considerations": ["No unauthorized access", "GDPR-compliant data collection"],
    "Tools": ["Tweepy", "Shodan", "Tor API", "Blockchain Explorers"]
}

# Save scope to JSON file
```

```
with open("osint_investigation_scope.json", "w") as file:
    json.dump(osint_scope, file, indent=4)

print("OSINT investigation scope saved successfully!")
```

✓ **Impact**: Automatically documents the OSINT investigation scope, ensuring clarity and consistency.

🚀 Conclusion: The Foundation of a Successful OSINT Operation

◆ A well-defined investigation scope is essential for efficient, ethical, and legal intelligence gathering.
◆ Asking the right scoping questions ensures relevant data collection and avoids wasted effort.
◆ Selecting the right tools based on scope improves automation and intelligence quality.

By setting a clear framework before launching an OSINT operation, analysts can improve efficiency, reduce risk, and extract actionable intelligence.

Next Step: Once the scope is defined, the next phase involves automating data collection and analysis to streamline OSINT workflows. 🚀

12.2 Selecting the Right OSINT Automation Tools

With a well-defined investigation scope, the next critical step is selecting the right OSINT automation tools. The choice of tools significantly impacts the efficiency, accuracy, and ethical compliance of intelligence gathering.

In this section, we will cover:

✓ Categories of OSINT automation tools

✓ Key factors for selecting the right tools

✓ Comparison of open-source vs. commercial OSINT tools

✓ Integrating multiple tools into an automated OSINT workflow

The right tools enable analysts to save time, extract relevant intelligence, and minimize manual effort in OSINT investigations.

🔎 12.2.1 Categories of OSINT Automation Tools

OSINT tools can be categorized based on data sources and use cases. Below are key categories:

✔ 1. Social Media Intelligence (SOCMINT)

Used for tracking social media activity, analyzing trends, and identifying influencers.

◆ Examples:

- **Tweepy** – Automates Twitter data collection
- **Facebook Graph API** – Extracts public Facebook data
- **Reddit API** – Scrapes discussions from Reddit
- **Social Links OSINT** – Advanced social media analytics

✔ 2. Search Engine & Web Scraping Tools

Used for gathering intelligence from Google Dorks, search engines, and public websites.

◆ Examples:

- **SerpAPI** – Automates Google search queries
- **Scrapy** – Advanced web scraping framework
- **BeautifulSoup** – Parses and extracts data from web pages
- **Google Dorks & Python** – Automates search queries

✔ 3. Domain, IP, & Network Intelligence

Helps investigate IP addresses, domains, subdomains, and DNS records.

◆ Examples:

- **Shodan API** – Finds exposed devices and vulnerabilities
- **WHOIS Lookup** – Identifies domain ownership details

- **VirusTotal API** – Scans URLs and files for threats
- **SecurityTrails API** – Provides historical DNS records

✔ 4. Dark Web Intelligence & Tor Monitoring

For tracking illicit activities, marketplaces, and forums on the dark web.

◆ Examples:

- **OnionScan** – Analyzes dark web sites for vulnerabilities
- **Tor API** – Automates crawling of onion sites
- **Hunchly** – Captures and archives online investigations
- **DarkTracer** – Monitors ransomware and dark web leaks

✔ 5. Data Leak & Breach Monitoring

Used for detecting leaked credentials, compromised accounts, and database dumps.

◆ Examples:

- **Have I Been Pwned API** – Checks for breached email accounts
- **DeHashed API** – Searches for leaked passwords & usernames
- **IntelX** – Advanced data breach search engine
- **LeakIX** – Monitors exposed databases & servers

✔ 6. Cryptocurrency Intelligence & Blockchain Analysis

Helps track cryptocurrency transactions linked to cybercrime.

◆ Examples:

- **Blockchain Explorers** – Traces Bitcoin and Ethereum transactions
- **Chainalysis API** – Investigates illicit crypto activities
- **CipherTrace** – Maps suspicious blockchain transactions
- **Elliptic** – Detects crypto fraud patterns

✔ 7. Image, Video & Metadata Analysis

Used for analyzing images, EXIF metadata, and reverse image searches.

◆ **Examples:**

- **ExifTool** – Extracts metadata from images
- **Google Reverse Image Search** – Identifies similar images
- **Yandex & TinEye** – Tracks duplicate images across the web
- **Amazon Rekognition** – AI-based image recognition & face detection

✓ 8. Automated Threat Intelligence & AI-Based Analysis

For real-time cyber threat monitoring and predictive analysis.

◆ **Examples:**

- **MISP (Malware Information Sharing Platform)** – Threat intelligence sharing
- **IBM X-Force Exchange** – Cyber threat database
- **AlienVault OTX** – Community-driven threat intelligence
- **Palo Alto AutoFocus** – AI-driven threat detection

🔎 **12.2.2 Key Factors for Selecting the Right OSINT Tool**

Choosing the best tool depends on several factors:

✓ 1. Investigation Objective

- Are you gathering intelligence from social media, dark web, or breach databases?
- Do you need real-time monitoring or historical data analysis?

✓ 2. Data Accessibility & API Support

- Does the tool provide an API for automation?
- Are there rate limits or paid tiers for API usage?

✓ 3. Ethical & Legal Compliance

- Does the tool collect data in a GDPR-compliant manner?
- Are there restrictions on scraping or data retention?

✓ 4. Open-Source vs. Commercial Tools

- Open-source tools (e.g., Maltego CE, Scrapy) are free but may require manual configuration.
- Paid tools (e.g., IBM X-Force, Chainalysis) provide better data access but require licensing.

🔎 12.2.3 Open-Source vs. Commercial OSINT Tools

Feature	Open-Source OSINT Tools	Commercial OSINT Tools
Cost	Free or low-cost	Subscription-based
Customization	High (can modify source code)	Limited (vendor-controlled)
Ease of Use	Requires technical skills	User-friendly interface
Data Access	Limited APIs & scraping	Direct access to intelligence feeds
Legal Risks	Higher (manual compliance needed)	Lower (vendors handle compliance)

✓ Example Use Case:

- A solo OSINT analyst may prefer open-source tools for flexibility.
- A corporate security team may invest in commercial tools for better legal compliance & data access.

🔎 12.2.4 Integrating Multiple OSINT Tools into an Automated Workflow

For advanced OSINT automation, analysts often integrate multiple tools into a single workflow.

✓ Example: Automating OSINT Data Collection with Python

This Python script automates data collection from various sources:

import requests

```
# Example: Fetching Twitter data using Tweepy
import tweepy

api_key = "your_api_key"
api_secret = "your_api_secret"
auth = tweepy.OAuthHandler(api_key, api_secret)
api = tweepy.API(auth)

tweets = api.search_tweets(q="cybersecurity", count=5)
for tweet in tweets:
    print(f"Tweet: {tweet.text}\n")

# Example: Fetching WHOIS data for a domain
domain = "example.com"
whois_url =
f"https://www.whoisxmlapi.com/api/v1?apiKey=your_api_key&domainName={domain}"

response = requests.get(whois_url)
whois_data = response.json()
print(f"Domain Owner: {whois_data['registrant']['name']}")
```

✔ **Impact**: Automates intelligence gathering from social media and domain records in a single script.

🚀 Conclusion: Selecting the Right Tools for Effective OSINT Automation

◆ Choosing the right OSINT tools is crucial for efficient intelligence gathering.
◆ Analysts should consider data sources, automation capabilities, and compliance when selecting tools.
◆ Integrating multiple tools enhances automation and saves time on intelligence workflows.

12.3 Collecting & Processing Large-Scale Data Efficiently

OSINT investigations often require collecting, processing, and analyzing vast amounts of data from various sources such as social media, public records, search engines, and breach databases. Handling this volume of information manually is impractical, time-consuming, and prone to errors.

To address these challenges, OSINT analysts must adopt efficient data collection and processing techniques using automation, optimized storage, and scalable workflows.

This chapter will cover:

✓ Strategies for large-scale data collection

✓ Optimizing API requests and web scraping for efficiency

✓ Data storage solutions for OSINT investigations

✓ Preprocessing and cleaning OSINT data for analysis

By implementing these techniques, analysts can speed up investigations, reduce resource consumption, and enhance intelligence quality.

🔎 12.3.1 Strategies for Large-Scale OSINT Data Collection

Collecting large-scale OSINT data requires a structured approach to avoid overwhelming network resources, storage capacity, or API rate limits. Below are key strategies:

✓ 1. Prioritizing High-Value Data Sources

◆ Not all data is useful—focus on sources with high intelligence value.
◆ **Example**: Instead of scraping entire Twitter timelines, focus on targeted hashtags, mentions, or geotagged tweets.

✓ 2. Using APIs Instead of Web Scraping Where Possible

◆ APIs provide structured data and are often more efficient than scraping.
◆ **Example**: Using the Twitter API instead of manually scraping tweets reduces CAPTCHA challenges and IP blocking.

◆ **Efficient API usage:**

- Use batch requests where possible (e.g., fetching 100 tweets per request instead of 1).
- Implement asynchronous requests to avoid delays.

✔ 3. Distributed Data Collection for Scalability

◈ Use distributed scraping frameworks to collect data in parallel.

◆ Example:

- Scrapy + Scrapy Cluster allows multiple machines to scrape large websites efficiently.
- Celery + RabbitMQ distributes API requests across multiple workers.

✔ 4. Handling API Rate Limits & Avoiding IP Bans

◈ Respect API rate limits by implementing cooldowns between requests.
◈ Use proxies & rotating IP addresses to avoid bans while scraping.

◆ Example:

Use Rotating Proxies in Python with requests library.

```
import requests
from itertools import cycle

proxy_list = ["http://proxy1.com", "http://proxy2.com"]
proxy_pool = cycle(proxy_list)

for i in range(10):
    proxy = next(proxy_pool)
    response = requests.get("https://targetwebsite.com", proxies={"http": proxy, "https":
proxy})
    print(response.status_code)
```

🔎 12.3.2 Optimizing API Requests & Web Scraping

✔ 1. Asynchronous Requests for Faster Data Retrieval

- ◆ Synchronous API calls slow down OSINT operations.
- ◆ **Solution**: Use asyncio and aiohttp to make parallel requests.

```
import asyncio
import aiohttp

async def fetch(url, session):
    async with session.get(url) as response:
        return await response.text()

async def main():
    urls = ["https://api.example.com/data1", "https://api.example.com/data2"]
    async with aiohttp.ClientSession() as session:
        tasks = [fetch(url, session) for url in urls]
        responses = await asyncio.gather(*tasks)
        print(responses)

asyncio.run(main())
```

✔ **Impact**: Reduces data collection time from minutes to seconds.

✔ 2. Scraping JavaScript-Rendered Pages Efficiently

- ◆ **Problem**: Some websites load content dynamically via JavaScript (e.g., Twitter, LinkedIn).
- ◆ **Solution**: Use Selenium or Playwright to automate browser interactions.

```
from selenium import webdriver

driver = webdriver.Chrome()
driver.get("https://example.com")
data = driver.page_source
print(data)
driver.quit()
```

✔ **Impact**: Captures dynamic content that traditional scrapers miss.

✓ 3. Extracting Specific Data Instead of Full Webpages

◆ Reduce processing time by extracting only relevant data elements.

◆ **Example**: Instead of saving entire web pages, extract headlines, timestamps, and author names using BeautifulSoup.

```
from bs4 import BeautifulSoup
import requests

response = requests.get("https://newswebsite.com")
soup = BeautifulSoup(response.text, "html.parser")

for article in soup.find_all("h2"):
    print(article.text)
```

✓ **Impact**: Reduces storage costs and processing time.

🔎 12.3.3 Data Storage Solutions for OSINT Investigations

✓ 1. Choosing the Right Database for OSINT Data

Different databases serve different purposes:

Database Type	Best For	Example Tools
Relational (SQL)	Structured OSINT data	MySQL, PostgreSQL
NoSQL (MongoDB, Elasticsearch)	Unstructured & large-scale text data	MongoDB, ElasticSearch
Graph Databases	Social network analysis	Neo4j
Time-Series Databases	Tracking threat intelligence over time	InfluxDB

✓ 2. Storing Data Efficiently with Compression

◆ Use Gzip or Parquet format to reduce storage size for large datasets.

```
import pandas as pd

df = pd.DataFrame(data)
df.to_parquet("osint_data.parquet", compression="gzip")
```

✓ **Impact**: Saves up to 70% storage space.

🔎 12.3.4 Preprocessing & Cleaning OSINT Data

Raw OSINT data is often messy, incomplete, or contains duplicate entries.

✓ 1. Removing Duplicates

```
import pandas as pd

df = pd.read_csv("osint_data.csv")
df = df.drop_duplicates()
df.to_csv("cleaned_osint_data.csv", index=False)
```

✓ **Impact**: Ensures accuracy and prevents data redundancy.

✓ 2. Extracting Meaningful Keywords from Text Data

♦ Convert unstructured text into actionable intelligence.

```
from sklearn.feature_extraction.text import TfidfVectorizer

documents = ["Threat actor group APT29 identified", "Phishing campaign detected in emails"]
vectorizer = TfidfVectorizer(stop_words="english")
vectors = vectorizer.fit_transform(documents)

print(vectorizer.get_feature_names_out())
```

✓ **Impact**: Helps in categorizing and prioritizing intelligence.

🚀 Conclusion: Scaling OSINT Data Collection & Processing

- ♦ Large-scale OSINT data collection requires automation, efficiency, and scalability.
- ♦ Use asynchronous API calls, web scraping optimizations, and distributed processing to handle vast data.
- ♦ Store data efficiently in SQL, NoSQL, or Graph databases, and compress large datasets to save space.
- ♦ Preprocessing techniques such as deduplication and keyword extraction improve data quality.

12.4 Challenges & Solutions in Automating OSINT Workflows

Automating OSINT workflows can significantly improve efficiency, but it also presents technical, ethical, and operational challenges. Issues such as data access restrictions, API rate limits, anti-scraping mechanisms, legal concerns, and data integrity must be addressed to build a sustainable and effective automation system.

In this chapter, we will explore:

- Common challenges in OSINT automation
- Technical solutions for overcoming these challenges
- Ethical and legal considerations in automated OSINT
- Best practices for building a resilient OSINT workflow

By understanding these challenges and their solutions, analysts can develop robust automation strategies that enhance intelligence-gathering efforts while remaining ethical and compliant.

12.4.1 Challenge 1: API Rate Limits & Access Restrictions

Problem

Many OSINT data sources, such as Twitter, Facebook, and Google, enforce API rate limits and require authentication. This restricts the amount of data that can be collected within a given time frame.

Solution: Efficient API Handling & Rate Limit Management

- **Batch Requests**: Fetch data in bulk instead of individual requests.

- **Caching Responses**: Store previously fetched data to minimize redundant requests.
- **Rate-Limiting Awareness**: Implement request delays or exponential backoff strategies.

Example: Using Exponential Backoff for API Calls in Python

```python
import time
import requests

def fetch_data_with_backoff(url, max_retries=5):
    for attempt in range(max_retries):
        response = requests.get(url)
        if response.status_code == 200:
            return response.json()
        elif response.status_code == 429:  # Rate limit exceeded
            wait_time = 2 ** attempt  # Exponential backoff
            print(f"Rate limit hit. Retrying in {wait_time} seconds...")
            time.sleep(wait_time)
        else:
            break  # Stop retrying on other errors

    return None  # Return None if all retries fail

data = fetch_data_with_backoff("https://api.example.com/data")
```

Impact: Prevents excessive API calls while maximizing data retrieval.

12.4.2 Challenge 2: Anti-Scraping & CAPTCHA Challenges

Problem

Websites often employ anti-scraping techniques, such as CAPTCHA verification, IP blocking, or JavaScript-based content loading, to prevent automated data collection.

Solution: Smart Scraping Techniques & Headless Browsers

- **Use Proxies & Rotate IPs**: Avoid detection by frequently changing IP addresses.
- **Headless Browsers & Selenium**: Load JavaScript-heavy pages dynamically.
- **CAPTCHA Solving Services**: Use AI-powered solvers when necessary.

Example: Using Selenium to Bypass JavaScript-Based Content Loading

```
from selenium import webdriver

options = webdriver.ChromeOptions()
options.add_argument("--headless")  # Run without opening a browser window
driver = webdriver.Chrome(options=options)

driver.get("https://example.com")
page_source = driver.page_source
driver.quit()

print(page_source)
```

Impact: Enables data extraction from dynamically loaded web pages.

12.4.3 Challenge 3: Handling Large-Scale Data Efficiently

Problem

OSINT investigations often involve processing huge datasets, leading to slow performance, high storage costs, and data duplication issues.

Solution: Distributed Processing & Optimized Storage

- **Use Asynchronous Processing**: Fetch and process data concurrently.
- **Compress Large Datasets**: Save storage space with formats like Parquet or Gzip.
- **Use Cloud Storage & NoSQL Databases**: Scale efficiently.

Example: Using Pandas to Process Large Data Efficiently

```
import pandas as pd

# Load CSV efficiently
df = pd.read_csv("large_osint_data.csv", chunksize=10000)  # Process in batches

# Process each chunk
for chunk in df:
    cleaned_chunk = chunk.drop_duplicates()
```

```
cleaned_chunk.to_parquet("cleaned_osint_data.parquet", compression="gzip")
```

Impact: Improves processing speed and reduces storage requirements.

12.4.4 Challenge 4: Ensuring Data Accuracy & Integrity

Problem

Automated OSINT tools may collect incomplete, outdated, or false information, leading to misleading intelligence.

Solution: Data Verification & Cross-Referencing

- **Use Multiple Sources**: Compare findings across different databases.
- **Automate Data Validation**: Identify inconsistencies in collected data.
- **Track Data Provenance**: Log where and when data was collected.

Example: Cross-Referencing Data from Multiple APIs

```
import requests

def check_data_consistency(email):
    api1 = requests.get(f"https://api1.com/check?email={email}").json()
    api2 = requests.get(f"https://api2.com/check?email={email}").json()

    return api1["result"] == api2["result"]  # True if both sources match

print(check_data_consistency("example@email.com"))
```

Impact: Reduces false positives and improves intelligence reliability.

12.4.5 Challenge 5: Ethical & Legal Considerations

Problem

OSINT automation must comply with privacy laws (e.g., GDPR, CCPA) and ethical guidelines. Unauthorized data collection could lead to legal consequences.

Solution: Implementing Ethical OSINT Practices

- **Follow Website Terms of Service**: Check what data collection is permitted.
- **Use Only Publicly Available Data**: Avoid private or restricted information.
- **Maintain Transparency**: Document data sources and methodology.

Impact: Ensures compliance and prevents legal risks.

12.4.6 Challenge 6: Maintaining OSINT Automation Over Time

Problem

OSINT tools, APIs, and websites frequently update, causing scripts to break.

Solution: Version Control & Automated Testing

- **Monitor API & Website Changes**: Regularly test scripts.
- **Use Version Control (GitHub, GitLab)**: Track script modifications.
- **Implement Error Handling**: Ensure scripts fail gracefully.

Example: Using Try-Except to Handle API Changes

```
try:
    response = requests.get("https://api.example.com/data")
    data = response.json()
except Exception as e:
    print(f"Error fetching data: {e}")
```

Impact: Prevents script failures due to unexpected API updates.

Conclusion: Building a Resilient OSINT Automation Workflow

Automating OSINT workflows comes with significant challenges, but these can be addressed using smart data collection strategies, optimized processing techniques, ethical compliance, and robust error handling.

Key Takeaways:

- Use API optimization & rate limit handling for efficient data retrieval.
- Implement anti-detection techniques to bypass scraping restrictions.
- Store data using scalable, compressed formats for efficiency.
- Cross-reference sources to ensure data accuracy & integrity.

- Stay ethical & legally compliant in OSINT investigations.
- Continuously monitor & update automation scripts to prevent failures.

By implementing these solutions, OSINT analysts can overcome automation challenges and build a resilient, scalable, and legally compliant intelligence-gathering workflow.

12.5 Final Report: Presenting Automated OSINT Findings

Once OSINT automation has collected and analyzed intelligence, the next critical step is presenting findings in a structured and actionable manner. A well-organized OSINT report enhances decision-making, threat assessment, and strategic planning. However, automating the reporting process presents unique challenges, including data visualization, contextual analysis, and ensuring clarity for non-technical stakeholders.

This chapter will cover:

- Key elements of an OSINT report
- Automating report generation using Python
- Best practices for visualizing intelligence data
- Ethical and operational considerations in intelligence reporting

By the end of this chapter, you will be able to create automated, professional OSINT reports that communicate intelligence findings effectively.

12.5.1 Key Elements of an OSINT Report

A well-structured OSINT report should include the following components:

Executive Summary

- Brief overview of the investigation's purpose and key findings.
- Focuses on actionable intelligence rather than technical details.

Data Sources & Collection Methods

- List of sources used (public databases, APIs, web scraping, etc.).
- Transparency in data collection methods for credibility.

Key Findings & Analysis

- Summary of threats, patterns, and anomalies identified.
- Includes contextual insights that help decision-making.

Visual Data Representation

- Graphs, charts, network maps, and timelines.
- Helps non-technical audiences interpret intelligence efficiently.

Risk Assessment & Recommendations

- Identifies potential risks based on intelligence findings.
- Provides actionable recommendations for mitigation.

Legal & Ethical Compliance

- Confirms that data was collected ethically and legally.
- Addresses any privacy concerns or legal constraints.

12.5.2 Automating Report Generation with Python

Manually compiling OSINT reports is time-consuming, but Python can automate report generation and export findings as structured documents (PDF, HTML, Markdown).

Solution: Using Python to Automate Report Creation

Example: Generating an OSINT Report in PDF Format

```python
from fpdf import FPDF

class OSINTReport(FPDF):
    def header(self):
        self.set_font("Arial", "B", 14)
        self.cell(200, 10, "Automated OSINT Report", ln=True, align="C")
        self.ln(10)

    def chapter_title(self, title):
        self.set_font("Arial", "B", 12)
        self.cell(0, 10, title, ln=True, align="L")
        self.ln(5)
```

```
def chapter_body(self, body):
    self.set_font("Arial", "", 10)
    self.multi_cell(0, 10, body)
    self.ln(5)


# Create report
report = OSINTReport()
report.add_page()
report.chapter_title("1. Executive Summary")
report.chapter_body("This OSINT investigation focused on tracking social media
disinformation campaigns...")

report.chapter_title("2. Key Findings")
report.chapter_body("Analysis revealed patterns in bot activity, with peak engagement
occurring at 2 AM UTC.")

report.output("OSINT_Report.pdf")
```

Impact: Automates structured reporting, ensuring consistency and efficiency.

12.5.3 Visualizing OSINT Data in Reports

Complex intelligence data must be presented clearly and visually to highlight patterns, connections, and trends.

Solution: Integrating Data Visualization into Reports

Example: Creating a Network Graph of OSINT Data Using NetworkX & Matplotlib

```
import networkx as nx
import matplotlib.pyplot as plt

# Create a graph
G = nx.Graph()
G.add_edges_from([("Threat Actor A", "Domain X"), ("Threat Actor A", "IP Address Y"),
        ("IP Address Y", "Leaked Database Z")])

# Draw the network
plt.figure(figsize=(8, 6))
```

```
nx.draw(G, with_labels=True, node_color="skyblue", edge_color="gray",
node_size=3000, font_size=10)
plt.title("OSINT Network Graph")
plt.savefig("osint_network_graph.png")  # Save as an image for reports
plt.show()
```

Impact: Highlights connections between entities for better intelligence interpretation.

12.5.4 Automating the Export of Intelligence Reports

To make intelligence findings easily shareable, reports should be automatically exported in multiple formats (PDF, HTML, CSV).

Solution: Converting Intelligence Reports to Various Formats

Example: Exporting OSINT Findings to a CSV File

```
import csv

data = [
    ["Threat Actor", "Associated Domain", "Risk Level"],
    ["Hacker Group X", "malicious-site.com", "High"],
    ["Anonymous User", "suspiciousforum.net", "Medium"],
]

with open("osint_findings.csv", "w", newline="") as file:
    writer = csv.writer(file)
    writer.writerows(data)

print("OSINT findings exported successfully!")
```

Impact: Enables structured data sharing for intelligence teams.

12.5.5 Ethical & Operational Considerations in OSINT Reporting

Automated OSINT reporting must remain ethical and legally compliant.

Common Pitfalls & How to Avoid Them

- **Including private or unauthorized data** → Only use publicly available sources.

- **Lack of source verification** → Cross-check intelligence across multiple datasets.

- **Failure to anonymize sensitive data** → Redact personal identifiers in reports.

- **Over-reliance on automation** → Always have human analysts validate critical intelligence.

Impact: Ensures intelligence reporting remains responsible and legally compliant.

Conclusion: Creating Actionable, Automated OSINT Reports

Automating OSINT reporting saves time, improves consistency, and enhances intelligence presentation. However, human validation remains crucial to ensure accuracy and context.

Key Takeaways:

- OSINT reports should be structured, clear, and actionable.
- Python can automate report generation (PDF, CSV, HTML).
- Data visualization tools (NetworkX, Matplotlib) enhance intelligence clarity.
- Exporting findings in multiple formats improves intelligence sharing.
- Ethical compliance is critical in intelligence reporting.

12.6 Lessons Learned & Future Trends in OSINT Automation

The automation of Open-Source Intelligence (OSINT) has revolutionized how analysts gather, process, and analyze data. From web scraping and API integrations to machine learning-driven intelligence analysis, OSINT automation has significantly improved efficiency, accuracy, and scalability. However, challenges such as anti-scraping mechanisms, ethical concerns, and evolving cyber threats continue to shape the field.

In this final chapter, we will reflect on key lessons learned from automating OSINT processes and explore emerging trends that will define the future of intelligence gathering.

12.6.1 Lessons Learned from OSINT Automation

Automation Saves Time but Requires Oversight

Key Insight: Automated tools significantly reduce manual effort, but they must be monitored for false positives, outdated data, or bias in AI-driven insights.

Example:

- A Python script automating Google Dorking may retrieve irrelevant or outdated results.
- **Solution**: Implement filtering mechanisms and periodic manual validation to ensure quality control.

API Limitations & Data Restrictions Are Constant Challenges

Key Insight: Many social media platforms and search engines restrict API access, making OSINT data collection challenging.

Example:

- Twitter has API rate limits and restricts access to certain types of user data.
- **Solution**: Use a combination of APIs, public datasets, and ethical scraping techniques to maximize intelligence gathering.

Ethical & Legal Considerations Must Guide OSINT Automation

Key Insight: Automated OSINT tools must comply with laws regarding privacy, data access, and cybersecurity regulations.

Example:

- Some OSINT tools scrape protected user data from websites, violating Terms of Service.
- **Solution**: Always ensure legality and transparency in OSINT operations.

Best Practices for Ethical OSINT Automation:

- Use only publicly available data.
- Obtain proper authorization when monitoring private sources.
- Avoid automation techniques that may violate website policies.

Machine Learning & AI Enhance OSINT But Have Limitations

Key Insight: AI-powered tools can detect patterns and anomalies, but they require quality training data and human oversight.

Example:

- Sentiment analysis models may misinterpret sarcasm or cultural nuances in social media intelligence.
- **Solution**: Combine AI-based analysis with human validation for accurate OSINT insights.

OSINT Dashboards Improve Decision-Making

Key Insight: Interactive dashboards allow analysts to visualize intelligence data in real-time, improving decision-making.

Example:

- A cyber threat intelligence dashboard aggregates and visualizes data from multiple sources (e.g., IP reputation scores, dark web activity, social media chatter).
- **Solution**: Use Streamlit, Flask, or Power BI to automate intelligence reporting in a structured, interactive format.

12.6.2 Future Trends in OSINT Automation

AI-Driven OSINT Investigations

What's Next?

- Machine learning will enhance entity recognition, pattern detection, and automated risk scoring.
- AI-based deepfake detection will become crucial in countering disinformation campaigns.

Example:

AI models trained on cyber threat intelligence datasets can automatically detect phishing domains, fake social media accounts, and bot networks.

Decentralized & Blockchain-Based OSINT

What's Next?

- Analysts will explore blockchain transactions to track cryptocurrency laundering and dark web activities.
- Decentralized OSINT tools will emerge to counter censorship and misinformation.

Example:

Tools like Elliptic and Chainalysis already track Bitcoin transactions linked to cybercrime activities.

Increased OSINT Use in Cyber Threat Intelligence (CTI)

What's Next?

- OSINT will play a crucial role in cyber threat intelligence (CTI) by tracking hacker forums, data breaches, and malware indicators.
- AI-powered OSINT tools will automatically identify cyber threats before they escalate.

Example:

Security teams will use automated dark web crawlers to monitor leaked credentials, ransomware discussions, and hacking toolkits.

Enhanced OSINT for Geospatial & Satellite Intelligence

What's Next?

- Automated satellite imagery analysis will improve geospatial intelligence (GEOINT).
- AI will detect military movements, deforestation, or environmental changes from satellite data.

Example:

Open-source projects like Sentinel Hub and Google Earth Engine provide automated monitoring for crisis response and national security.

Autonomous OSINT Bots & Virtual Analysts

What's Next?

- AI-powered OSINT chatbots will assist in real-time threat intelligence gathering.
- Automated OSINT bots will collect and analyze intelligence without human intervention.

Example:

An OSINT chatbot integrated into a threat intelligence platform can instantly provide information on a suspected cyber threat.

Final Thoughts: The Future of OSINT Automation

As OSINT automation evolves, intelligence analysts must adapt to new technologies, data sources, and challenges. The combination of AI, blockchain, geospatial intelligence, and automated dashboards will redefine how intelligence is gathered and used in cybersecurity, law enforcement, national security, and corporate intelligence.

Key Takeaways from OSINT Automation:

- Automation enhances OSINT efficiency but requires oversight.
- API restrictions and anti-scraping measures present ongoing challenges.
- Ethical and legal compliance is essential in OSINT investigations.
- Machine learning improves OSINT analysis but has limitations.
- Future OSINT trends include AI, blockchain intelligence, and geospatial automation.

In the ever-evolving world of Open-Source Intelligence (OSINT), manual investigations can be time-consuming and inefficient. Automating intelligence gathering with Python and APIs allows analysts to collect, process, and analyze vast amounts of data quickly and accurately. By leveraging scripting and automation, OSINT professionals can enhance their investigations, uncover hidden patterns, and extract intelligence at scale.

OSINT Automation: Python & APIs for Intelligence Gathering is your comprehensive guide to using programming and automation tools to streamline OSINT workflows. Whether you're an investigator, cybersecurity analyst, journalist, or intelligence professional, this book provides hands-on techniques to automate data collection, social media monitoring, web scraping, and more.

What You'll Learn in This Book

- **Introduction to OSINT Automation**: Understand the benefits of automating intelligence gathering and how Python enhances OSINT investigations.
- **Python Basics for OSINT Analysts**: Learn essential Python programming skills for data collection and analysis.
- **Web Scraping & Data Extraction**: Use Python libraries like BeautifulSoup and Scrapy to extract information from websites and online databases.
- **API Integration for OSINT**: Leverage public and private APIs to gather intelligence from social media, domain records, and online platforms.
- **Automating Social Media Investigations**: Monitor Twitter, Facebook, LinkedIn, and other platforms using Python scripts.
- **Data Cleaning & Processing**: Organize and filter OSINT data using Pandas and other Python data-processing tools.
- **Geolocation & Image Analysis Automation**: Automate reverse image searches and analyze geospatial data with Python.
- **Dark Web & Threat Intelligence Automation**: Use Python to monitor dark web marketplaces, forums, and hacker activity.
- **Real-Time OSINT Alerts & Dashboards**: Build automated alert systems and visualization dashboards to track intelligence in real-time.
- **Ethical & Legal Considerations in OSINT Automation**: Ensure responsible and lawful use of automation tools in investigations.

Packed with hands-on coding examples, real-world case studies, and ready-to-use Python scripts, OSINT Automation is an essential resource for any OSINT professional looking to scale their intelligence-gathering capabilities. Whether you're new to coding or an experienced programmer, this book will help you master OSINT automation and take your investigations to the next level.

Thank you for reading **OSINT Automation: Python & APIs for Intelligence Gathering**. Automating OSINT investigations is a game-changer, allowing intelligence professionals to work faster, uncover deeper insights, and tackle large-scale data challenges. By learning how to integrate Python and APIs into your workflow, you are future-proofing your OSINT skills and staying ahead in the intelligence field.

We encourage you to use these techniques ethically and responsibly. Automation is a powerful tool, but with great power comes great responsibility. The OSINT community thrives on curiosity, integrity, and the pursuit of truth, and we are grateful to have you as part of this journey.

If you found this book valuable, we'd love to hear your feedback! Your experiences and suggestions help us improve future editions and provide even more valuable resources for OSINT professionals.

Stay curious, stay ethical, and keep automating.

Continue Your OSINT Journey

Expand your skills with the rest of The **OSINT Analyst Series**:

- **OSINT Foundations**: The Beginner's Guide to Open-Source Intelligence
- **The OSINT Search Mastery**: Hacking Search Engines for Intelligence
- **OSINT People Finder**: Advanced Techniques for Online Investigations
- **Social Media OSINT**: Tracking Digital Footprints
- **Image & Geolocation Intelligence**: Reverse Searching and Mapping
- **Domain, Website & Cyber Investigations with OSINT**
- **Email & Dark Web Investigations**: Tracking Leaks & Breaches
- **OSINT Threat Intel**: Investigating Hackers, Breaches, and Cyber Risks
- **Corporate OSINT**: Business Intelligence & Competitive Analysis
- **Investigating Disinformation & Fake News with OSINT**
- **OSINT for Deep & Dark Web**: Techniques for Cybercrime Investigations
- **OSINT Detective**: Digital Tools & Techniques for Criminal Investigations
- **Advanced OSINT Case Studies**: Real-World Investigations
- **The Ethical OSINT Investigator**: Privacy, Legal Risks & Best Practices

We look forward to seeing you in the next book!

Happy investigating and automating!